The Socialist
Industrial State

Also by David Lane

The Roots of Russian Communism (1969 and 1975)
Politics and Society in the USSR (1970)
The End of Inequality? Social Stratification under State Socialism (1971)
Social Groups in Polish Society (1973). With George Kolankiewicz

The Socialist Industrial State

Towards a Political Sociology of State Socialism

DAVID LANE

Fellow of Emmanuel College, Cambridge

London   George Allen & Unwin Ltd

Ruskin House   Museum Street

First published in 1976

© George Allen & Unwin Ltd 1976

ISBN 0 04 320111 3

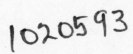

Printed in Great Britain
in 10 point Times Roman type
by Acolortone Ltd, Ipswich
Composition by Linocomp Ltd
Marcham, Oxon.

For Christel

Contents

PART THREE: THE SOCIAL STUCTURE

Figures

Tables

Introduction

Before beginning the study of the social system I have chosen to call 'state socialism', it is necessary to define the term and to describe the societies to which it is held to apply. A *society* may be defined as a behavioural system having three components: a distinct set of central or dominant value and beliefs, a number of social institutions, and patterns of interactions between individuals and institutions. What, then, are the distinguishing features of state socialism? The dominant values are those of Marxism-Leninism, and the peculiar institutions of the system stem from the state-owned means of production which determine man's relationship to property. The values laid down in the charter of the society are those of socialism: that is, a system of beliefs focused on the ultimate perfectibility of man, on the determining influence of class forces operating through the laws of historical and dialectical materialism. In state-socialist societies, the dominant institution is the Communist Party, which is considered to lead the working class and provides an authoritative interpretation of the laws of historical development, which in turn legitimate the Party's own political power. The appellation *state* focuses on the central role played by government and Party institutions in the process of these societies: not only do ownership and control of the means of production legally reside with the state, but it has the authority to mobilise the population to achieve the goals defined in the 'official charter'. In the patterns of interactions between institutions, the state (government and ruling party) plays a dominant role. Let us now turn from analytical concepts to consider some historical generalisations.

While we shall consider important differences in the culture, the level of economic development and the political processes of different state-socialist societies, the historical developments of these states share many common features. First, the communists came to power in an alliance with other social-democratic or popular parties, and with the consolidation of the revolution such parties were weakened as independent political groups: they have been banned – as in Soviet Russia, amalgamated with the Communist Party – as was the fate of most social-democratic parties in East European countries, or reduced to the role of political interest groups subservient to the ruling party. Second, the process of revolution includes an attack on right-wing liberal-democratic groups: nationalisation deprived the bourgeoisie of industrial property and land and was often accompanied by political violence – by civil war, by terror. Third, a land reform at first gave to the peasantry the rights over the land they worked, though this later gave way to the collectivisation of agriculture (Poland and Yugoslavia being two important exceptions). Fourth, political policy is decided within the Communist Party and is often accompanied by internal conflict – by purges and political violence; politics remain endemic to state-socialist society. Fifth, economically, with the exception of Eastern Germany (GDR) and Czechoslovakia, all state-socialist countries were, relative to those of the advanced West, at a low level of economic development and they all pursued policies of rapid and extensive industrialisation. Sixth, following the consolidation of political power and parallel to the industrialisation drive, a cultural revolution was instituted which involved the introduction of mass education, widespread development of communications and the comprehensive development of social services.

The notion of state socialism may be contrasted with its linguistic opposites. Democratic socialism as in Sweden is a social system in which there is a plurality of institutions, including political parties, and in which the government does not play a dominant role and operates in a context of private property. Syndicalist socialism emphasises the devolution of power, limited state activity, and particularly workers' control. The term state *capitalism* will be discussed in detail later. In the first instance, however, it is regarded as inappropriate because 'capitalism' is associated with private appropriation of the means of production, and the term state capitalism has also been used to refer to societies in which the state has controlled private trade: as in Russia during the New Economic Policy, in wartime European states, such as Germany and the United Kingdom, and in countries such as Tsarist Russia where the state itself had a considerable stake in industrial ownership.

Widely conceived, state-socialist society includes such diverse countries as the Soviet Union, China, Poland, North Korea, Yugoslavia and Cuba. These may be grouped into European (including Cuba) and Asian powers (see Ionescu, 1967: 5). Politically they may be grouped into societies which came to power without direct intervention of Soviet troops – Yugoslavia, Albania, Czechoslovakia, China, North Vietnam, North Korea and Cuba – and those that did have such support – Poland, Rumania, Hungary, Eastern Germany (German Democratic Republic), Bulgaria. The governments of these latter countries, at least in their formative stages, were very much dependent on the direct or indirect presence of the Soviet Army.

In this book the Soviet Union has been selected as a central type of state-socialist system. This is because the values and goals of Marxism–Leninism and the particular institutions, the form of economy and polity, were first adopted in Soviet Russia. At present the USSR has the largest gross national product and most powerful armed forces of all state-socialist countries.* She has the most clear-cut socio-political formation of this type and (with Czechoslovakia) her constitution defines the structural form as 'socialist' which is not yet the case with other societies.† It is worthwhile to emphasise that state-socialist countries are relatively poor. It has been estimated that China (in 1969) had an average yearly per capita gross national product of £40, North Korea £110, Cuba £128, Poland £387, the USSR £489 and East Germany £619. By comparison, the United Kingdom's GNP was £825, Western Germany's £1,252 and that of the USA £1,943. Other countries which have followed the Soviet Union's path have been modelled on her and some are, or have been, to a considerable extent politically dependent on her. At the beginning of the 1970s 1,371 million people (about a third of the world's population) lived in state-socialist societies, including $42\frac{1}{2}$ million politically active Communist Party members (Mickiewicz, 1973: 222).

Consideration of such countries would bring out their varying cultural character or historical experience and its impact on the socio-political system copied from, or imposed by, the Soviet Union. Such a task, involving detailed and systematic study of such diverse cultures as China and Hungary, is beyond the scope of this book. The central concern here is to identify the peculiar features of a state-socialist system, to determine its motive forces and to attempt to explain the relationships between its various parts. For this purpose we shall concentrate on the USSR, though comparisons and contrasts will be made with some other state-socialist countries.

Such contrasts, it is hoped, will enable one to discern that Marxist-Leninist parties, which all share more or less similar values, come to power in societies which already have their own cultural values and are at differing levels of economic development. The interaction of the ruling Party seeking to further social change along Marxist-Leninist lines with the traditional economic and cultural institutions gives rise to variation in the structure and processes of these societies. It is important, therefore, not to assume that the activity in these states is 'socialist' because the leading Party is Marxist-Leninist. The internal processes and structures of these states may be the result of traditional values or may be attributed to the low

---

*But the USSR has been overtaken in the absolute strength of her Communist Party, the USSR having 14·8 million members (1973) and China 17 million (1968).

†Since 1975, the People's Republic of China is officially described as a socialist state of proletarian dictatorship.

level of economic forces, or may be determined by the conditions in which the communist revolution occurred.

The values (Marxism-Leninism) and institutions (Communist Party and centralised government) which I have described as 'dominant' are taken from the point of view of the incumbents of political power, of the established political order, and are, I believe, accepted by the majority of the citizens of these countries. Alternative interpretations stress different values and institutions. Many, especially in the West during the Cold War, considered state-socialist societies to be totalitarian, and they stressed the role of the police and the regimentation of the individual. Others take as a point of departure the low level of productive forces and regard the state as carrying out a capitalist revolution, and the political and economic rulers as forming a ruling class. Yet another group emphasises the process of change and considers that state-socialist society is a modernising society.

It is the purpose of this book to examine in detail these various conceptual models. In the first part we shall consider meta-theories (that is, sets of orientating statements about a society) of state-socialist society from a conceptual point of view. In the second part we shall examine the institutional framework and conflict between various groupings in the political system and then turn to discuss some counterpoints to the Soviet model which have developed in China, Yugoslavia and Czechoslovakia. In the third part we shall discuss the 'outcomes' of the political system in the form of the nature of social stratification and social mobility. Hence generalisations are made in Part One which are taken up in later parts of the book.

Part One

META-THEORIES OF STATE SOCIALISM

1
Marxist Approaches

Every society is held together more or less by a system of values. Such values define what is 'sacred' in the society: they define the allegiances which man *should* have, they legitimate the distribution of power and justify the unequal division of wealth and status. The political rulers and the mass of the population are bound together by allegiances to these values, for no society is held together solely by force. A society's ideology or belief system attempts to legitimate its political system and to routinise values into obedience by the population. All societies, including state-socialist ones, have ideologies: 'Human societies secrete ideology as the very element and atmosphere indispensable to their historical respiration and life' (Althusser, 1969: 232). Under state socialism, the institutions of society, such as schools, political party, the family, are more or less linked to these values and the direction of social change is justified by them. The value system also acts as a constraint on the political elites: it defines the terms within which the rulers operate and plays a part in formulating policy.

A major distinction must be grasped between Marxism in western capitalist society, where it is critical of and destructive to the dominant ideology, and Marxism-Leninism in state-socialist society, where it legitimates the established order. The ideology of Marxism-Leninism, which developed in the USSR under Stalin, should not be equated with the writings of Marx and Lenin. It is qualitatively something different. Marxism-Leninism, then, is not merely an ideology which condones the domination of a ruling clique, but a value system which both guides and legitimates the activity of the ruling groups. In socialist societies the idea of a classless society lives in their ideology and men must be conditioned and transformed to achieve it. As Althusser has put it: 'In a classless society ideology is the relay whereby, and the element in which, the relation between men and their conditions of existence is lived to the profit of all men.'

It must be emphasised that the central value system of a society or its ideology is not the actual set of beliefs which *all* the citizens hold in that society, and it does not describe the political processes which take place. Certain groups or classes may oppose some or even all elements of the ideology and may wish to replace it with an alternative. The dominant value system in such a society is what the ruling class or ruling elites define as the normative order; it is the official charter which attempts to direct the activity of the society.

Many writers adopting different political stances emphasise the importance of the 'ruling ideas'. Daniel Bell, for instance, considers ideology in the Soviet Union to be of crucial significance and describes it as 'a self-conscious set of directives to change the society in accordance with a generalised theoretical doctrine'; 'ideological activism' he sees as a parallel to the American value system characterised by Talcott Parsons as one of 'instrumental activism' (Bell, 1966 : 81, 174). In defining what is legitimate, by the same token, it specifies what is illegitimate and justifies the sanctions which are exerted against those who violate its charter. It should be made clear that the extent of social integration and the kinds of conflict which occur cannot be known directly from a study of the central or dominant value system but only from an empirical study of the processes of the social system. Recognition of the importance of ideology does not entail confusing it with the actual structure and processes of society. The critical evaluation of ideology and its impact on society and the ways it transforms (or prevents the transformation) of the social structure to achieve certain goals, are some of the most important tasks for study by sociologists. A discussion of the dominant or central system of values serves as a *point of reference* for analysing the structure and process of the system.

It should be emphasised that the discussion of Marxism-Leninism and other models which follow is not intended to be a description of the way the system actually works. Such description follows in the second and third parts of the book.

The Legitimating Function of Marxism-Leninism

The institutions and processes of all state-socialist societies are predicated on the doctrine of Marxism-Leninism. The legitimacy of the system, in its own terms, based on the theoretical analysis of society carried out by Marx and Lenin as interpreted by the ideological and political elites of a given society. This means that the doctrine of Marxism-Leninism is assumed to be the only true science of society. As the writings of Marx and Lenin are open to more than one interpretation, a second important assumption is that the only true account of their theories can be made by the Communist Party

These two assumptions are in Durkheim's sense 'sacred' and under-pin the evolution of the official ideology. In capitalist-type societies the dominant value system is not defined in theoretical terms: in the United States and in France the statements of the Constitution are the nearest one has to an official charter – and these have to be in-terpreted in conjunction with other generalised values such as Christianity. In state-socialist societies the content of the central value system is more clear-cut. In the Soviet Union, it may be ex-amined in official pronouncements and in the expositions contained in books such as *Fundamentals of Marxism (Osnovy Marksizma-Leninizma*; 1961), *Fundamentals of Scientific Communism (Osnovy nauchnogo kommunizma*; 1969) and *Marxist-Leninist Philosophy (Marksistsko-Leninskaya filosofiya*; 1972). These books, which are carefully composed by the Party elite, serve the purpose of selecting from the writings of Marx and Lenin those ideas which legitimate the structure and processes of the Soviet state. Until the split between the USSR and China these pronouncements were accepted by all states in the Communist bloc; and even since it, most of the essential viewpoints have been generally held.

What, then, are the distinguishing features of the official value system of Marxism-Leninism? They may be itemised as follows. First, Lenin's acceptance of the unity of the thought of Marx and Engels which in practice emphasises Engels's interpretation of the 'mature' rather than the 'young' Marx and entails an emphasis on economic structures and class formations. Second, the acceptance of Lenin's theory of imperialism which gives underdeveloped countries an important, if not decisive, role in revolutionary activity in the twentieth century. Third, the addition to Marxist analysis of Lenin's theory of the Party as the articulator of the working class's interest. These components must be seen as forming an organic whole rather than, as is sometimes the practice, being considered in isolation. Hence the Party is seen as applying the laws of historical materialism as defined by Marx and Engels and it cannot realistically and socio-logically be analysed as an organisational structure independently of its goals.

These views underpin the Marxist-Leninist interpretation of history and legitimate the actions of the Soviet leaders. In this light, the October Revolution in Russia made Soviet Russia, after a period of the dictatorship of the proletariat, the first socialist society in world history. The Marxist-Leninist argument is that capitalism must be analysed on a world scale. Lenin's law of uneven development of the 'world system of imperialism' justifies the breaking down of capitalism at its 'weakest link'. That is where the economic and political contradictions become 'particularly acute', and in such countries 'the ruling classes prove incapable of coping with the revolutionary movement' (Kuusinen, 604). The 'front of imperialism' was broken first in Tsarist Russia. Then in Soviet Russia, the basis of a socialist society was built, thereby 'skipping' the full development of the capitalist stage. It is true that in Marx's original writing, the rise of a socialist system was not thought to occur in the less economically developed countries. Soviet Marxists, however, take the view that an imperialist interpretation of capitalism entails the working out of the laws of capitalist development in a way unforeseen by Marx – nevertheless, they still follow the sequence of the stages of historical development (primitive-communist, slave, feudal, capitalist, socialist). What distinguishes Leninism from Marxism is not that it stresses the 'voluntarist' aspect of Marxist thought as suggested by Bochenski (1966: 62) but the fact that the socialist revolution should be carried out by the Communist Party and in a society which had not completed the bourgeois stage of development. We might emphasise here that Lenin's contribution to Marxist theory involved devising first the law of uneven development which posed the possibility of the evolution of societies missing out the complete capitalist stage, and second, the development of the political party as an instrument of the working class to carry out the proletarian revolution.

The Marxist-Leninist Party is given a central place in the theory of all state-socialist societies. The essential task of the Party is to express 'the basic interests of the working class and to lead it to complete victory' (Kuusinen, 408). The Party is composed of a 'vanguard' of the working class, that is of class-conscious communists. It forms alliances with other parties and groups – especially sections of the peasantry – to overthrow capitalism. The Party's organisational structure is characterised by centralised leadership which unites revolutionary forces to achieve the goal of revolution. 'Absolute centralisation and the strictest discipline of the proletariat constitute one of the fundamental conditions for victory over the bourgeoisie' (Lenin, cited by Kuusinen, 412). The Party's centralism, however, is tempered by democratic participation – the election of the leading Party bodies and their accountability to Party organisations. Leninists (at least in Russia) have no confidence in the spontaneity of the working class to perceive its own class interests, and therefore the Party has to channel the workers' activity into the revolutionary cause. Even with the maturation of socialism, the Party is necessary to articulate and to aggregate the interest of the working class. Students of political theory may note that Lenin and his followers suggest a solution to Rousseau's problem of how the 'general will' of a society is defined and recognised: it is the interest of the working class expressed through the Party.

The Dictatorship of the Working Class: the People's Democracy

These ideas shape the Marxist-Leninist conception of the form of their own society. It is theoretically possible for societies under certain conditions to move to socialism without first completing the full stage of capitalism. This, however, involves an intermediary or transitional stage. In the USSR this social formation was called the dictatorship of the proletariat. This transitional stage lasted in the Soviet Union until 1936. In other state-socialist societies its legal title is that of a People's Republic, which is not quite the same thing as dictatorship of the proletariat. The importance of this stage in the contemporary world is that most of the countries in Eastern Europe (Czechoslovakia is a notable exception) are still passing through it. These states, then, are not yet socialist but, headed by their Communist Parties,* are either creating the preconditions for the development of socialism or are actively building it.

During this period, the class struggle continues and may even become more acute. A workers' state apparatus is strengthened and becomes, as it were, the executive arm of the proletariat and the Communist Party seeks to consolidate its position of power by eliminating class opposition. In doing so, it may form alliances with other classes (such as the poor peasantry) and strata (for instance the employed intelligentsia), thus giving rise to a 'people's democracy' (not all 'the people' are members of the working class). The task of 'socialist construction' follows the consolidation of power and is characterised by state control of most industry and other social institutions. The theoretical nature of the stage of transition may be illustrated by considering the 1954 Constitution of the People's Republic of China.

In the Maoist view it may take several generations and continual struggle on the part of the Party to build a socialist society. In China, the Communist revolution is considered to be the culmination of the struggle of the Chinese *people* against oppression. Though this revolution was led by the Party of the working class, it was more than a proletarian revolution and its popular character left its imprint on the social order which was created in 1949. The preamble to the Constitution of the People's Republic of China (1954) makes clear that it is a 'people's democratic dictatorship'. The Communist Party of China, which seeks to bring about the 'socialist industrialisation' of the country, leads 'all democratic classes, democratic parties and groups, and people's organisations'. In 1963 there were nine political

---

*By 'Communist Party' is meant the ruling Marxist-Leninist Party. (In Poland, for instance, its name is Polish United Workers' Party; in the German Democratic Republic, Socialist Unity Party.)

parties in existence (the Communist Party of China, the Revolutionary Committe of the Kuomintang, the China Democratic League, the China Democratic National Construction Association, the China Association for Promoting Democracy, the Chinese Peasants' and Workers' Democratic Party, the China Chih Kung Tang, the Chiu San Society, and the Taiwan Democratic Self-Government League). These parties, of course, accept the leadership of the Communist Party and its general objectives. The first article of the 1954 Constitution defines the Republic as a 'people's democratic state led by the working class and based on the alliance of workers and peasants'. Like the Soviet Union, the People's Republic has state and co-operative forms of ownership, but in addition it also until recently had 'ownership by individual working people and capitalist ownership' (Article 5). Thus the law protected the 'right of peasants to own land and other means of production' (Article 8) and 'the right of capitalists to own means of production and other capital' (Article 10).

The Constitution of 1975 presents a radically changed picture. The People's Republic is regarded as 'a socialist state of proletarian dictatorship' and the Chinese Communist Party is the 'core of leadership of the whole Chinese people'. No rights to capitalist forms of ownership are mentioned and the main categories of ownership are socialist ownership by the whole people and socialist collective ownership by masses of working people. The Chairman of the Party is also head of state and commander of the armed forces.

Similar conditions have existed in other People's Democracies and reflect, beside economic position, the cultural heritage of particular countries. In Poland, for instance, not only is the class of private entrepreneurs important but also the intelligentsia still keeps much of its prestige and life-style inherited from pre-socialist Poland (Szczepanski 1970: Chapter 6). Polish sociologists regard the intelligentsia as something more than a specialised stratum of the working class.

It is in this heterogeneous class context that the Marxist-Leninist Party is conceived of as leading the society forward to socialism. Official Marxism-Leninism accepts the existence of antagonistic contradictions; and the state, as an instrument of the dictatorship of the proletariat, plays an important role in resolving them. With the advent of socialist society antagonistic classes (those based on private property) disappear, the dictatorship of the proletariat by the Communist Party becomes transformed into a leadership function, and the oppressive role of the state begins to wither away. The relatnioship between the basis and the superstructure of the society is considered to reach a high level of congruity. The Soviet Union was the first and is the most developed model of 'a Marxist-Leninist *socialist* society. Let us therefore turn to consider its legitimating ideology.

Socialist Society

The Soviet Union since 1936 has been a *socialist* society; it has a 'Socialist mode of production . . . based on social ownership of the means of production'. The abolition of private ownership of the means of production and its replacement by 'state socialist property' and control of the 'production process *of the entire national economy on a country-wide scale*' (Kuusinen, 694) create the basis of a socialist mode of production. On this view, the means of production are owned and directed by those who take part in the productive process, and therefore there can be no class conflict between owners and workers and there can be no class exploitation. 'Since they jointly own social property and jointly participate in the social production process, all peoples are equal and their relations are based on the principles of comradely co-operation and mutual assistance' (Kuusinen, 695). Surplus value and class exploitation cannot exist under Soviet socialism 'because the means of production belong to the working people . . . who cannot exploit themselves'; and surplus product is utilised for the benefit of the people as a whole. It should be emphasised that in Marxist terms 'the basis' of the socialist system, according to the official ideology, is state ownership and control of the means of production. 'On behalf of society, the state directs the whole of the social production as a single process. While the state remains the owner of the means of production, it places the means of production at the disposal of various collective bodies for their use. In saying that under socialism people consciously direct their own social development, one has in mind that they do this through the Party and state, whose function it is *to lead and organise the socialist economy*' (Kuusinen, 696).

Given the determining role derived from Marxist theory of the basis in relation to the superstructure, it too therefore has a socialist character. The political superstructure, the state (made up of government and the Communist Party) is brought into 'agreement' with the economic base; this was put clearly by Stalin when in 1936 he wrote that there was a perfect correspondence between basis and superstructure. The Communist Party in the USSR is the only party because it is the expression of the unitary will of the working class. The institutions in the superstructure are socialist and congruent with the basis. Here, we shall illustrate this contention by considering the Soviet view of the state, the family and the social phenomenon of 'alienation'. (The nature of social stratification will be considered in more detail below; see Chapter 7).

Under Soviet socialism, the state '*loses the character of an instrument of class suppression*' (Kuusinen: 734), and with the progress of socialist construction the class struggle becomes weaker and there is no need for a state as an instrument of oppression. All citizens have the right to vote and stand for election. The state, however, does not vanish but takes on a new socialist form. It takes upon itself the task of 'public leadership of the economy, social relations and cultural development'. Also, socialism is only the first stage of development of communist society and therefore the state safeguards the political interests of socialist society by protecting 'public and personal property and cuts short anti-social actions dangerous to the socialist system'. The state is also necessary as an agency of defence against the capitalist world and has to 'combat spies, saboteurs, and other subversive elements sent in by imperialists'. The state under socialism, then, has an important economic role: it controls planning and development, it has a cultural and educational function and it safeguards socialist property. The overriding goal of the government and Party is that of building a communist society. It may be pointed out that in Soviet theory there is an explicit shift from the classical Marxist emphasis on the 'withering away' of the state, to its assumption of *administrative* functions under socialism.

A similar approach may be found in Soviet analysis of other parts of the superstructure. In the case of the family, for instance, the socialist revolution swept away the old bourgeois form of monogamy and put in its place a 'new form of monogamy'. (*Marksistsko-leninskaya filosofiya: istoricheski materializm*: chapter XI, 263. Lane, 1970: chapter 11.) Under capitalism, family relations are dominated by the needs of private property which militate against the expression of true love in the family. With the development of communism the chief function of the family becomes procreation and upbringing of children and mutual love between the family's members (*Osnovy nauchnogo kommunizma*, chapter 16, 357). Previous forms of inequality between husband and wife including rights over children have been legally abolished. Changes involving woman's emancipation, her participation in industry, in politics, and in education are linked to the economic changes carried out by the revolution. (The *actual* position of women is discussed later in this book: see Chapter 7, below.)

The notion of alienation is treated in a similar way. Its existence in society is explained in terms of what Skolimowski (1971: 26) calls a 'right wing version' of Marxism. In contrast to the work of modern West European Marxists, alienation finds little place in the thought of Soviet theorists concerned with socialist society. (The word 'alienation' (*otchuzhdenie*) does not warrant even a chapter sub-head in the three primers mentioned at the beginning of this chapter.) Alienation can exist only in capitalist society, where it is caused by the laws of capitalism based on private property and economic exploitation. Igor Kon clearly states that a Marxist 'socio-economic analysis [regards] the employee's alienation from the means of production as the derivative of private ownership and the social division of labor' (Kon, 1969: 147). He points out that in Marx's later writings, 'the worker's very attitude towards work is derived from the objective social processes associated with the private ownership and the social division of labor' (*ibid*, 160). Soviet writers see 'alienation' as something exceptional in Soviet society, having its roots in capitalism, and consider that it will disappear completely with the attainment of full communism.

This brief review illustrates how changes in the base lead to changes in the superstructure: a socialist base gives rise to an equally socialist superstructure. Given this congruence, how does social change occur? Soviet ideologists do not deny that societies should be analysed dialectically. Indeed they assert that in social life, in human thought and in nature, 'development proceeds in such a way that opposite, mutually exclusive sides or tendencies reveal themselves in an object . . . Development is the "struggle of opposites" ' (Lenin, cited by Kuusinen, 94). In Soviet society change proceeds not through *antagonistic* contradictions (such as between workers and capitalists) but through *non-antagonistic* ones. This distinction is in keeping with the line of argument outlined above. The Soviet Union is a socialist society in which 'the basic interests of classes and social groups coincide. [Contradictions] are not resolved through class struggle but through the joint efforts of friendly classes, of all social strata, under the leadership of the Marxist-Leninist Party' (Kuusinen, 98). The sources of non-antagonistic contradictions which remain are derived from the different forms of property (state and collective), types of labour (manual and non-manual), uneven development of town and country and the persistence of pre-revolutionary and capitalistic mores. Hence the explanation of the existence of such phenomena as crime or Christian religion in Soviet society is couched either in terms of such non-antagonistic contradictions, of the immaturity of the person concerned (imperfect socialisation) or of the persistence of pre-Soviet norms: resulting conflict may be resolved not by a major clash but through, say, education (see Connor, 1972). The laws of motion of societies are being fulfilled in Soviet society which is moving from socialism to full communism in which there will be 'complete equality of people' (*Osnovy nauchnogo-kommunizma*, 236).

Before proceeding to consider criticisms of this ideology, we may summarise some of its principal characteristics as noted above. This 'official' description of Soviet society is similar to the description made by many structural functionalists of Western liberal-democratic societies. Marxism-Leninism is a central value system rather than a 'dominant' ideology as conceived of by Marxists. There is no fundamental conflict which could tear apart the society, though there are 'deviations' from the central value system. The need for 'politics', in the sense of making social arrangements or mobilising people and resources, continues. The social system depicted in Soviet theory is very similar to Parsons's 'ideal type' of industrial society. One might draw attention to the fact that the Soviet Marxist view of the USSR and the Parsonian approach to the structure of American society are similar and might be conceived of as providing a kind of ideological 'convergence'. This does not mean, of course, that the structures of the society are the same. On the other hand, from a Marxist perspective, Soviet socialism is not an 'ideal' communist society: the state continues as an institution; social inequality is justified by the division of labour; the Party does not wither away but continues as an organ which leads the people: there are no forms of direct rule, such as workers' control. Marxism-Leninism cannot be equated with the original writings of Marx and Lenin; it is something more than that.

Marxist Criticisms of the Soviet Form of Socialism

The Soviet interpretation of state socialism has led to a reaction from many Marxists in the West, from Chinese communists and to a lesser extent from Yugoslav socialists.* Many socialists have abhorred the practices of Stalinist Russia and see them not as aberrations in an essentially socialist society but as symptoms indicating the negation of socialism. Soviet ideology is seen as an intellectual smokescreen blocking the perception of Soviet reality. The Yugoslavs regard the domination of the state apparatus as a necessary condition for the achievement of socialism, but emphasise that it is a transitional form and should lead to greater participation by the masses. Others, such as the Chinese, have few objections to Stalin but believe that the USSR has more recently reverted to a form of capitalism. Such critics seek to analyse Soviet society in terms of Marxism and therefore to expose the falsity of the Soviet claim to socialism on the basis of its own legitimating value system. From this viewpoint, ideology has the role of blinding men to social reality; it manipulates the masses; it is a tool of suppression of the ruling groups. In contrast to Althusser's view (see above, p. 19), it is not for 'the profit of all men', but for the profit of some at the expense of others.

It must be admitted that no comprehensive interpretation of Soviet

*Titoism is not pursued in this chapter but is considered below in Chapter 6.

society from such a Marxist viewpoint has been attempted. This does not mean to say that various critical works have not applied Marxist theory to economy or politics or social structure, but no single work or group of works attempts to refute Soviet Marxism-Leninism in terms of dialectical and historical materialism, and to analyse the structure of Soviet and world society seen through the prism of scientific communism. Anti-Soviet Marxism, however, does provide a number of significant and important criticisms of state socialist societies. (Most of these works do not distinguish between the Soviet Union and other socialist societies.) Here we shall group these analyses according to the various political standpoints which are partly defined by their relationship to, and analysis of, the USSR. Some writers do not come within the parameters of any particular political grouping and therefore they are included where their argument makes it seem most appropriate. The two major types of these Marxist criticisms are those of bureaucratic state capitalism, of which Maoism is one variation, and the transitional economy of a workers' state. Writing on these two models is not as comprehensive and consistent as the Soviet model and it should be borne in mind that the various writers cited often do not agree with each other on all aspects of the analyses of state socialism. The purpose here is to construct generic types of argument.

Bureaucratic State Capitalism

Herbert Marcuse has provided one of the most elegant statements of the state capitalist thesis. Marcuse seeks to refute the theory that the 'socialist state is the proletariat constituted as the ruling class'. In practice, argues Marcuse, there is no unity between subject and object, between state and citizen.

> The Soviet state exercises throughout political and governmental functions against the proletariat itself; domination remains a specialised function in the division of labour and is as such the monopoly of a political, economic and military bureaucracy. This function is perpetuated by the centralised authoritarian organisation of the productive process, directed by groups which determine the needs of society (the social product and its distribution) independently of the collective control of the ruled population. (Marcuse, 1958: 105.)

It is clearly not Marcuse's view that the Soviet state is acting in the interest of the proletariat while the latter has insufficient conciousness to perceive its own class interest. The state bureaucracy has a 'caste character' and it has a 'vital interest in maintaining and enhancing its privileged position'.

These points have been elaborated by the International Socialism group, and particularly by one of its specialists on the Soviet Union, Tony Cliff (1964, 1974). He attempts, by way of a Marxist historical account, an explanation of the forces inherent in what he calls 'dialectical historical development' by which the 'subjective intention' of building socialism in one country 'became the foundation of the building of state capitalism' (Cliff, 1964 : 107). Essentially, in my view, Cliff's argument is the traditional Menshevik one, but with some important embellishments. The Mensheviks were wont to quote Marx's famous statement that : 'No social order ever disappears before all the productive forces, for which there is room in it, have been developed; and new, higher relations of production never appear before the material conditions of their existence have matured in the womb of the old society' (*Critique of Political Economy*). Hence, as capitalism had only recently started in Russia, the October Revolution could not be, in a Marxist sense, a socialist one. Citing Engels, Cliff points out that the division of society into a ruling and a ruled class, an exploiting and an exploited class, is the 'necessary outcome of the low development of production hitherto'. At the 'root of the division [of society] into classes' is the 'law of the division of labour'. In Tsarist Russia the level of the productive forces was extremely low and the October Revolution 'put an end to the remnants of feudalism' and 'gave tremendous lever to the development of the productive forces'. Cliff turns to the mode of production, to the level of technology, as a conditioning factor in the analysis of societal development. 'The *central* problem in post-October Russia with its low level of national income . . . [has been] the fulfilment of the bourgeois tasks' of the development of the productive forces (*ibid*, 106).

Cliff recognises that the working masses and, at least in the early years after the Revolution, even the leaders of the Soviet state did not intend to bring about a form of capitalism : 'They thought the Five-year Plans would take Russia far in the direction of socialism'. But the 'historical mission of the bourgeoisie', in 'outright contradiction to the wishes and hopes of the actors themselves', had to be carried out by the Soviet bureaucracy. The Soviet leaders were forced into this position because the Russian Revolution did not spread to the advanced capitalist West. Hence, unlike the Mensheviks, Cliff justifies the October Revolution because it was conceived of by Lenin as the vanguard of the world revolution but, as the revolution was not consummated on a world scale, the working class in Russia lost power to the bourgeoisie (Cliff 1974 : Chapter 4). Had the revolution taken on an international character, the result would have been different, for the level of development was higher in West Europe and the help which Russia's (ruling) working class might have been given would have obviated the need for the rise of a ruling bourgeoisie in the USSR. In Cliff's view, with the advent of the First Five Year Plan which sought to industrialise Soviet Russia, the bureaucracy became a ruling class. The bureaucracy had to accumulate capital as a first priority, and this led to the abolition of 'all remnants of workers' control', to the introduction of coercion in the labour process, to the atomisation of the working class and to the forcing of 'all social-political life into a totalitarian mould' (Cliff, 1964 : 107). During the process of capital accumulation the bureaucracy, as a consequence of its function, took on the character of a ruling class. It became the 'oppressor of the workers', it made 'use of its social supremacy in the relations of production in order to gain advantages for itself in the relations of distribution'. Cliff takes a clearly historical determinist position : industrialisation and the collectivisation of agriculture 'in a backward country under conditions of siege transforms the bureau-cracy from a layer which is under the direct and indirect pressure and control of the proletariat, into a ruling class, into the manager of [to quote Engels] "the general business of society: the direction of labour, affairs of state, justice, science, art and so forth" '. State capitalism, then, is 'the extreme theoretical limit which capitalism can reach' and is the 'extreme opposite of socialism' (*ibid*, 113).

Having grasped the inner logic of Cliff's position, various other aspects of state-socialist society fall neatly into place. The state bureaucracy is a ruling class because of the dominant role it plays in the production process. Control of the means of production is effectively in the hands of the bureaucrats as a collective. The rela-tions between the workers and the bureaucrats is exploitive. The state is an instrument of oppression, with the bureaucrats extracting surplus value from the working class (see Cliff, 1964 : Chapter 6). Though state capitalist theorists do not detail these points, the social institutions, such as the family and the educational system, operate as under capitalism. Alienation as a social relationship occurs because of the continuation of the essentially exploitative relations between the masses and the ruling class. The official ideology of Soviet society manipulates and enslaves. Cliff's argument is the exact obverse of the Soviet Marxist. State capitalist society is based on class conflict and class exploitation.

Maoist Counterpoint

Since some time following the Twentieth Congress of the CPSU, in 1956, the Chinese Communist Party has come to accept many con-clusions similar to those of the state capitalists about the nature of the Soviet Union. But the arguments adopted are quite different. It is not denied that the Soviet Union under Stalin was a socialist society.

This may be clearly demonstrated by study of Mao's works. The Soviet Union was for a long time the model which the Chinese Communists followed: 'In the more than one hundred years since the birth of Marxism, it was only through the example of the Russian Bolsheviks in leading the October Revolution, in leading socialist construction and in defeating fascist aggression that revolutionary parties of a new type were formed and developed in the world' (Mao Tse-Tung, 'Revolutionary Forces of the World Unite . . .', 284). In 1939, Mao clearly recognised Stalin as the 'commander of the revolutionary front'. 'Comrade Stalin is the leader of the world revolution.' His contribution to the development of Marxism-Leninism was to produce 'a very clear, concrete and living doctrine for the oppressed people of the whole world. This is the complete doctrine of establishing a revolutionary front, overthrowing imperialism, overthrowing capitalism and establishing a socialist society' (Mao Tse-Tung, *Stalin is our Commander*, 426, 428). There can be no doubt that, until after the death of Stalin, Mao considered the USSR to be the first socialist society. In *On Contradiction* (334) he writes: 'The proletariat . . . is a new force which . . . becomes an independent class playing the leading role in history, and finally seizes political power and becomes the ruling class. Thereupon the nature of society changes and the old capitalist society becomes the new socialist society. This is the path already taken by the Soviet Union, and the path that all other countries will inevitably take.'

In the Chinese Maoist view, after the fall of Stalin, and with the consolidation of Khruschev's rule, a restoration of capitalism occurred in the USSR. The Chinese Communist Party opposed the Soviet leadership's policy of the 'complete negation of Stalin' and the thesis of 'peaceful transition to socialism' (*The Origin and Development of the Differences . . .*, 1963: 6). While the Chinese recognised that Stalin made mistakes, he 'expressed the will and aspirations of the people and proved himself an outstanding Marxist-Leninist fighter. . . . By pursuing [Stalin's policy] the Communist Party of the Soviet Union brought about the triumph of socialism in the Soviet Union in the war against Hitler. . . .' In 1956, after Khruschev's anti-Stalin speech, Mao is said to have acknowledged that 'Stalin's merits outweighed his faults' (cited in Schram, 1966: 286). In the way that he deplored Stalin's rule, Khrushchev 'negated the dictatorship of the proletariat and the fundamental theories of Marxism-Leninism'. Krushchev is also accused of revising both Lenin's theory of imperialism and his doctrine on war and peace: and Khrushchev's (and his successor Brezhnev's) views on peaceful coexistence were strongly denounced on the grounds that they involve 'collaboration with US imperialism and the settlement of world

problems by the heads of the Soviet Union and the United States'.
The *Programme of the CPSU* is considered 'a revisionist programme
for the preservation or restoration of capitalism' (*The Origin and
Development*, 43). What then are the social dynamics which lead
to this restoration?

Chinese theorists explain the degeneration of Soviet Marxism by
reference to the nature of the process of the revolutionary transformation of a society. Such a process is very long and drawn out –
for the 'complete victory of socialism' one must think of a time period
of 'five or ten generations or even longer' (*On Khrushchev's Phoney
Communism* . . . , 1964: 12). It is impossible to build socialism in a
short time period because the bourgeoisie persists both at home and
abroad and this creates contradictions in the society seeking to build
socialism. Also, 'In their present level of economic development all
socialist countries are still far, far removed from the higher stage of
communism. . . . Therefore, it will take a long, long time to eliminate
the class difference between worker and peasant. And until this
difference is eliminated, it is impossible to say that society is classless
or that there is no longer any need for the dictatorship of the
proletariat' ('A Proposal Concerning the General Line . . .', 1963: 17).
Under these circumstances, even at the *socialist* stage, 'the dictatorship of the proletariat is absolutely necessary . . . before the advent
of a full communist society' (*On Khrushchev's* . . . , 13. See also: 'A
Proposal . . .', 1963: 16–17). The class struggle continues in socialist
countries after the nationalisation of the means of production: 'in all
socialist countries without exception, there are classes and class
struggle. There is the struggle between the socialist and the capitalist
roads, the question of carrying the socialist revolution through to the
end, and the question of preventing the restoration of capitalism'
(*On Khrushchev's* . . . , 13). Thus in China, the collectivisation of
agriculture, completed in 1956, entailed the formation of a socialist
economy but this in turn did *not* mean (as it had been assumed in the
USSR) the end of the class struggle: a state of 'permanent revolution'
characterised the period of transition from socialism to communism.
(See below, Chapter 6.)

In Soviet society, according to the Chinese Communist Party, 'The
old bourgeoisie and other exploiting classes . . . survived after industry
had been nationalised and agriculture collectivised'. Stalin prema-
turely declared in 1936 that the USSR was free from class conflicts
and 'one-sidedly stressed the internal homogeneity of socialist society
and overlooked its contradictions' (*ibid*, 15). An English Maoist,
Professor George Thomson (1971), points out that Stalin did not
recognise the fact that if non-antagonistic contradictions are wrongly
handled they may become antagonistic ones. From this point of view,

in the sequence of the succession of the different modes of production, a society may miss out the full capitalist stage, enter the socialist and then 'slip back' to the bourgeois capitalist. It fell to Khrushchev, however, to push through a 'series of revisionist policies' which have led to the growth of capitalism in the USSR. He has supported a 'class that is antagonistic to the proletariat, [its members] belong to the bourgeoisie' (*On Khrushchev's* . . . , 19). The reform started by Khrushchev and continued by Brezhnev 'sabotages the socialist planned economy, applies the capitalist principle of profit, develops capitalist free competition and undermines socialist ownership by the whole people'. Under his rule the privileged bourgeois stratum gained control of the Party, the government and other institutions; and this group 'appropriates the fruits of the Soviet people's labour. . . . They live the parasitical and decadent life of the bourgeoisie' (*ibid*, 30. See also Chang Peng-Ya, 1966). By 1970 the Chinese went as far as to call Soviet revisionism 'fascist' (*Leninism or Social Imperialism*, 7), and the 'new-type bureaucratic monopoly capitalist class has turned socialist ownership into ownership by capitalist roaders and turned the socialist economy into a capitalist economy and a state monopoly capitalist economy'.

The foregoing analysis may be applied to various institutions of Soviet society. For example, the Soviet state cannot be a 'state of the whole people'. Every state is a 'dictatorship of a definite class' (*On Khrushchev's* . . . , 34) and thus the Soviet state, which has destroyed the dictatorship of the proletariat, represents the dictatorship of the bourgeoisie. These conclusions are in fact very similar to those of the International Socialist Group, though of course the appraisal of Stalin is quite different.

Let us now turn to consider what supporters of these views consider to be the dynamics of bureaucratic state socialism. A discussion between Sweezy and Bettelheim (1971) concerning the significance of the Soviet invasion of Czechoslovakia highlights some of the forces at work in state-socialist society. Both Sweezy and Bettelheim accept the view that the juridical form of property relations (public ownership) does not entail socialist property relations. In Sweezy's view capitalism is built into the social system by virtue of 'the control of enterprises in the enterprises themselves, co-ordination through the market, and reliance on material incentives – these three factors, taken together, make inevitable a strong tendency toward an economic order which, whatever one may choose to call it, functions more and more like capitalism' (1971 : 4). The contradictions in the system of state capitalism – of which the slowing down of the economic rate of growth is but one symptom – may be resolved by a greater reliance on the discipline of the market and greater incentives for profit. Hence 'once profit and efficiency at the plant and enter-prise level have been elevated to the status of supreme values, managements will inevitably strive for closer association with those (the West) who are most advanced and proficient in putting these values into practice'. Both Sweezy and Bettelheim regard the adop-tion of market forms in Eastern Europe as a movement on the road (or further along the road) to capitalism. Bettelheim, in exposing its 'ideological character', argues that market socialism 'indicates an ideology which favours a considerable development of market rela-tionships, when in fact such a development (which is possible only under the domination of a bourgeoisie) leads to the full restoration of capitalism' (*ibid*, 17–18). The development of 'market socialism' is only a further rationalisation of capitalism in these countries which is in the interests of the ruling class.

What, then, is the way in which class conflict between the ruling class and the working class may be resolved? Reform is not an appropriate means of change. Only a revolution can liberate the working class. Both Bettelheim and Sweezy look to a revitalised Communist Party as a mechanism of change and they advocate a Chinese-style 'cultural revolution' to enable the working class, through the Party, to reassert socialist aims and to put the society back on the path to socialism. Cliff has a similar – but rather longer-term – policy. 'Only when the anger and resentment embedded in the hearts of the masses accumulates till it is ready to burst, will the masses break out in revolt. . . . The final chapter can be written only by the masses, self-mobilised, conscious of socialist aims and the methods of their achievement and led by a revolutionary Marxist party' (Cliff, 1964: 349). The state-capitalist view would seem to entail a social, economic and political revolution. Marcuse is more ambiguous. In *One Dimensional Man*, he recognises that the ruling strata in the Soviet system are 'separable from the production process – that is, they are replaceable without exploding the basic institutions of society'. But he sees the transition to a 'mature and free industrial society' to be 'a revolutionary rather than evolutionary process, even on the foundation of a fully nationalised and planned economy' (Marcuse, 1968: 49).

The major criticisms of the Soviet state and the Soviet conception of socialism levied by state-capitalist theorists may be summed up under six headings. Firstly, the means of production are not at a level superior to those of advanced capitalist societies: the October Revolution created conditions for the development of the capitalist mode of production. Secondly, socialist relations of production do not simply follow from the state ownership through nationalisation of the means of production. Thirdly, state ownership of the means of production may give rise to a ruling class deriving its power from *control* of the means of production. Fourthly, a revolution embracing the economic, political and cultural realms is necessary to liberate the working class. Fifthly, Maoist theorists emphasise the necessity of the dictatorship of the proletariat continuing through the socialist stage. Sixthly, International Socialists stress the importance of the world character of the socialist revolution; revolution in the western capitalist states must accompany change in the Soviet bloc and China.

Transitional Economy of a Workers' State

While Soviet Marxists and state-capitalist theorists may be seen as taking Marxist, yet diametrically opposed, positions on the nature of the Soviet Union, there remains yet a third group of Marxists which takes up a position between these extremes. The intellectual heritage of Trotsky underpins this viewpoint which is supported by his followers in the Fourth International.* The concept of a 'workers' state' was developed by Trotsky and the elaboration of the thesis of the transitional economy has been carried out by Ernest Mandel.

Trotsky was most concerned with the sociology (and particularly the class character) of the Soviet Union. In both the *Revolution Betrayed* (1936) and *The USSR: Non-Proletarian and Non-Bourgeois State?* (1937), Trotsky justified the October Revolution while at the same time criticising Soviet society under Stalin. In contrast to the Menshevik interpretation, Trotsky accepts the Leninist law of combined development which justifies the socialist revolution taking place at the 'weakest link of capitalism' (Trotsky: 1936, chapter 1). And, like Soviet Marxists, Trotsky sees the working class through the Party carrying out *socialist* industrialisation without going through the capitalist stage. The social structure of Soviet society under Stalin is determined by the relations of production. 'The nationalisation of the land, the means of industrial production, transport and exchange, together with the monopoly of foreign trade, constitute the basis of the Soviet social structure. Through these relations, established by the proletarian revolution, the nature of the Soviet Union as a proletarian state is for us basically defined' (1936: 248). Trotsky is quite clear that the Soviet bureaucracy cannot be

*In the 1970s the Fourth International is split into several political groups. Only one is considered here, the International Marxist Group. The other important Party in Britain adopting a similar view is the Workers' Revolutionary Party.

NOT

accurately described as 'state capitalist'. 'The bureaucracy has neither stocks nor bonds. It is recruited, supplemented and renewed in the manner of an administrative hierarchy, independently of any special property relations of its own. The individual bureaucrat cannot transmit to his heirs his rights in the exploitation of the state apparatus. The bureaucracy enjoys its privileges under the form of the abuse of power' (1936: 249–50). Trotsky brings out the fact that state-capitalist theorists in attempting a *Marxist* analysis reach a theoretical *impasse*. They are unable to provide a Marxist analysis of the ruling class. Marcuse, for example, admits that in terms of its relation to the means of production, the Soviet bureaucracy is not a class (1968: 105 n), for the 'traditional sources of economic power are not available to the Soviet bureaucracy; it does not own the nationalised means of production'. Hence 'control' of the means of production Marcuse sees as the 'decisive factor' (*ibid*, 110). But Marcuse fails to pinpoint any *class* groups which account for the dynamic of Soviet society. Rather he pictures a 'top ruling group' composed of representatives from various bureaucracies (economic, political, management, army, Party) and this group is subject to two other forces: 'the Central Plan', and 'the competitive terror'. Cliff is even more general and identifies the '*Russian bureaucracy* [as] "owning" . . . the state and controlling the process of accumulation . . .' (Cliff, 1974: 169). It is unclear where the bureaucracy starts and ends and no analysis of different bureaucratic institutions (police, government, Party) is given. The possibility of bureaucratic power being independent of class power is not considered.

Since Trotsky's death, the workers' state thesis has been further developed by Ernest Mandel. Mandel's view is that the Soviet Union 'does not display any of the *fundamental* aspects of capitalist economy' (Mandel, 1968: 560). He points out that 'primitive accumulation' was achieved by a 'forcible levy' on the consumption of workers and peasants. The distinguishing factor of the process of *capitalist* accumulation is the aim of producing more surplus value. 'Profit remains the purpose and driving force of capitalist production' which in turn is based on competition and the quest for markets. 'It is this competition that determines the *anarchy* of capitalist production.' In the Soviet system, however, Mandel points out that accumulation is for producing *use-values*. It is based on central planning which decides the level and rate of growth of production and accumulation. 'Artificial limitation of production, agricultural Malthusianism, suppression of technical inventions . . . periodical crises of "over-production", partial stoppage of production, or even destruction of part of production . . . are not to be found in the Soviet economy, and this has been so since 1927 . . . for a third of a century' (*ibid*, pp. 561–2. More precisely, nearly half a century in 1975). For Mandel, the Soviet economy has a 'non-capitalist mode of production' but a 'basically bourgeois mode of distribution'. The utilisation of 'profit' and material incentives in the Soviet economy are not, as other state-capitalist theorists and some Maoists have argued, an indication of the persistence of capitalism but should be interpreted as a means of optimising resource utilisation (Mandel, 1969 : 14).

An important political conclusion stems from this analysis : in international politics, states of the Soviet type are to be supported when in conflict against capitalist states. The International Socialism group, on the other hand, has condemned both 'Moscow and Washington'; but as Mandel (1969 : 20) has succinctly pointed out, advocates of the 'state capitalist' theory have no logical basis for supporting the South-Vietnamese Liberation Front (the 'nucleus' of a 'bureaucratic class') and they refused to support North Korea and China against the Americans in the Korean War. They argued that a victory for North Korea would reduce Korea to a bureaucratic pattern of Soviet Russia. . . . At the same time the immediate result of the victory of Stalinism in Korea would be the liquidation of the independent socialist movement and the disorienting of the socialist vanguard . . . we can therefore give no support to either camp since the war will not achieve the declared aims of either side' (V. Karalasingham, 1971 : 78).

According to Mandel, societies modelled on the Soviet type are 'transitional'; they are half-way between capitalism and socialism. They are not socialist because 'socialism means a classless society', and in the USSR there is 'still partial commodity production, not yet universal production for use, there is still money, there are still social conflicts, and there is still a state' (Mandel, 1969 : 17). This formulation brings the workers' state theorists closer to the analysis of Soviet Marxists. There are, however, many differences between them. These followers of Trotsky emphasise the fact that the Soviet Union has not achieved a socialist form of social relations (as distinct from socialist forms of ownership); they point particularly to the 'parasitic role' of the bureaucracy which is a 'monstrous and continually growing social distortion, which in turn becomes the source of malignant growths in society' (Trotsky, 1936 : 236). The bureaucracy stands apart from and is counterposed to the working class and the rank and file of the Party – in contrast to Soviet theory, where there is a unity of interests.

The origins of this lack of congruence are to be found in the backward state of Russia, in the low level of its productive forces and in the undeveloped 'consciousness' of its working class, together with the impact of western imperialism. 'What is non-socialist in the

USSR – extensive social inequality, bureaucratic privilege, lack of self-determination for the producers, etc. – represents a product of the country's *capitalist* past and *capitalist* environment' (Mandel, 1968: 564–5. A combination of these factors, particularly the small working class and the isolation of the USSR after October 1917, enabled a bureaucratic clique to gain control of the country.

Trotsky and Mandel, like Chinese Communists, point to the difficulties of building socialism and to the long time-scale which is involved. Mandel discusses the way in which individual forms of consciousness may continue for thousands of years after the material conditions which give rise to them have gone. He points out that in Europe, 'The peculiar ideas of the Catholic Church, born out of material conditions of feudalism, still have a powerful impact a thousand years after their formation . . .' (Mandel, 1969: 24 n). Trotsky, in discussing the changes which took place in the family under the early Soviet regime (1936: chapter 7), shows that to overcome 'the thousand year old fetters' greater resources and a higher level of culture were required than the Soviet state possessed. This economic and cultural backwardness was responsible for creating 'a cruel reaction' in the form of a retreat from the socialist family in the 1930s. The contradictions in Soviet society do not stem from a mechanistic economic determinism, but are accounted for by the interaction of economic, political and cultural factors. From this point of view, a *political* revolution is necessary to dislodge the degenerate ruling stratum, and this does not require a wider explosion of the social structure and social institutions. Internal developments such as the maturation of the economy, the growing class consciousness of the working class, may result in a regeneration of the Communist Party which is capable of purging itself.

Marxism and Soviet Society

The above discussion of various Marxist explanations of the USSR highlights the flexibility with which Marxist doctrine may be applied. While Marxists in analysing western capitalist or feudal society may disagree about the particulars of these types of society, it can only be considered incredible that in the case of state-socialist society one theory can lead to such completely contradictory conclusions, not merely about aspects of the regime, but about its fundamental character in terms of the Marxist typology. How can we account for these divergent viewpoints? In the first place, any doubts about the sincerity and honesty of the various theorists should be excluded from the analysis. Such an explanation can only be psychologistic and moralistic. It is more profitable, first: to clarify the assumptions on which particular models are dependent; second: to consider the method of analysis which is utilised; and third: to indicate what is valuable about the various viewpoints.

One of the greatest divisions between the various Marxist schools is the extent to which Lenin's development of Marxism is accepted. The rejection of Leninism* by the International Socialism group lies behind much of its argumentation. Its propositions rest on a view of Marxism which emphasises the *level* of development of the productive forces and the need to complete capitalism before beginning socialism. Given the fact that the Soviet Union and other state-socialist societies have not reached the full development of the bourgeois mode, they cannot by definition be 'socialist'. The struggle for socialism is seen to lie primarily (not exclusively) with the proletariat of advanced western societies. It is considered to be impossible to build 'socialism in one country', because the bourgeois order operates on a world scale and will undermine – economically, politically and morally – the social order of one country. Also, Marxist opponents of the form of these societies often reject Lenin's theory of democratic centralism. It is contended by such writers that communist parties cannot *act on* the working class to develop its consciousness but that consciousness develops spontaneously and that a socialist revolution will grow *out of* the working class.

These two assumptions have very important implications for political action in the twentieth century. They entail standing outside the major political upheavals in the Third World in so far as any revolutionary movement is linked to Soviet power or aspires to its model. The general political orientation of Lenin, Stalin and Mao is repudiated. Even the views of Trotsky, at least as far as the Soviet Union is concerned, are rejected. This is not necessarily reprehensible; it may very well be that a return to the classical Marxism of the nineteenth century is desirable and it may also be the case that the destiny of the world proletariat lies in a revolution led by the working class of the advanced industrial societies of Europe and the USA. It is not, however, a Leninist viewpoint.

These objections do not apply to the Chinese Party's analysis, and writers such as Bettelheim and Sweezy believe that a regeneration of the working class (through the Party) may occur in the 'state capitalist' societies. Bettelheim particularly stresses the 'existence of the domination of the proletariat, of the dictatorship of the proletariat', and decentralisation and reliance on the market is opposed. Three objections may be made to these views and these will be taken up more fully later.

First, it is not at all clear whether a cultural revolution like the

*By Lenin*ism*, I mean the adaptation of Lenin's thoughts by the political leaders of state-socialist societies (see Lane: 1974).

Chinese is at all appropriate to the societies of the East European type. Much of the activity of the cultural revolution is meant to break centuries-old habits and to mobilise the people into a frame of mind for social and political development. The countries of Eastern Europe have a quite different social structure and political culture. Even if a mobilising agency, such as the Red Guards, could be found (which is unlikely), the effects of such activity would only create resentment among the population and would not in these conditions sharpen the popular 'consciousness'. Second, it is important to bear in mind here that the historical experience of China and the Soviet Union was quite different. In the latter, the working class played a more direct role in the revolution than it did in China where the revolutionary movement had a strong national liberation element in the struggle against imperialism and foreign invaders. In the Soviet Union, the land was nationalised immediately at the time of the revolution, whereas in China the peasants were given legal right to the land by the first Constitution; unlike China, the Soviet Union never gave compensation for loss of property and has had no class of private capitalists since the end of the New Economic Policy. Hence the social and political context of social change is quite different and must be related to the policies adopted. The economic problems of countries such as the Soviet Union and Czechoslovakia stem from an economy much more advanced and complex than that in China, and the class structure of these societies is more homogeneous than it is in China. In a more economically advanced society, the greater utilisation of a market may be an important step towards socialism. It may function under socialism as a technical device, allocating resources. As long as shortages exist some mechanism must be devised to allocate resources (see Nove: 1972). A market is a device or a mechanism which is appropriate under conditions of scarcity for reconciling demand and supply through the formation of prices. It does not necessarily involve class exploitation. It is possible to make a distinction between the class nature of markets under capitalism and the technical role of markets under socialism. This essential distinction is usually not made by Marxist critics of markets in state-socialist society.

Third, the 'Maoist' line is largely a criticism of post-Stalinist Soviet policies; it fails to locate any dynamic of class structure or institutional change which is significantly different from the Stalin era. In other words, there does not seem to have been, in this writer's opinion, any *restoration* of capitalist forms. The dynamics of Soviet society have been largely a projection forward of processes started in the Stalin era. The role of the Party, the state machinery, the system of distribution of rewards are developments of the system existing under Stalin rather than fundamental new departures. Indeed, it is under Mao that the leading role of the Party has (at least for a time) been challenged, and that an alliance between the leader and other social groups (the army and youth) has replaced the hegemony of the Party (see below, chapter 6).

The political and social order I have defined as 'state socialism' is not by any means an ideal socialist society and the claim that it is a workers' state undergoing the transition to socialism seems to be a more accurate description of its character than that either of Soviet Marxism or state capitalism. While one may not *complete* the building of socialism in one country, there is no reason why it may not be *commenced* in one country. The Soviet model is a positive example of planned economic advance to societies which are about to undergo rapid industrialisation. The notion of the workers' state and the Soviet Marxist thesis concerning the property relations of Soviet socialism would seem to me to be irrefutable. But critics who concentrate on exposing bourgeois forms of distribution do so at the expense of ignoring the socialist relations of production. The view adopted here is that the Soviet Union is only partially 'socialist' and that the contradictions in Soviet society are of more importance than is granted by Soviet theorists. The political control inherent in a bureaucracy in a Weberian sense, and the continuation of practices having their roots in bourgeois and feudal modes of production into the socialist stage would appear to be most important.

The International Marxist Group's analysis, however, is also deficient in that it exaggerates the primary role of the 'bureaucracy' in the degeneration of the USSR. While there is no doubt that bureaucratism does militate against democratic control, this must not detract from the fact that centralised administration has been a major instrument in ensuring industrialisation and social change. Also, the forms of political participation developed in the USSR are not completely meaningless and contain some genuine forms of public involvement. The Soviet Union has developed methods of ensuring the commitment of the population to the political order and of mobilising the masses. The dynamics of Soviet society cannot be explained by the bureaucracy seeking to exploit the working class and to promote its own wealth, privilege and political power. The overriding values are derived from Marxist theory, which provides an ideological motivation to build an industrial society leading to a classless society. The bureaucracy has an ideological commitment which conditions its activity; it is limited by the social expectations of the working class. Such conditioning factors make the bureaucracy act in a way quite different from a profit-maximising bourgeoisie, or from the state in a western capitalist system.

One of the most unsatisfactory parts of the Soviet and of workers' state theories is the explanation of the process by which a socialist order degenerated. The Soviet analysis of the 'cult of personality' during the Stalin era is particularly weak. In this respect International Socialism's explanation is a logical one – the society concerned was *never* socialist and therefore no degeneration could have taken place. It seems clear that a formal Marxist explanation is inadequate. An interesting point of departure is suggested by Mao Tse-Tung, Trotsky and Mandel when they consider the influences of cultural factors in shaping the structure of transitional societies. Even with a fundamental change in property relations Mao Tse-Tung recognises that it might take five or ten generations to build a socialist society. Clearly the roles of the superstructure of ideas, of the family and of political culture have a determining influence on the formation of the personality which have not been sufficiently considered by many Marxist writers. Mandel's distinction between the socialist form of production and the bourgeois form of distribution indicates that it may be apposite to utilise concepts developed in relation to bourgeois forms of society to aid our understanding of the structure and processes of state socialism. This will be attempted later. But before turning to consider in empirical detail state-socialist societies, it is necessary to complete our study of typologies of state-socialist society by consideration of the notion of 'totalitarianism'.

2

Non-Marxist
Meta-Theories

Totalitarianism as an Explanation of State-Socialist Society
In the Western world, 'totalitarianism' is by far the most pervasive
and politicallly important interpretation of the USSR and other
states modelled on her. It is considered here to be a meta-theory, that
is, a set of orientating statements to society. Its role, especially during
the Cold War, has often been as a kind of 'counter ideology' to that
of Soviet Marxism. It has provided a legitimation of the foreign
policies of western capitalist states in their confrontation with the
Soviet Union and her allies. But totalitarianism purports to be more
than a description of Soviet-type societies. It is held by some writers
to be a phenomenon of the development of urban industrial society
applicable in an extreme form to Nazi Germany and to states of the
Soviet type. This viewpoint, adopted by C. J. Friedrich and Leonard
Schapiro, by definition puts liberal democratic states (such as Britain
and the USA) at the opposite end of a continuum from state-
socialist states (such as the USSR). In the former the individual has
certain 'private' areas of autonomy which are absent in the latter.
Other writers, such as Herbert Marcuse, go even further and regard
totalitarianism as a more general tendency of modern society resulting from class exploitation coupled to modern technology and including both Western capitalist society and what such writers sometimes refer to as the 'state-capitalism' of the USSR. In this book, we
shall consider both the model associated with the work of Friedrich
and Brzezinski (1965) and the more generally applicable theory of
Marcuse (1968) and Ellul (1965).*

A totalitarian social system has been defined by Friedrich (Friedrich, Curtis and Barber, 1969: 136) as 'a system of autocratic rule
for realising totalist intentions under modern technical and political

*See also a Soviet dissident version, below, p. 111.

conditions'. Friedrich's definition emphasises control by the ruling elite. Arendt draws our attention to the other side of the coin by discussing the state of the masses. For her, totalitarianism is 'the permanent domination of each single individual in each and every sphere of life' (Arendt, 1966: 326). Literature on utopias such as *Brave New World* and *1984* vividly brings out the fact that only the technological conditions of modern society allow totalitarianism to occur through three major forms of control; in Friedrich's words – 'a totalist ideology, a party reinforced by a secret police, and monopoly control of the three major forms of inter-personal confrontation in an industrial society [weapons, communications, and work]' (Friedrich, 1972: 251).

Unlike Marxism, which attributes political power to the owners of the means of production, totalitarianism is a theory which gives to politics (in the shape of Party/state control of the means of manipulation and coercion) a place of supremacy in the social system. For totalitarian theorists, police terror and the concentration camp have a similar status to that of the relations of production for Marxists. So much has the study of politics dominated the study of totalitarianism, that there has been little sociological study of the concept. This is reflected in the distinction between political science and political sociology made by Bendix and Lipset in 1957: 'Political science starts with the state and examines how it affects society, while political sociology starts with society and examines how it affects the state, i.e. the formal institutions for the distribution and exercise of power' (1957: 87). As it was generally held that in totalitarian countries there was by definition scarcely any influence on 'the state' by society, it followed that there could in theory be no such thing as a political sociology of Soviet-type societies.

The Scope and Values of Rule

In analysing the concept of totalitarianism we may distinguish between scope and values. The *scope* of activity of the polity involves its penetration into all areas of social life and the breakdown of the boundaries between them and the polity. The scope of activity is predicated on the *values* held by the rulers which in totalitarian theory are essentially malevolent and involve the exploitation of the masses. In a totalitarian state, the ends of the dominant ruling class or elite require for their realisation the total subservience of the population and the complete subordination of other goals, such as individual freedom, and values (such as found in law or religion). Theorists supporting the totalitarian theory deny that this ends-means relationship is legitimate as it would be in parliamentary democracies in times of world war. Rather they point to the actual exploitation of the masses by the ruling elite or ruling class which does not seek to provide conditions for human liberation but to perpetuate and institutionalise its own particular privilege.

Hence totalitarianism is not only concerned with the totality of political penetration but implies a form of 'false consciousness' on the part of the masses who may accept the totalitarian state and a form of exploitation on the part of the rulers. This distinction enables us to differentiate between statism and totalitarianism. In the former, there is much state activity which furthers human development, whereas under totalitarianism all-inclusive state activity denies the goal of human liberation, and the values of the political rulers are malevolent. Hence totalitarian theorists overcome the apparent differences in ideology and form of ownership between Fascist (or even capitalist) and state-socialist regimes by pointing to the similarities of wide state control linked to a common manipulation of the masses to the benefit of the rulers. Given this common feature, the institutional arrangements and legitimating ideologies between types of totalitarian society may differ. Applied to the Soviet Union, totalitarianism is said to be furthered by one dominant political party under the command of the leader, more or less complete state control of the productive forces, means of violence and communication and an 'official' ideology (Marxism-Leninism) which promises, in an unspecified future, a society of human perfection. Implicit in the writing of theorists of totalitarianism is the view that the process of politics excludes interest groups but involves a conscious 'massification' of the population, either through coercion and terror or by manipulation. This massification, however, is not complete and certain 'islands of separateness' (the family, churches, universities, the arts) (Friedrich and Brzezinski, 1965 : 279–329) continue which are not fully penetrated by the political elites; these are small, isolated and, as it were, unconnected with the happenings in the main stream of society.

What remains unclear in the writing of writers such as Arendt and Friedrich is precisely the ends to which the policies of totalitarian leaders are directed. Apparently, maintaining their own power with the maximum degree of massification is the major goal. As Burrowes has aptly pointed out : 'It is possible to read *The Origins of Totalitarianism* without getting the slightest inkling that the political events and processes that are described in detail were paralleled by – much less systematically related to – the rapid and radical modernization of most aspects of Soviet society' (Burrowes, 276). Individualism and pluralism are values held in high esteem by such theorists but they fail to consider whether policies based on these values are practical under the circumstances which face countries experiencing early industrialisation (such as the USSR and China) or facing internal economic ruin (such as Weimar Germany). Also, an historical and comparative dimension is often lacking in their work: they fail to acknowledge particular periods in the history of parliamentary societies when the masses were (or are) severely exploited by their ruling classes (say during the enclosures in England) nor do they take account of the ways in which minorities may be oppressed in plural societies. Individualism and pluralist political and social arrangements do not necessarily promote equality and the development of all social groups: they may institutionalise the privileges of some and the backwardness of others (say, the Blacks in the United States). More importantly, this group of totalitarian writers fails to recognise that the distribution of property and political power is so uneven in liberal-democratic states that some sections of the population may also be grossly exploited. Theorists of totalitarianism fail to say how the interests of the masses may be articulated under that system, how they may be channelled into political change: they have a pessimistic view of man, not only of the incumbents of power but also of the masses.

The Role of Technology

As noted above, totalitarianism is seen by some commentators to be a form of political rule appropriate only to an advanced and technological society. The classic study by Friedrich and Brzezinski (1965: 24) makes explicit this relationship: '. . . totalitarian societies appear to be merely exaggerations, but nonetheless logical exaggerations of the technological state of modern society'. This idea is generalised by other theorists to apply also to western capitalist-type societies. Jacques Ellul, for example, has emphasised the ways in which 'technique' is ever expanding, being extended to all domains of life and becoming ultimately common to capitalist and communist states (1965: 284). Ellul sees 'technique' as the independent causal factor. Marcuse, moreover, adds to technological dominance a bureaucratic element leading to political domination. In an advanced industrial society, asserts Marcuse, 'The productive apparatus tends to become totalitarian to the extent to which it determines not only the socially needed occupations, skills and attitudes but also individual needs and aspirations. . . . Technology serves to institute new, more effective and more pleasant forms of social control and social cohesion' (Marcuse, 1968: 13). Capitalist and communist-type systems tend to converge to a totalitarian type characterised by their technological character. The imposition of rationality through complex organisations and scientific management is regarded by Marcuse as an insidious form of political domination pervading the fabric of society and alienating man (see Habermas, 1971 : 81ff). As the Soviet Union develops its industrial base, Marcuse sees the 'underlying population' becoming 'more firmly . . . tied to the various ruling bureaucracies'. From this viewpoint, then, the management of advanced industrial society through bureaucratic formations and ideology negates democratic control (either socialist or liberal) of the process of society. The industrial process excludes any ideology which does not promote it : '. . . in both camps non-operational ideas are non-behavioural and submissive. . . . Thus emerges a pattern of *one-dimensional thought and behaviour* in which ideas, aspirations and objectives that, by their content, transcend the established universe of discourse and action are either repelled or reduced to terms of this universe' (Marcuse, 1968 : 28, 27).

At first sight it might appear plausible that the technological conditions of modern society make state control of the individual more possible than in a non-technocratic society. Political control in a pre-technocratic society is much more diffuse than it needs to be in an advanced society. The development of large-scale economic and political units requires integrating institutions unknown in pre-technocratic societies. It is true that only an advanced industrial state can make and deliver nuclear warheads, whereas in pre-technocratic societies individual men had more equal access to weapons. Similarly, control of media, of communication and of the economy is of a different scale in a modern society, compared to a pre-modern one. These different forms of constraint, however, may be misleading, for other things may affect the individual in a pre-technological society : traditional forms of control such as religon or the economic power of feudal lords may act as compulsively on the individual as does the state in a technological society. Slavery is a traditional, not a modern institution. Wittfogel (1957) has argued the case that total power may be wielded in Asiatic or Oriental types of society. The character of the political order described by Wittfogel – the lack of balance between political institutions and the ineffective 'checks' of 'mores and beliefs' – would appear to be similar to the kind of political regime that writers such as Arendt and Friedrich have in mind (see Wittfogel, 1957 : chapter 4). The case is not being argued here for a pre-modern form of totalitarianism : rather attention is being drawn to the fact that forms of extreme oppression of the masses have existed in societies at a relatively low technological level. It is certainly not a self-evident proposition that such societies of an intermediate type are inherently more pluralist, have more enlightened rulers and a freer population than those with an advanced technology. Indeed, a case may be made that in modern industrial societies the problem of ensuring the compliance of the population to a ruling group is more difficult than in pre-modern ones.

In non-industrial societies the social structure is segmented and the units are homologous. That is, social units grow by duplicating each other and institutions (particularly the family) are multi-functional. Political control over the heads of kin groupings, there-fore, ensures the allegiance of family groups. In modern industrial societies, segmentalism gives way to structural differentiation in-volving division of activities in a society in a functional way. The evolution of social institutions entails splitting up the functions per-formed in simple societies by the family, and their replacement by institutions such as the educational system and the economy operating relatively autonomously. In these circumstances, not only economic classes but also professional groups, such as scientists, writers, teachers and doctors, form their own view of the public good and articulate their particular interests. Paradoxically, Marcuse's own work is a good example of the non-totalitarian nature of modern capitalism: the penalty for such dissent as his against the system in the Middle Ages would have been death. Ruling groups become dependent on the various functional groups and have to take account of their interests. It becomes more difficult, not less, for the ruling groups to maintain effective control of the population. Com-munications, for example, are international and transcend geo-graphical areas and political boundaries. Universal literacy which characterises industrial states gives far greater access to science, culture and 'deviant ideas' than that known in pre-modern society. In practice, it is impossible for governments to encapsulate their own citizens and it is notoriously difficult for them to root out either political or criminal deviance.

Criticisms of the Totalitarian Syndrome

The discussion so far has been relatively theoretical. Let us now indicate in the light of empirical knowledge some of the deficiencies of totalitarian theory as applied to the six 'basic' features of totali-tarianism spelled out by Friedrich and Brzezinski (1956: 9–10). These are: an official ideology embracing 'all vital aspects of man's existence'; a single mass Party typically led by one man; a system of terroristic police control; a technologically conditioned monopoly of all means of effective mass communication; a similar monopoly of effective armed combat; and central direction and control of the en-tire economy. Firstly, it is doubtful whether ideology in fact does embrace 'all vital aspects of man's existence'. Marxism-Leninism, for instance, has been shown to be largely redundant when it comes to explanation in the natural sciences though Lysenkoism is a notable exception (see D. Bell, 1966) and the actual structure and process of social institutions, such as the family or industrial enterprises, cannot be understood solely by reference to the 'official ideology'. Secondly, the 'dictator' is no longer a supreme ruler in the USSR. In fact, one might suggest that the British Prime Minister has greater capabilities for political leadership (though a narrower scope) than has the present General Secretary of the Communist Party of the Soviet Union, who is limited in his ability to select the membership of the Politbureau. Thirdly, the notion of 'terroristic police control' utilised against 'arbitrarily selected classes of the population' is not a feature of contemporary state socialism. While terror has been a political process in such societies it has not been institutionalised. Fourthly, the control of communication is not absolute; the 'underground' press, oral communication and foreign sources of news are important alternatives to the officially sponsored agencies. It must be conceded, however, that the media of communication are less open than they are in liberal-democratic societies. Fifthly, the monopoly of the 'means of effective armed combat' would appear to be nothing special to the USSR but a characteristic of all modern states – except perhaps the USA where the persistence of a 'frontier mentality' gives to individuals the right to own firearms. Sixthly, central control and direction of the 'entire economy' would appear to be a major distinction, though in practice this is limited by the existence of a labour market, a 'free market' in certain agricultural products and by a gradual introduction of 'market' elements in the economy to complement centralised planning.

Criticisms of a more general nature may also be made. The assumption that political elites are malevolent in intention is not universally true. It might be argued that the principal aim of the Soviet political elite has been to industrialise the USSR; Party hegemony and state control have been means to this end, rather than simply being used to further the interests of the political elites. The motor forces controlling social and economic change should be conceived of as central to the social system of the USSR (see Churchward, 1967). The wider extent of government activity and control is a major distinction compared to capitalist countries. Here this difference is considered to be a form of statism rather than totalitarianism (compare Hollander, 1973). The notion of total domination by technology is overdrawn. Technology itself is controlled by men and may be utilised not only to enslave but also to create conditions of freedom. Under state socialism, the absence of production for private profit and of a market system playing a major role in allocating resources allows for the greater utilisation of technology for beneficial human ends rather than for private profit. The techno-logical forms of control do not in fact result in either total or uniform political forms of dominance: Marcuse's own work would not be available at all (let alone in a cheap paperback edition) if his analysis was correct; in the USSR, the existence of 'dissident' groups is com-pletely counter to the totalitarian view.

Theorists of totalitarianism provide no alternative; they see no hope of man controlling his own destiny: it is a pessimistic theory of man. Marcuse sees change originating from 'the subtsratum of out-casts and outsiders', but it seems most unrealistic to expect that sig-nificant political change will come from this quarter. The orientation of the totalitarian viewpoint is one of unchangeability in the political and social system. As Chalmers Johnson (1970) has pointed out, the model does not rule out change, but the alterations in the system are relatively minor involving changes of leadership, or the mobilisation of the population to meet various crises such as wars. Johnson lists four types of change not allowed for by the model: first, those in the political system involving a movement from a dictatorship to col-lective leadership; second, the decline of terror as an instrument of compliance; third, changes in the economic system from a centralised command economy to 'market socialism'; and fourth, changes from the status of 'satellite' to 'client state' or to a 'national Communist state' (1970: 3–4). Totalitarian theory postulates a static form of society, whereas state-socialist societies have been characterised by rapid social and economic change. Structural differentiation in an advanced society creates a group structure and the individuation of interests not only among the population but also among the elite. The notion that the USSR is ruled by an omnipotent and omniscient leader or a unitary party elite is unrealistic.

Finally, it should also be noted that there is an incipient contradic-tion between those countries which are seen as being most totalitarian and their technological character. Stalin's Russia, for instance, was predominantly a rural and agricultural country and Communist China is one of the most poorly endowed technologically and at pre-sent is nearest to fulfilling some of the requirements of totalitarianism. If the level of technology is the defining characteristic, then modern Germany and Italy should be more totalitarian than Hitler's Ger-many or Mussolini's Italy. The kind of political domination by the state that many totalitarian theorists have in mind would seem to be more appropriate to societies which are *developing* an advanced mode of production (and this might include certain African and Asian states).

The view of the author is that no modern society is totalitarian in the sense of the state exercising total control as discussed above. State power has never been all-inclusive as totalitarian theorists have assumed. Even under Stalin, the state had insufficient resources to penetrate widely to all areas of Soviet society. In the countryside and particularly in the non-Russian republics where the Party was relatively weak, traditional ways of life were less disturbed and less subject to political control. With the maturation of the Soviet Union as an industrial state, social differentiation of the population has developed to such an extent that 'political penetration' cannot be considered total. Perhaps most important of all, the *institutionalisation* of the kind of political power wielded by Stalin cannot be taken for granted as assumed by writers advocating the totalitarian syndrome. As the Soviet Union advances in time towards 1984, its features become less like those depicted in *1984*. The substantive difference between the Soviet Union under Stalin and today is that in the earlier period political activity was subordinated to the goals of economic development and the maintenance of Soviet power. Since the fall of Stalin, the Soviet Union has become more institutionally differentiated, the number of goals which are pursued by the government has increased and the political system has moved from ruthlessly pursuing a limited number of goals to aggregating many interests. The political style has moved from a reliance on terror and ideology to methods involving manipulation and material incentives as under capitalism.

In answer to 'technocratic totalitarians', such as Marcuse, it is held here that there are important differences between the Soviet Union and liberal-democratic states such as the United States and Great Britain. While undoubtedly state-socialist and capitalist societies have much in common, they are not the same type of society. At a fairly superficial level, the width of the activity of the government apparatus is greater in the Soviet Union than it is in advanced modern capitalist states, and the fact that the industrial order is directly controlled by the government has important ramifications which affect the nature of the social system. Differences stemming from the party system are exaggerated by liberal theorists. While ruling communist parties are monopolistic, the dominant political parties in western democratic states do not differ much over *major* questions concerning the arrangement of capitalist societies : while there are important differences between them, no large political party in 'stable democratic' countries can be seen as a threat to the integrity of capitalist society. It is not inconceivable that the differences which manifest themselves between, say, the British Parliamentary Labour and Conservative parties could be accommodated within one single political party. What does influence the structure of the state-socialist social system is the process of party penetration and party control through the *nomenklatura* (discussed below, p. 78) of important positions in all institutions of Soviet society. The only analogous process to this in capitalist societies is ascription on the basis of the ownership of private property. This points to another major difference between capitalism and state socialism which is obscured by theorists of totalitarianism : the fact that political power is largely influenced by private economic interests under capitalism, whereas the analogous institution is the Communist Party under socialism. The *possibilities* for popular participation and control of political power would appear to be greater under the latter rather than the former system because control of economic power in principle is public, not private. Both Marcuse and Friedrich emphasise the manipulative role of ideology. While there are undoubtedly forms of ideological manipulation in capitalist and state-socialist societies, this should not blind one to important differences in the value systems pertaining to these different types of society.

The approach adopted by the present writer is that the Soviet political apparatus, like that of other state-socialist societies, has mobilised the population to a greater extent than is the case in parliamentary democracies even in times of war. Historically, the Soviet Union and other communist states are distinguished by the pursuit of the goal of industrial development to the exclusion of other competing goals. The mobilisation of the population is closely linked to industrial growth : the ends which the elites seek to achieve are associated with the development of an advanced industrial society. Thus it is not true to assert that the relationship between mass and elite is predominantly exploitive. State power in the USSR has been concerned with a form of *developmental mobilisation*; it has been used to change the rural character of the population to an urban one, to enforce a high level of saving, to raise the level of industrialisation, to induce values of work discipline and to introduce both mass literacy and a comprehensive system of education. Such mobilisation has geared the population to the demands of social change. While these tasks are to some extent shared by other non-communist developing societies, they differ in that the Communist rulers nationalised much of industry and farming is collectivised. It is not denied that oppression of individuals and groups has taken place (and has occurred illegitimately) but it is contended that force is an intrinsic element of revolutionary change, and is utilised in an attempt (which has not been completely successful) to ensure societal integration and the kind of social and economic change desired by the political elites. Also, central control has been employed to break down traditional privileges and to create greater opportunities and equality for groups traditionally underprivileged – as, for example, the peasants during the Cultural Revolution in China or the indigenous population in the Central Asian Republics of the USSR. Rather than placing the USSR among the states who deny welfare to the population, the effects of the activity of the political rulers have increased welfare: compared to the situation under pre-communist rulers there is greater economic and educational equality, a longer life expectancy and far greater social and political stability. One other major political difference which has to be brought out when comparing the communist form of modernisation process to other forms of directed social change is the saliency of its belief system: comparatively, communist beliefs are held more seriously by the political elites and a conscious effort is made to indoctrinate the population. The elites are less corrupt and more altruistic than the ones they replaced and those to be found in nationalist-type modernisation regimes.

Convergence to a Common Type of Industrial Society

One variant of totalitarianism (that of Marcuse) is a type of convergence thesis: it is postulated that with the attrition of democratic participation and with the demise of the market in the economy, the United States becomes more like the USSR; at the same time, the rise of technology in the USSR with its attendant growth of bureaucracy and the ideology of technical rationality entails this country becoming more like the USA. There is a double convergence towards totalitarianism. Yet another and perhaps more widely recognised convergence thesis is that which posits the view that there is an evolutionary tendency for societies to converge to a single type of *industrial* society. Most of the comparisons which are made show the similarities between the USSR and the USA. Sorokin (1944 : 26) as early as 1944 stressed the similarity of psychological, cultural and social values between the USA and the USSR, and in 1949 Parsons (1964a: 333) described 'capitalist and socialist industrialisms . . . as variants of a single fundamental type'. More recently Clark Kerr (1962 : 46), Galbraith (1967) and Parsons (1960, 1971) have attempted to develop the notion of an 'industrial society' in which the homogenisation of the social structure is brought out. One implication of this theory is that Marxist-type analyses as discussed above are irrelevant to the understanding of the structure and dynamics of industrial societies.

The convergence thesis is much more than a cataloguing of similarities. We may define convergence as a process by which heterogeneous cultures, characterising different societies, develop and change in the direction of greater likeness one to another until eventually they adopt similar arrangements for the performance of important social functions. This definition involves three major assumptions. First, that there is a 'process of change': convergence is concerned with the social dynamics of change, not with the description of a static state. Second, that societies remain relatively independent and autonomous as behavioural entities; they do not merge into a common single behavioural unit – socialist and capitalist states retain distinct personalities. Third, that with the passage of time they become in important ways more alike; it is not a necessary condition that the converging societies become identical in all respects.

		USA		
		Becoming different	*Remaining the same*	*Becoming similar*
		1	2	3
	Becoming different	Double divergence	Single divergence	——
USSR		4	5	6
	Remaining the same	Single divergence	Static	Single convergence
		7	8	9
	Becoming similar	——	Single convergence	Double convergence

Figure 1. Single and double forms of divergence and convergence*

It would be misleading to assume that convergence is a simple concept and much of the criticism of it is misplaced because the implications of the notion are not understood. Excluding the possibility of parallel change, Fig. 1 shows six possible combinations of change between two societies: these range from double divergence (box 1), through single divergence (boxes 2 and 4), single convergence (boxes 6 and 8) and double convergence (box 9). Discussion of convergence, then, must distinguish which institutions or processes are becoming alike and the respects in which each society is changing. For it is possible that there may be divergence and convergence occurring simultaneously.

The theory which underpins the views of many convergence writers is evolutionism. The clearest recent statement of this position has been put by Talcott Parsons. His thesis is that world history has moved through three stages: primitive, intermediate and modern (1966: 26). The fundamental criterion of evaluating change in these societies is that of 'evolving adaptive capacity' (1971: 26–7). This is a much wider concept than the Marxist notion of the mode of

*Parallel change is ignored.

production. As in Marxism, changes in the mode of production, which make 'a wider range of resources . . . available to social units', is one important element. Parsons, however, applies the notion of evolving adaptive capacity to structural differentiation and value generalisation. By this he means that a social system at a more advanced stage of development has by definition more highly differentiated and specialised components enabling it to cope. Similarly, changes need to take place in the integrating mechanisms to permit the 'inclusion' of the new units into a societal community; new forms of solidarity need to be devised and changes in value generalisation are necessary to legitimate the new units. Thus, according to Parsons, the development of the productive forces (the movement from stone to metal, for instance) is dependent on adaptations in the value, political and social systems. Without such corresponding changes, evolution will not occur and society may collapse and may revert to a more primitive state.

Parsons explicitly, and other 'convergence' writers often implicitly, assume that world history is moving different societies to copy the structural and functional features of American society. 'The United States' new type of societal community, more than any other single factor, justifies our assigning it the lead in the latest phase of modernisation. . . . American society has gone farther than any comparable large-scale society in its dissociation from the older ascriptive inequalities and [towards] the institutionalisation of a basically egalitarian pattern' (1971: 114). The United States as the most advanced industrial society becomes a model for the rest of the world. Parsons seems clear that the possibilities of creating an essentially different kind of society are limited. One of the most important consequences of the increasing division of labour is the necessary development of social and political differentiation which are not compatible with totalitarianism. Parsons argues that communist societies are likely to become more like those of the western world because of the 'centrifugal' effect on the social system of differentiation in the economy, science and the arts. 'It can . . . be definitely said that the further this differentiation of the social structure proceeds, the more difficult it becomes to press it into the mould of a rigid line of authority from the top down' (1964b: 397–8). Or as Kerr has rather dramatically described it: 'The empire of industrialism will embrace the whole world; and such similarities as it decrees will penetrate the outermost points of its sphere of influence and its sphere comes to be universal' (Kerr: 46).

As far as the convergence of the USA and the USSR are concerned, box 8 (Fig. 1) would appear to be most apposite to Parsons's model. Parsons stresses the growing similarities at the functional level and he has made it explicit that the institutional arrangements, particularly the organisation of the state and political institutions, may differ between the USA and the USSR. He distinguishes 'between a type [of industrial society] which does and . . . which does not rely most heavily on political agency in the developmental and industrial management contexts'. The Soviet Union is the paradigmatic example of such reliance whereas the USA and Great Britain are at the other extreme. 'The broad ideological division between "capitalistic" and "socialistic" models of the industrial society reflect the ways in which the role of government is differentially conceived' (Parsons, 1960: 21). Galbraith, however, stresses the fact that 'planning must replace the market' for the efficient operation of the industrial system in the West (Galbraith, 1967: 389). He sees the growth of enterprise autonomy in both systems – independence from the bureaucracy under state socialism being analogous to the 'exclusion of the capitalist from effective power' in Western societies (*ibid*, 390).

Industrialism

The idea of an 'industrial society', though not new, was articulated most forcefully in the 1960s and became counterposed to the dominant Soviet interpretation of Marxism, which through the spokesmen of world communist parties analysed the world in terms of a rather rigid kind of economic determinism, positing the objective class struggle and the economic crises of capitalism. Opponents of this view put forward a battery of arguments. First, it was denied that the abolition of the capitalist class in the Russian October Revolution had led to a qualitatively superior type of civilisation (socialism) and that in fact the economic, political and social characteristics of the Soviet Union had much in common with those of advanced capitalist states. The political international *detente* between Soviet communism and American capitalism, it was pointed out, is further evidence that 'irreconcilable contradictions' do not stem from the class system of capitalism and socialism. Secondly, the traditional Marxian argument concerning the crash of the capitalist economic system appeared to be no longer true; the general economic stabilisation of the capitalist world seemed to be a permanent feature of post-Keynesian economics, and this helped to explain the decline of overt class struggle in the capitalist west.

The eased atmosphere of international relations created a congenial political environment for the reception of such ideas. In the early 1950s in the West, the ideological climate would not have ensured the widespread dissemination and acceptance of the convergence thesis; a similar state of affairs persists to the present day in the USSR where such views are at least officially violently opposed. Also western social science was producing empirical studies which were favourable to an industrial society analysis: Weberian and structural-functional analysis largely excludes class conflict analysis.

What, then, is the evidence to which such convergence theorists refer? Parallels were perceived in the highly developed division of labour giving rise to a hierarchy of statuses and political, economic and social elites. Structural differentiation, it was argued, led to a decline of the roles of the family and to the development of specialised institutions, such as the educational system and the industrial enterprise. The value system of an industrial system puts great emphasis on the instrumentality of work, a striving for mastery of the environment, for individual advancement and status differentiation. Large-scale production required central planning, state control and greater power to technocrats at the plant level. The economy is dominated by *manufacturing* industry, the semi-skilled worker and engineer; economic growth is a major objective (Bell, 1974: 117). The radical's conception of a utopian order, of a higher form of democracy, of a classless society, it was held, had largely met with no response from the masses, and intellectuals were becoming absorbed within the framework of their own society (Bell, 1961: 398). Convergence theorists said that a value system linked to the exigencies of industrialism had replaced the utopianism of revolutionaries and radicals. Politics had become more an affair of 'managing' an industrial society than the expression of the class struggle. The bureaucratic system of organisation with salaried officials bound by rules and promoting specific goals had replaced the individualist entrepreneur's pursuit of profit and the commissar's strivings for a classless society. With the development of an urban culture social relations also change. The anonymity of the city with its specialised functional arrangements (industrial and residential segregation, pop culture and mass media) become symbols of urban life transcending geographical, ideological and political divisions.

Research on the Soviet Union suggested that many of those developments were true for that country. Both Inkeles and Bauer (1959) and Brzezinski and Huntington (1964) in books concerned with the social and political system of the Soviet Union report similarities concerning values, institutions and social stratification (see also Lane, 1971). Even in the study of the political systems some commentators have pointed to similarities. This view concerning the politics of Eastern Europe has been put by Ionescu: 'No society, and especially no contemporary society, is so politically underdeveloped as not to contain, and reproduce within itself, the perennial conflict of power. No contemporary society can, on the one hand, run all the complex activities of the state, political, cultural, social and economic, exclusively, by its own ubiquitous and omniscient servants, without collaboration and bargains with, or checks by, other interest groups' (Ionescu, 3–4). This assumes that in state-socialist societies the process of social differentiation results in systems of exchange between interest groups. Such writers then recognise structural divergence (in the organisation of political parties and parliaments) but point to functional similarities.

Criticisms of Convergence
These views have precipitated a reaction from some sociologists. The most notable opponent of the industrial society thesis is Goldthorpe who in a celebrated article argued that social stratification and economic order are subject to '*political* regulation' and that totalitarianism and industrialism may coexist. In a crucial passage he asserts: 'The experience of Soviet society can be taken as indicating that the structural and functional imperatives of an industrial order are not so stringent as to prevent quite wide variations in patterns of social stratification, nor to prohibit the systematic manipulation of social inequalities by a regime commanding modern administrative resources and under no constraints from an organised opposition or rule of law' (Goldthorpe, 657–8). Goldthorpe argues specifically against the convergence thesis as it applies to social stratification. He considers three major propositions: differentiation, consistency, mobility. After considering developments in these areas in western societies, Goldthorpe concludes that empirical findings do not substantiate convergence. With regard to differentiation, he denies that there is any 'process in industrialism' which ensures a 'continuing egalitarian trend'. By 'consistency', Goldthorpe refers to the tendency for the relative position of persons and groups to be the same or similar in different industrial societies. Against this he argues that status does not automatically follow changes in economic position, and thus the achievement of 'middle incomes' does not result in ' "middle class" ways of life or of "middle class" status'. He also argues that 'occupational roles with similar economic rewards may in some instances be quite differently related to the exercise of authority'. Lastly, Goldthorpe takes issue with the proposition of convergence theory that mobility in industrial societies is high, that it is dependent on achievement rather than ascription and that educational systems are crucial in the allocation process. Goldthorpe contends that, in fact, industrial societies differ considerably when the range and frequency of mobility are taken into consideration. Patterns of social mobility cannot be understood, he argues, 'simply in terms of

occupational structure', for educational and cultural values have important effects on the system of stratification (*ibid*, 654–5).

In reply to Goldthorpe it may be pointed out that many of his strictures would be accepted by many 'convergence' writers and do not add up to a convincing case against the proposition (see Dunning and Hopper, 1966). The Parsonian model outlined above makes it quite clear that political regulation in the Soviet Union has given and does give shape to different institutional forms. Goldthorpe draws largely on the work of Inkeles and Bauer (1958) to substantiate his points concerning the Soviet Union. This study, however, refers in many places to the ways in which industrial society develops its own logic and transcends political cultures, though these writers do bring out the ways in which the state subordinates individuals to it. They say that the totalitarian model denies 'the validity of a private sphere of life as against the complete or *total* subordination of the individual and institutions to the purpose of the state . . .' (Inkeles and Bauer, 385). It is in this context that they make clear that : 'The distinctive features of Soviet totalitarianism have for so long commanded our attention that we have lost our awareness of an equally basic fact. The substratum on which the distinctive Soviet features are built is after all a large-scale industrial order which shares many features in common with the large-scale industrial order in other national states of Europe and indeed Asia' (Inkeles and Bauer, 383). The useful service which this book provides is to highlight the fact that state-socialist society is different in *some* but not *all* respects to that of capitalism.

Critics of the industrial society thesis are open to the charge that they knock down a theory of 'convergence' that only a simplistic 'convergence theorist' would put forward. What is at issue is not whether any two or more societies are 'the same', but whether they are becoming more alike and in what respects they are becoming alike. What such theorists stress is that compared to other *types of society* (such as ancient or feudal) 'an industrial society must at some time have given special emphasis to the development of the economy and hence have accorded to the economy a place of special prominence in the structure of the society' (Parsons, 1960 : 13). An industrial society is distinguished by the fact that in the mastery of the environment, economic considerations and political mobilisation of resources have a primacy over other considerations (pleasure, religion, personality interests, integration) (Parsons, 1960 : 13). This does not mean to say that one may not differentiate between main types of industrial society nor does it mean that educational and cultural systems may not influence the nature of the system of stratification.

If the notion that the 'convergence' of industrial societies means that they are alike in all respects then it is clearly an untenable thesis. Such a view is a crude form of technological determinism. In fact, most theorists of convergence admit that there are important modifications and divergencies from an ideal typical model of industrial society. Two kinds of modification may be noted here. First is the fact that the diffusion of technology passes through a *cultural filter*; technology is lodged in different cultural contexts and this results in different forms of social life (Weinberg, 1969: 12). Second, that capitalism works through a more or less pronounced market mechanism and is organised for private profit, whereas under state socialism, industrialism is ordered by the political institutions. Within these limits are to be placed Galbraith's views concerning the strengthening of the role of the technocracy and of the power of the individual production enterprise. A much more realistic approach is to conceive of there being limited forms of convergence in addition to cultural difference and even divergence.

Feldman and Moore (1962: 146) suggest that convergence is limited to some 'core' elements of the industrial system. They regard all industrial systems as having the following:

(a) a factory system of production;
(b) a stratification system based on the division of labour and a hierarchy of skills;
(c) extensive commercialisation of goods and services and their transfer through the market;
(d) educational systems capable of filling the various niches in the occupational and stratification system.

This seems to be a much more realistic approach, but it may be objected that the traits of the system described above are again subject to considerable variation. A 'factory system' may be quite different in various cultural settings (see Dore (1973) on the cultural context of the British and Japanese factory), and the market is not a characteristic of state-socialist systems in the way that it is of capitalist.

Study of modern capitalism and state socialism leads one to conclude that there is no one path for the evolution of industrial societies. Taking the model of convergence outlined above, an important area of divergence between the two societies is on the level of political and civil disorder. This would appear to be on the increase in western capitalist societies while it appears to be low and relatively constant in state-socialist ones. In the economy there is some double convergence: the economy of the USSR is adopting more processes associated with commodity (though not capital) exchange, the USA over time is moving towards greater central co-ordination and control. In other spheres there is some single convergence: the Soviet Union is becoming more urbanised, the family is losing some of its roles – as a work unit on the farm, for instance.

The major drawback of the convergence approach is that it is often separated from a theory of social change. The dynamic class characteristics of societies are either ignored or relegated to a minor place. We must bear in mind that capitalist societies have a class system with two major classes and private firms which are run for profit through a market – which the state seeks to influence – whereas state-socialist societies have a more or less unitary economic class system, with state ownership and central planning. These relations of production provide the dynamics in the two systems. As the actual levels of the productive forces become more equal (through the catching-up of the Soviet Union) it is inevitable that many aspects of the two societies will appear to 'converge' to Feldman and Moore's 'core' elements. The major divergence, however, must be sought in the nature of the class systems and associated property forms of the two types of society: they are a source of latent instability under capitalism but of social consensus under state socialism.

3
A Developmental Approach

We have discussed the various theoretical approaches to the analysis of state-socialist societies and have found them to be lacking in many respects. While each theory provides some valuable insight, none provides us with a model with which we may do justice to the complexity of the kind of society we are studying. We have criticised the Soviet Marxist model because it gives no prominent place to conflict and does not adequately show how under socialism the politics of the society intermesh with the social structure and social change. The state-capitalist and totalitarian approaches clearly emphasise the role of a ruling class and ruling elite respectively. But the former does not satisfactorily define the nature of the ruling class and the latter does not explain the values and motivations of the rulers. Both these theories exaggerate the role of violence and neglect consensus. The industrial society theory brings out the ways in which a common technology influences social institutions such as the educational system; but it lacks a social or class dynamic and glosses over the fact that property classes characterising capitalist society have no counterpart in state-socialist society. The workers' state theory gives prominence to the class nature of Soviet society and brings out the role of values in economic change and social development. Whilst recent thinkers, such as Mandel, have recognised the role of culture and of historical experience, a *sociology* of state-socialist society has not been attempted; the nature of consensus under state socialism is little explored and too many ills of the system are attributed to 'bureaucracy'. In searching for an approach to guide research into the nature of state socialism, we need a model which incorporates culture and values and is sensitive to the role of politics and the nature of the economy. It must also be able to deal with conflict within the parameters of the system – rather than conventional Marxist theory which sees conflict as exploding the society.

It seems to me that it is unrealistic to search for one all-inclusive theory which will 'explain' the various historical trajectories taken by, and the social structures and political processes of, such diverse societies as the USSR, China and Czechoslovakia. Following Dahrendorf (1958: 125–6), it is much more fruitful to distinguish between the epochs in the histories of those societies which were characterised by revolutionary struggle and those concerned, to use their own terms, with the construction of socialism. The revolutionary process seems best explained by the theory of class struggle devised by Marx and applied by Lenin. The revolutions in these societies were class revolutions, and these defined the over-arching values of the societies which the communists sought to create. In the new social system which the political rulers sought to form, these values determined to a large extent the motivational commitments, the forms of social ownership and social control which were encouraged and the political and economic structures which were set up. But they did not do so completely. The values, practices and structures of the pre-revolutionary society continued and these not only existed in conjunction with the new socialist social formation, but also interacted to some extent and shaped the contours of the society. We feel justified in defining state-socialist societies as transitional, between the traditional or capitalist and socialist formations. Many of the problems facing these societies require a more detailed analysis of the 'superstructure' than is conventionally found in Marxist writings. This is because the essentially 'explosive' nature of the class struggle which Marxists point to in pre-socialist societies does not exist in socialist ones, though various forms of conflict do. Mandel has pointed out that many aspects of these societies are similar in character to those found in capitalist societies: for example, the 'bourgeois' form of distribution. It is felt that many aspects of sociological theory developed in relation to capitalist society can usefully be applied to the state-socialist. Many of the deficiencies of these approaches to *capitalist* society are irrelevant when socialist societies are considered. One of the major criticisms of contemporary structural functional analysis made by Marxists and others is that the model excludes class-conflict analysis; it is also said that there is an inherent circularity of reasoning in the functionalist argument. These criticisms are less applicable to our study because we recognise the unitary class nature of state-socialist society and its domination by the values of the Communist Party. We are also able to locate the development of the society historically in the evolution from a multi-class to a unitary class society. No theoretical or empirical reasons have been put forward which substantiate the view that a ruling and an exploited class exist. This does not mean to say that there are no competing social interests, nor residuals of class groups, but it is held that such interests and residuals may be satisfactorily handled by a functional-structural paradigm. Much of the approach adopted here is derived from the work of Talcott Parsons. This has been utilised as a heuristic device to order the facts and has been adapted to meet the problems confronting socialist societies. Let us briefly indicate those parts of the Parsonian model which seem relevant to our concerns.

The basic orientation of Parsons is to suppose that for social systems to operate efficiently and effectively four major functions must be performed; or, put another way, society must solve four problems. These are: *pattern maintenance* (L), involving the motivation of individuals and the control of tension within the system; it is concerned with the process by which values are internalised by individuals through socialisation. *Integration* (I) has to do with maintaining the wholeness of the system; social control, particularly through law, provides mechanisms by which order and integration are maintained. *Goal attainment* (G) is the process of the co-operative organisation of resources which is necessary to achieve collective goals for the society. *Adaptation* (A) is concerned with the adjustment of society to the physical environment, with role differentiation and the division of labour. These four functions help to identify the four main sub-systems which make up a society. These functions are performed (at the societal level) by various concrete social institutions such as industrial enterprises, churches, schools, families, police, government departments.

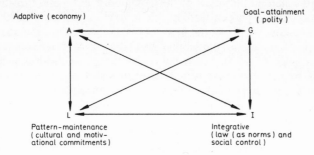

Figure 2. Parsons's social interchange system

Parsons has been concerned with the nature of exchange between these functional components of social systems. He considers societies to be in a kind of moving equilibrium in which these components ideally balance or become congruent. Reciprocated forms of exchange take place between the four sub-systems of a society as in

Fig. 2.* Note that no one structure dominates these exchange processes: mutual interaction and adjustment is the characteristic of this model. Parsons's model may be regarded as the sociological equivalent of Marshall's perfect competition theory of the economy. This, of course, has led to the widely voiced criticism that Parsons is ethno-centric and ideologically motivated in seeking to allege a fundamental harmony of American society.

A second major assumption of the Parsonian model is the cybernetic hierarchy of control. This conceives of a hierarchy of controls in which 'systems high in information but low in energy regulate other systems higher in energy but lower in information' (1966: 9). At the apex of a society is the pattern maintenance sub-system (L) concerned with maintaining institutionalised cultural patterns; the functions performed here are the articulation of the values of the society. In state-socialist society, Marxism-Leninism is the highest system of values. These are enforced by the integrative sub-system. Here values are expressed in norms and laws which are enforced by and against the members of a society; the maintenance of order precedes that of goal attainment. Socialist law, political indoctrination and education are forms of social control directly reflecting the values of 'official' Marxism-Leninism. These are negative as expressed in the form of labour camps involving punishments of deviants and positive in the sense that definite codes of conduct are devised to which individuals are expected to conform. The polity is concerned with the function of organising effective collective action to attain general social goals (i.e. those defined in the value system). Here the state in the shape of the Communist Party and the government apparatus plays a leading role in devising means of achieving general goals. Finally in the hierarchy of control comes the adaptive system which includes the economy and the forms of technology. The processes going on here are linked by the polity (which allocates goals), by the integrative sub-system (through laws of property and contract) to the guiding values of the society. The cybernetic hierarchy, then, has the form LIGA.

The Parsonian model, the starkest details of which are outlined above, should be regarded as an 'ideal type'. It does *not* refer to any existing society (though Parsons believes that the USA comes closest to it). In practice the exchanges between the various sub-systems are by no means reciprocated. Parsons is concerned to show how a modern society may operate most efficiently and effectively. It is also important to note that Parsons draws attention to necessary conditions for the evolution of social systems. To achieve particular

*A simplified version of the chart which appears in Bendix and Lipset, 'On the Concept of Political Power' (1968: 262).

ideal social arrangements (say, communist society), integrative and political institutions must be devised to achieve this goal. Without appropriate institutions the goals cannot be realised and the society may collapse. Parsons, for instance, explains the decline of the Roman Empire by reference to the lack of a dynamic religious system which could legitimate the social system (1966: 92). Hence the Parsonian system helps identify possible causes of decline or decay as well as necessary conditions for growth and efficient performance.

The idea of a cybernetic hierarchy of control might be distinguished from the notion of primacy of different *institutional* structures. In the United States, primacy is given to the pursuit of the goal of economic productivity and profitability. This gives primacy to the economy. In the Soviet Union, on the other hand, Marxism-Leninism establishes the primacy of the Party and the political apparatus (the state) which determines collective goals. By taking account of the priority afforded to various institutions we may pinpoint *whose* interests dominate in a given social order and counteract a tendency of Parsons to assume that values are *always* prior to interests and that social change originates from values. Values, however, may be rationalisations of particular group interests and may be routinised into ideologies which create conformity among a dominated class.

The social system of the Soviet Union may be described as a state-directed form of socialist modernisation. This phrase brings out the fact that the values of the system are socialist, that the goals involve change in the direction of modernisation, and that the instrument of change is the political system (Party–government). Contrary to the views of totalitarian theorists, the values of Marxism-Leninism are given some prominence as determinants of action. On the other hand, institutional functional primacy is located with the polity which brings out a major distinction between state-socialist and capitalist societies. In terms of the Parsonian interchange model, exchange between the various sub-systems is controlled by the polity – though there is feedback between it and the other sub-systems. This exchange (or lack of it) has varied over time and directs attention to tensions in the social system. The model includes not only tensions between ideal goals (such as egalitarianism) and economic efficiency (the need for income differentials), but also helps one to identify conflicts between various institutional interests – those concerned with value articulation (Party ideologists), enforcement (police), goal attainment (government ministries) and the economy (managerial groups).

The pattern of exchanges varies through time. A diachronic study of the communist type of social transformation leads one to conclude that following a communist seizure of political power a period of social disequilibrium occurs: initially the pre-revolutionary sub-systems are isolated and brought under the control of the polity more or less in keeping with the values of the revolutionaries. But after the initial revolutionary upheaval there is a tendency over time for the revolutionary goals to be modified. Actual policies come to be more the result of a social process of exchange between different societal demands rather than determined solely by ideology. Also a process of osmosis takes place whereby the orientations socialised by the old regime modify the social goals of the revolutionary leaders. The general trend of family policy in the USSR, for instance, has been away from casting the family in a revolutionary role towards the conservation of the family. Also, the process of education has moved away from being child-centred and libertarian towards fulfilling the needs of industry. Movements such as the Cultural Revolution in China seek to arrest this tendency and to reassert the ideological and revolutionary component. The pull of the past may also be analysed in terms of this model, for the structures ensuring patterns of integration (such as in Russia the police) have been established a long time and come to be taken for granted by the incumbents of power.*

We saw earlier that while some theorists have emphasised that modern urban industrial civilisation gives to political elites the possibility of total control over man, they have ignored the structural differentiation of modern society which results in the specialisation of human activities. Science, medicine, law, the economy, and literature, for instance, satisfy different aspects of the functional requisites of societies and if subjected to political control operate less efficiently – as political interference in biology in the Soviet Union has shown. This is especially so as societies develop and become more complex. The USSR after the October Revolution was at a relatively low level of industrial development and socially undifferentiated with a large, segmentalised peasant population. It was a heterogeneous society with conflicting value systems. The aim of terror and police activity was to weaken the traditional customs and belief systems so that the values of the new order could be transmitted and so that rapid social change could occur. During this process of domination by the communist elites certain political goals have been pursued at the expense of functional requisies of other sub-systems. In Russia in the 1930s, political control of the countryside was maintained at the cost of chaos in the countryside, and involved peasants slaughtering livestock. But such dominance has limits : unless agriculture can be made to flourish and unless people are given a fairly reasonable

*For an historical description which bears out this point, see E. H. Carr (1958).

expectation that a satisfactory life will continue in the future, society will disintegrate.

The populations of the USSR and of most of the socialist states of Eastern Europe in the 1970s are not organised on the basis of segmentalisation, but are structurally differentiated. It is not now a simple process for the Party elite to 'control' writers or scientists and at the same time to ensure their creative participation in the social order. A modern industrial society, therefore, should be regarded as providing the necessary conditions for pluralism in the sense of exchange between sub-systems rather than 'totalitarian' control, though such exchange does not entail a political order of the liberal-democratic type.

In practice, the process of policy-making is not shaped exclusively by the 'official' values but also by demands originating in the various sub-systems. Hence the understanding of state-socialist society would be furthered by giving less attention to the 'outputs' of the political elite and more to consideration of other social elites each having eminence in a certain sphere and each playing a particular functional role (see S. Keller, 1963). This is a plea for progress from the perspective of political science to that of political sociology. For in addition to the political elite which, in state-socialist societies, is particularly concerned with goal articulation, there are the scientific, economic, military and cultural elites performing important but different roles. But these groups develop their own notion of the public good and attempt to establish boundaries beyond which the political elite may not penetrate.

Social integration is strengthened by a 'pop' culture elite, by the cult of astronauts, by the success of sportsmen and teams, by socialist rituals (encouraged by the political elites), such as wedding ceremonies and homage to Lenin in the Mausoleum. A sense of personal participation is achieved by mass participation in sports, by May Day celebrations and such extravaganzas (in the 1960s) as the Soviet Twist. The attachment by the young to western 'pop' stars and jazz was once regarded as incongruent with 'communist values' in the Soviet Union and Eastern Europe. (Even now, such forms of bourgeois decadence attract the wrath of Chinese communists.) But the current *laissez-faire* attitude of the Soviet and East European political elites to such activity is indicative of their realisation that it is politically harmless and a valuable contribution to tension-release and personal satisfaction.

This approach to state socialist society has the advantage that it takes account of historically determined ethno-national cultural factors, recognises the group formations of an urban-industrial society, and puts into perspective the importance of the Communist

Party in a socialist state. Initially, after a socialist revolution, the Party is an institution which articulates the overriding values. At the societal level, it seeks to translate these values into social action through the sub-systems of integration, goal attainment and adaptation. As the internalised values of the population are largely traditional, the Party as an institution seeks to penetrate the structures to try to ensure the implementation of new values. Hence Party control appears ubiquitous. Through time, however, the traditional structures performing the various functions influence the values of the political elites and 'socialism' takes on some of the cultural values of the society in which it is implanted. This is given 'official' recognition in the policy of different national roads to socialism. Also, the population to some extent internalises the values articulated by the political elites, and the need for Party penetration declines. At the same time, structural differentiation increases and exchange between the various sub-systems becomes more reciprocated. The society is less 'politicised' in the sense that formal political agencies are less directly involved in performing the roles of integration and adaptation. The danger here is that certain interest groups lodged in crucial functional position such as the economy or cultural apparatus seek to legitimate their own power by reference to values which are inconsistent with those of the Party theoreticians. In such cases the Party elites react either through a 'cultural revolution', as in China, or by accommodating the demands into a new theoretical and institutional framework, as suggested by the Czechoslovak reformers in 1968.

The politics of state-socialist societies involves struggles about the definition of goals and are also concerned with the putting into effect of these goals. In the latter sense politics is concerned with 'effective collective action in the attainment of the goals of collectivities' (Parsons, 1963: 241). From this point of view power is a generalised capacity to secure the performance in a society of collective goals. This is a much wider notion than that of some political scientists who regard power as the capacity to get one's way in the face of the opposition of others and who stress the use of sanctions by the power-wielders against the powerless. In the case of state-socialist societies, study of political power has been concentrated on the struggle for power between contending personalities and groups, rather than as the medium concerned with effectively mobilising resources to achieve collective goals. The polity in state-socialist societies has furthered a particular form of developmental mobilisation.

Part Two

POLITICAL SYSTEM
AND PROCESS

4

The Political System and Culture

The Political Structure
The key to the understanding of the political system of state socialism is to recognise that the major goal defined by the state is that of modernisation and development. All modern polities are concerned with development in that they encourage economic growth and desire to improve general welfare. State-socialist societies, however, put a much greater emphasis on modernisation, and this includes not only economic growth but a much wider consideration of social change. The element of truth in the totalitarian model is that it recognises the centrality of the political system. Also, the 'official' theory of these societies emphasises the goal of building socialism. In practice 'building socialism' involves in the first instance the polity directing and co-ordinating resources (human and material) to achieve, at the quickest possible speed, the industrialisation of the country and the other associated processes – urbanisation, and occupational, educational and political change. The political institutions play a dominant role in three major ways: first, they allocate high levels of investment ('forced saving') to ensure economic growth; second, they propagate the diffusion of secular and rational norms linked to the general orientation of science; and third, they also seek to change the personality system by creating a new 'communist man'. Mobilisation and development are multi-dimensional in scope and include changes in the economic, institutional and personality systems. The distinguishing feature about such changes under state socialism is that the polity plays a much more dominant role in these processes than it does in the more advanced stages of capitalism.

We might generalise that state-socialist (or 'communist') political systems have certain common characteristics: they all see modernisation as a dominant political goal, as a precondition for building communism; they are legitimated in terms of social class; and the structures of their leading political institutions, based on the principle of democratic centralism, are similar. It should be empha- sised, however, that it should not be assumed that the application of the terms 'state-socialist' or 'communist' political system to all societies which are led by a single Marxist-Leninist political party means that these societies are alike. The actual political order of each society is made up of a unique constellation of historical and social components which give each society and its political system an individual cultural character. For example, the Chinese Party fought a revolutionary war for a very long period before it achieved power in an economically most backward country. In Poland and in Eastern Germany (now the German Democratic Republic), on the other hand, the indigenous Communist Party was either very small or non-existent and initially the communist state was largely dependent on the Soviet Red Army; these societies, too, had a much more highly developed industrial infra-structure. One can see in- tuitively that different kinds of political policies are appropriate to China, Poland and Eastern Germany (GDR) and also that the social support and political cultures generally of these societies are variable and not identical.

Nevertheless, the political institutions of these and other socialist states have been copied from the Soviet model and bear its imprint. Soviet institutions in turn were shaped in many respects by the ex- perience of pre-revolutionary Russia. In Tsarist Russia there was no liberal-democratic political structure or process and the Communist Party (then called the Russian Social Democratic Labour Party) had led a clandestine existence. In destroying the political structures in- herited from Tsarist Russia, the Party played a leading role and initially it directed the administration of the Soviet order. The execu- tors of the Revolution were commissars appointed by, and responsible to, the Party, and the legitimacy of the Soviet order originated from it. This is quite unlike the system in parliamentary regimes where political sovereignty resides in the electorate and which by various means evolves representative political institutions. Marxists regard the political institutions of a society as a reflection of its *class* struc- ture. Hence Soviet Marxists, who think of their society as socialist and having no contradictory classes, conceive of the political structure as expressing the unitary will of the working class as expressed by the Communist Party. The resolution of conflicting interests which are manifest in heterogeneous capitalist society is not regarded as a major function of the political system, and procedures for aggregating 'pres- sure group' activity and mechanisms for adjusting group conflicts find no formal place in the institutional structure. Indeed recognition of such partial interests is regarded as weakening the general will of the working class as expressed by the Communist Party.

In most communist states in Eastern Europe outside the Soviet Union, the ruling party was formed in the early years of the regime from the previously separate communist and social-democratic parties. Also the ruling party flourishes with other quasi-independent political groups such as in Poland, for example, the Peasant Party and the Catholic Church. Such groups are indications that 'non-socialist' elements in the form of private landowners and religious beliefs persist. In China, the communists for a very long time led a national liberation struggle among the peasantry in which they were joined by some of the bourgeois and petty-bourgeois strata. While the legitimacy of the claim to power by the ruling communist elites was justified in class terms as in Soviet Russia, the actual social structure of Poland and China and its political manifestation were quite different.

The political institutions common to these societies and charged with guiding and managing their affairs may be divided into five major groupings: first, the Communist Party and associated organisations such as the Komsomol (young Communists) and Pioneers (schoolchildren's organisation); second, the government executive or bureaucracy including ministries concerned with industrial, police, military and cultural affairs; third, popularly elected soviets (representative parliamentary-type bodies) functioning at all levels of the political system; fourth, other 'pro-regime' mass associations such as trade unions; and fifth, organisations which are in one way or another non-socialist, such as churches and non-communist parties. Here we shall describe briefly the structure of the political institutions as a preliminary to the discussion of the political process.

The Party plays a key role in the functioning of the political system. By virtue of its being the leading political institution it seeks to control administrative bodies by determining policy at the highest level and enforcing it at lower levels. This draws attention to the official organisational principle of democratic centralism which seeks to promote the election of leading committees from the bottom to the top, dual subordination of executive bodies both to higher bodies and to bodies which elect them, the subordination of the minority to majority decision, and the subservience of lower bodies to higher ones. The highest political body is the Politbureau (sometimes in the past called the Presidium) which is composed of about a dozen men. Below it comes the Central Committee which technically elects it and to which it is legally responsible. Next comes the Congress of the Party. The Central Committee of the Party has its own secretariat with bureaux concerned with all aspects of political and social life. These bureaux help to formulate policies and keep a general oversight over the day-to-day running of the Party. Control of the secretariat by the General Secretary gives him a crucial position of power in the political apparatus. The Party secretariat sanctions appointments to all major posts through its cadres department which controls the *nomenklatura* (lists of positions in the administration which cannot be filled without Party consent). For some posts, officials are appointed by the Party, whereas for others the approval of, or ratification by, a Party body is all that is necessary. Party oversight pertains not only to some 3 million posts having administrative and executive importance but also to elective posts in the soviets, unions, and collective farms and to delegates to conferences (Harasymiw, 511). Such control of personnel puts the Party in an extremely powerful position.

The government is separate from the Party. It is hierarchically organised and made up of ministries (and other bodies, such as planning offices and banks) headed by ministers composing the Council of Ministers. These executive bodies are theoretically answerable to the hierarchy of soviets which are elected popularly. Also, in keeping with the doctrine of dual subordination, lower administrative bodies are obliged to follow directives from higher ones. The Supreme Soviet of the USSR is formally the chief legislative body; the ministries are answerable to it and ministers are elected by it. In practice, however, the soviets exercise little actual control over the activities of ministries. This does not mean that individual deputies are unable to take up grievances against ministerial bodies or that they are without influence. But it does mean that soviets as such do not exercise the same kind of control or veto over the administration which is the prerogative of Parliament or Congress, in different ways, in the United States and Britain. In theory, the executive should be in harmony with Party and soviets; in practice, ministries may develop wills of their own and may lose sight of the general purpose of their work. Conflict between interests located in and across Party and state institutions is one of the incipient problems of the political system.

The soviets ostensibly are similar in appearance to western parliaments or councils. But they do not have, and do not seek to create, the same kind of political power as do their western counterparts. In theory, they are the elected, popular, political organs of all social strata – not just the working class. Before the Revolution in Russia, they were originally revolutionary strike committees made up of representatives of the Bolsheviks and other parties and groups; this mixed composition – party and non-party – still continues. Soviets now function in order to mobilise the public in support (active and passive) of the Soviet state. They build into the system an outlet for the political participation of citizens who for one reason or another are not Party members. The soviets are directly elected bodies and are organised at local, regional and national levels. The Party utilises them to exert influence rather than, as in western states, to 'capture' parliamentary institutions via the electoral system. The elections, too, have a different function: to expose the population to political media, to increase political commitment and to demonstrate political loyalty. In this way they contribute to the functioning of the political system.

Finally, there are institutions which are not formally part of the state or ruling Party, but which defend and articulate social interests. Such interests accept the general political arrangements of communist power and seek actively to further it. Soviet trade unions, for example, do not 'oppose' the employer as do unions in Western Europe; they seek to assist in the carrying out of national economic plans and to further the workers' interests through organisation or social services; they are closely integrated with Party and government. Other non-communist parties and churches which exist more or less accept the parameters of the social order (though some illegal dissident groups oppose the communist system). They are regarded as transitional by the incumbents of power and should disappear with the evolution of socialism. In the meantime, such institutions often exert considerable pressure on the ruling political elites.

The various institutions and groups concerned with the operation of the social system of state socialism articulate individual interests which are expressed within the framework of the political system. Such interests and the conflict generated may be analysed at various levels. Elsewhere (Lane, 1970: chapter 8) I have suggested that interest-group activity be considered at five different levels: that of the political elites; of the institutional groups (such as the *Komsomol*); of 'loyal dissenters' (such as professions); of amorphous social groupings (such as peasants, or consumers); and, outside these 'official' groupings, of dissident activity which calls for modifications of, or changes in, the processes or structures of the institutional system. There may be demands for significant structural alterations defined by their proponents in liberal-democratic or in Marxist-Leninist terms, or more typically, interests may require the enforcement of particular rights which are constitutionally legitimate but which have been abrogated by the political elites.

Following Talcott Parsons, we might generalise about the hierarchy of control in the political system in the following way. In theory, at the highest level, the society is guided by Marxist-Leninist theory. The Party turns these general values into political policies. The ministries and mass organisations put into effect these ideas; they are strong in power but weak in ideas. The soviets ensure integration of the system and link the political with the social system. In practice, the system does not work in this way; or, at best, it operates imperfectly. Values may be ambiguous, they may lose their binding force. Individual and group interests develop in different parts of the system, thus 'blocking' the execution of high-level Party policy. Social and political interests arise which conflict with each other. Before discussing the ways in which the leadership attempts to accommodate these problems, let us consider some of the major causes of strain and analyse some of the main ways in which they are manifested.

The political system will be analysed in the following pages in three main ways: in terms first of supportive and deviant orientations in the political culture; second, of 'systemic contradiction' and forms of dissent; and third, of institutional and group conflict between the elites (chapter 5). In chapter 6 we shall consider three important and distinctive political and social movements which involve structural deviations from the model evolved in the USSR, these being workers' management in Yugoslavia, the Chinese Cultural Revolution and the Czechoslovak Reform Movement. Finally, in Part Three we shall discuss the social pattern of rewards and the impact of the political system on that of social stratification.

Political Culture

In analysing the political system, the general orientations of the population are widely recognised as important determinants of the political process (Almond and Verba, 1963). Here we shall follow Pye and Verba's definition of political culture as 'the system of empirical beliefs, expressions, symbols and values which defines the situation in which political action takes place' (Pye and Verba, 1963: 513). Almond and Verba identify three types of political culture: parochial, subject and participant. These are concerned essentially with different patterns of individual orientation to politics. The *parochial* culture is one in which there are no specialised political roles and in which individuals have no expectations of activity on their behalf by a political system. The *subject* political culture involves a passive relationship to politics: an awareness of government and its activity but little participation in it; this culture involves an orientation to the output of a political system. In the *participant culture,* individuals have an active interest in government activity and are involved in policy-making. Here citizens have an orientation to both the input and the output of the system. It should be emphasised that these three main types of culture are not mutually exclusive. On the contrary, actual political systems are typified by their heterogeneity. This may occur at various levels. The individual may have a mix of participant, subject and parochial orientations; and a participant culture will contain, in addition to active participants, those with parochial and subject orientations. In the three cultures defined above the kinds of orientation specified are typical or dominant.

Another important distinction made by Almond and Verba is that the political culture and the structures of the political system may or may not be congruent. Thus a subject political culture would be congruent with 'a centralised authoritarian structure' (1963: 21). Under such circumstances the political system is stable, for citizens' expectations coincide with the nature of the political institutions. Where there is incongruence there may be apathy or 'alienation'. In the former case members of a community may be indifferent to the political system, whereas in the latter they have a negative evaluation and the political system is rejected. Where negative evaluations are strong there may be a likelihood of political instability.

In practice, societies have mixed political cultures. (In some cases, in revolutionary situations, there may even be dual political institutions: these are ignored here.) In a *subject-parochial* culture a part of the population has allegiance to a tribal or village authority, whereas another part has a commitment to a more specialised central government structure. A *subject-participant* culture is one where part of the population has specialised input orientations and 'activist self-orientations' whereas the remainder has passive self-orientations. Political cultures may remain mixed for a long period.

Some time has been spent in outlining a political culture approach to political systems because it suggests lines of enquiry in the analysis of the political system of state socialism. It suggests tensions, sources of strain and forms of duality between various groups of citizens and between citizens and the political system. Societies undergoing rapid change should be characterised as heterogeneous rather than as monolithic as suggested by the totalitarian syndrome. The view of the present writer is that the political cultures of state-socialist societies vary greatly. They need to be considered historically and regionally, though the lack of data makes this a task beyond the scope of this book. The lack of a temporal dimension obscures the dynamic character of Soviet-type political systems. Over the past fifty years of Soviet power the political culture has shifted from a predominantly parochial-subject culture to a subject-participant one. China is currently undergoing this change. It is also important to bring out the fact of regional variation. The Soviet Union alone includes many diverse cultures ranging from the European Russia to the Asian Kazakh. The latter, at the time of the Revolution, had a parochial culture; the role of the predominantly

Russian Bolsheviks was to try to superimpose a distinctly subject-political culture on it (see Lane, 1975). A cultural revolution may be conceived of as the political imposition of a new set of symbols and values; its incidence is at the level of the individual – it affects his internalised feelings towards, and evaluations of, society and his attitudes towards his fellow men and the political order.

It is impossible to define the content of the orientations of the population of state-socialist society with the high level of sophistication which is possible with research in western societies (see Mann, 1970). Such work is highly dependent on social surveys, and those done in state-socialist societies emphasise the congruity between the beliefs of the population and the dominant values of Marxism-Leninism. Bearing this in mind, we may describe, following Parkin and Mann (1970), two major sets of values: those which are dominant and supportive of the legitimating ideology and the political elites; and 'destructive' values shared by deviants who in various ways oppose the ruling elites and their ideology.

Political Supports
The Bolsheviks were political activists and their ideology encouraged political participation. The regime under Stalin was a mobilisation regime *par excellence.* The party and state bombarded the population with political messages and sought to mobilise the population to take a positive role in carrying out the industrialisation of the country. There can be no doubt that a participant political culture was developed under Stalin for *supporters of the Soviet order.* The individual orientations that make up the participant political culture include a knowledge of the political system, its history and its 'constitutional' characteristics, and an awareness of the self as an active member of the political system (Almond and Verba, 16–17). In all these areas the Soviet *activist* had a positive evaluation of the activity of the political system and a positive allegiance. Of course, many Soviet citizens during the Stalin era did not have positive affective or evaluative orientations to the political output. But these oppositional groups, and Stalinist policy to eliminate them, have been over-emphasised in western writing on the Soviet Union. They were a component of the political culture and were strongly alienated. While Party members and other supporters of the Soviet order constituted a participant culture, the masses who were being mobilised in the massive industrialisation campaigns and were forming the new working class and urban population constituted a subject political culture. They were manifestly aware of the output of the system but had little, if any, input orientations. Soviet policy, how-

ever, was to involve such persons in campaigns and in other various forms of audience participation.

The maturation of the industrial system also led to changes in the political culture in the post-Stalin period. The process of industrialisation led to the creation of a large technical intelligentsia. For example, the educational system underwent massive changes. Mass literacy was a priority of education policy, and measured literacy increased from 44 per cent of the population in 1924 to 99·7 per cent in 1970. Changes in the occupational and educational structure of the population (involving the growth and formation of a scientific, technical and cultural intelligentsia) created its own demands on the system. It seems reasonable to assume that the potential for participation by the population was enhanced. The Soviet political system may be characterised by a tension between groups forming the subject and the participant sub-cultures. Almond and Verba, discussing a different situation, put this very clearly when they write that authoritarian-orientated groups, in competing with democratic ones, must develop a 'defensive political infra-structure of their own' (1963: 26). The examples in *The Civic Culture* relate to instances in which authoritarian governments have alternated with democratic ones (i.e. France, Germany, Italy). But there is no theoretical reason why the balance between authoritarian and democratic groups should not change within a polity, without a change of legal government. The balance of forces may change between 'liberals' and 'conservatives', and policy therefore may fluctuate.

This is what seems to have happened in the socialist states of Eastern Europe. During the 'Stalin' period the groups with specialist input orientations and activist self-orientations were mainly in the Party. Since then, however, to use Almond and Verba's words, 'participant orientations' have spread among only a part of the population and structural conditions prevent 'the participant-oriented stratum of the population' becoming a 'competent, self-confident, experienced body of citizens. They tend to remain democratic aspirants' (*ibid*, 25). In other words, the authoritarian structure remains tied to the political elites which claim legitimacy whereas 'participant orientation' to politics has spread to many other groups.

The rigid centralised political system devised to implement rapid industrialisation now becomes redundant when its major task has been completed. It comes into conflict with participant-oriented groups. These in turn, without a well-based democratic societal infra-structure, lack confidence in pushing their creative group interests. What we have here is a political system which is not congruent with the political culture. Changes in state-socialist societies since 1956 may be explained by the fluctuating influence of these groups. The political changes started by Khrushchev in the USSR, by Gomulka and Gierek in Poland, by Dubcek in Czechoslovakia, by Kadar in Hungary, and by Ceausescu in Rumania have all been attempts to reconcile this new 'demand structure' to the hegemony of the traditional political elites. In all these societies, the social structure has become more differentiated, and the groups highly antagonistic to the socialist regime have declined in number and significance. Allegiance to the regime has grown and the objective need for rigid political control has declined. The society is more diverse, more specialised, and new groups such as the scientific intelligentsia develop their own expectations. These groups are the basis of the democratic-participant infra-structure; they have manifest and latent 'input orientations'; their interests often (not always) clash with the various elites who safeguard the more authoritarian aspects of the political structure. This is reflected, as we shall consider below, in clashes between institutional interests, and in demands for greater differentiation of rewards.

The study of the political culture in western societies has utilised mainly social survey data to establish the orientations of the public to the political system. In the study of state-socialist society one is considerably hampered by the absence of comprehensive studies of attitudes. A major investigation which may be utilised for our purposes is *The Soviet Citizen* (Inkeles and Bauer, 1959), a book based on some 3,000 questionnaires completed by Soviet refugees who had left the USSR during the Second World War. These data are invaluable for the light they throw on popular attitudes during the Stalin period. For more recent periods, Soviet surveys, whilst not devised for our purpose, can also be utilised to illuminate individuals' opinions about, and attitudes to, the Soviet system.

Interpretation of Inkeles and Bauer's data enables one to say quite convincingly that the ex-citizens had many well-defined attitudes to the Soviet system. As the interviews were conducted in Western Europe and America it is perhaps rather surprising that the data suggest that the majority of the respondents accepted the Soviet system as a whole. The following question was put: 'Suppose that the Bolshevist regime were removed and a new government came to power. What things in the present system would you want to keep in the new one?' Of the intelligentsia, only 19 per cent said: 'Keep nothing'; the figures for white-collar employees were 23 per cent, for skilled workers 29 per cent, for ordinary workers 33 per cent and for collective farm peasants, 32 per cent. The authors of the study point out that 'there appears to be a deep-rooted expectation among Soviet citizens that their government and society will provide extensive social welfare benefits, including job security, universal education, medical care, and other securities and guarantees. This attitude is found in virtually all individuals with almost no variation from social group to social group' (1959: 236). Even government ownership and control of industry was 'overwhelmingly supported' by the former Soviet citizens. Support of state ownership and control was strongest in the 'basic areas of the economy': 85 per cent favoured state control of heavy industry, and 87 per cent state ownership and control of transport and communication (*ibid*, 243). This would seem to suggest that the expectations of a large proportion of the Soviet population were 'congruent' with, rather than alienated from, certain aspects of the Soviet system.

The institution which was most consistently opposed by the Soviet refugees was the collective farm. The proportion of responses *spontaneously* citing features of the Soviet regime they would replace if it could be changed was highest for the collective farm. The rankings of elements disliked also bring out differences in orientations between social groups, as shown in Table 1.

Table 1

Rankings of features of Bolshevik regime spontaneously cited to be changed, by social group

Feature	Intelligentsia	Skilled workers	Collective farm peasants
Collective farm system	2	1	1
'Absolutist' state organisation	3	2	4
Terror and injustice	1	3	3
Absence of private initiative	4	$5\frac{1}{2}$	5
Labour conditions	5	4	6
'Communism' and Bolshevik ideology	6	$5\frac{1}{2}$	2

Adapted from Inkeles and Bauer (1959: 245).

The table is interesting because it shows that 'terror and injustice', which figures prominently in western criticism of the Stalin regime, were particularly strongly felt by the intelligentsia (members of which, of course, write books). Ideology came very low down the scale both for skilled workers and for the intelligentsia; the collective farmers were more strongly opposed to ideology, possible because Orthodoxy was stronger in the countryside. It is also important to note the relatively low rankings given to private initiative and to labour conditions.

The citizens' orientation to government may also be ascertained from some of the questions. They were asked whether they would prefer a government which 'guarantees freedom but does not assure them of a job, or one which guaranteed a decent standard of living but not personal rights'. The respondents had high expectations of personal rights, for between 80 per cent and 90 per cent of each social group chose a government which secured personal rights. This evidence would suggest that the citizens not only had expectations of government activity but had definite expectations that this activity should both be limited and geared to meet their own individual interests. They therefore had more than a passive orientation to the output of the political system. Inkeles and Bauer sum up citizens' expectations in the following way. The Soviet citizen, they say, would favour 'a paternalist state, with extremely wide powers which it vigorously exercised to guide and control the nation's destiny, but which yet served the interests of the citizen benignly, which respected his personal dignity and left him with a certain amount of individual freedom of desire and a feeling of security from *arbitrary* interference and punishment' (*ibid*, 247).

There is a certain ambivalence in the attitude of the respondents to civil liberties. While, on the one hand, they declared themselves in principle in favour of civil liberties – freedom of speech, of association – on the other, when pressed about specific situations, their support for civil liberties 'melted away' and they favoured government intervention. Inkeles and Bauer interpret the data in terms of the American creed of an opposition between civil liberties and government intervention; European socialists, however, would perceive no such contradiction and would regard it as legitimate for a government to promote actively the conditions for freedom. It is also interesting to note that there was considerable opposition, especially by the lower classes, to criticism of the government: only a third of the respondents thought it right to criticise the government. (The orientations of Soviet citizens, on the basis of these data, were not unlike those of American citizens in 1954 when only 37 per cent thought it right to make speeches against churches and religion (Stouffer, 1955: chapter 2, cited by Inkeles and Bauer, 247).) Hence the 'input' orientations of Soviet citizens and Americans to the state and to religion respectively are not totally different. In the Soviet Union reverence for the Tsar on the part of the masses was transferred to Stalin. Ex-Soviet citizens particularly had greater expectations of the government's acting for the good of the citizens. 'A strong central government is assumed as giving the nation direction and purpose, as providing the stimulus for improvement and advancement, and as facilitating the economic features of the welfare state which are so strongly devised' (Inkeles and Bauer, 250). The test of a good government, as shown by the interview data, was in its capacity to promote the common good, to foster public welfare and not to interfere in certain 'private' areas (e.g. movements of the individual). The Soviet citizen, then, even under Stalin, had a sense of what the government should do to promote the general welfare. If this bond between government and citizen was broken, the citizen felt it legitimate to adopt an attitude of non-cooperation and 'to treat his government as alien or illegitimate' (*ibid*, 251).

One might distinguish between the attitudes of the population to the Soviet order as such and to particular Soviet leaders. It was found that the younger respondents were more inclined to favour the institutional structure of Soviet society than older ones; younger groups, too, felt that 'things would have been better if the leadership had been different' (*ibid*, 254). One may generalise that discontent and alienation were not focused on the whole range of institutions; orientations were such that expectations of government activity for the benefit of the citizens were quite high. When such expectations were not met, alienation ensued; but such alienation was not of a blanket kind and was often directed against the political leadership.

It is important to consider differences between generations. Younger people who have grown up after the Revolution provide a more dynamic indicator of changes in the expectations of the population. Inkeles and Bauer conclude that the younger people were more favourably disposed to the institutional structure of Soviet society (state-ownership, control, planning and welfare institutions). Even though they were opposed to the collective farm, they were 'not as firmly and unanimously against the kolkhoz [collective farm] system as the older generation'. The pre-revolutionary generation particularly was much more hostile to the Soviet regime than those who had grown up with it. Inkeles and Bauer show that each successive age group in the population 'seems to take the Soviet order more for granted'. They found that of people in the sample born before 1900, 82 per cent said that they had always been opposed to the Soviet system; of those born after 1920, 45 per cent said that they had once been in favour of the system. The authors of the survey point out that their response rates tended to underestimate support for the regime, for the following reasons: first, the 'situational pressures' on the respondents (such as desire for residence in the West) make it likely that they would have responded negatively about the regime; second, the emigrés were probably actually more anti-Soviet than the Soviet population as a whole; and third, the sample did not include the youngest age groups of the population. Nevertheless, and even with these caveats, the authors conclude that 'the overwhelming majority of Soviet youth initially are supporters of the regime' (Inkeles and Bauer, 274). These conclusions are perhaps surprising to many western students who have been led to believe that the Soviet population under Stalin was almost completely hostile to the communist order.

While it seems reasonable inference that the younger age groups referred to by Inkeles and Bauer would with maturation keep these more positive attitudes, the research is strictly limited to age groups who were exposed to Soviet communism during the Stalin era. To complete our picture we would require a comparative study of Soviet citizens in the 1960s. No such work has been done in the USSR. The best the writer can do is to indicate some general attitudes to society which may be gleaned from various sources. The reader should bear in mind the fact that we are dealing mainly with 'supports'; later we shall consider more negative attitudes.

A study of Jewish emigrants from the USSR conducted in 1972 shows that they were not alienated on all counts. Over 90 per cent of those surveyed ($N = 437$) felt that 'the material life of the average Soviet citizen had improved over the past twenty-five years' (Ross, 1974: 113). Over 67 per cent thought that Soviet politics could be understood (i.e. according to Ross there was no evidence of alienation in the sense of incomprehensibility of the political world); over 67 per cent thought that officials 'really have the interests of the people at heart and . . . really try to help them'. (The alienated aspects are described below, p. 114.)

Another important source of information on Soviet public opinion is to be found in polls conducted in the USSR. (For a review of the polls conducted, see Weinberg, 1974: chapter 6.) The results of the respondents' replies have not been comprehensively published and it is likely that dissenting views have not been given their true significance. In general, as reported by Weinberg, the results of the polls are not very penetrating and show that public opinion is in support of the Soviet government's policy. For instance, one study showed that the majority of people thought that mankind would succeed in averting war because of 'the downfall or the "senility" of capitalism, Soviet rocketry, her technological and scientific strength, or the staunch policy of the CPSU and the government' (Weinberg, 1974: 85). A study of youth found that young people were patriotic, resolute, loved their homeland and liked the collectivism of Soviet society. 'Negative characteristics' among young people were held to be drunkenness, hooliganism, worship of foreign fashions, music and dancing. Another survey showed great identification of youth with Soviet power. The best expressions of achievements in arts and sciences were the CPSU Programme (most important document),

Lenin (great man of the epoch) and Yuri Gagarin (greatest exploit of twentieth century) (*ibid*, 94). G. D. Hollander, in a study devoted to the Soviet mass media, concludes that 'there are indications that most Soviets basically do not question the legitimacy of the regime and most of its political messages' (Hollander, 1972: 187). The published results of these polls leave a rather unsatisfactory impression in the observer's mind. As the role of the press is to 'lead' public opinion, it seems likely that only positive messages to achieve desired state policy will be published and that opinions which are highly critical of the official line will be intensively studied by the relevant elites but not publicised. This should not be taken to mean that criticism of the elites is not made publicly; it refers to the kind of criticism. Hollander has analysed a sample of letters to two Soviet newspapers (*Izvestiya* and *Zarya Vostoka*) in the years 1956, 1959, 1962 and 1965. In dividing the correspondents' comments into 'negative', 'neutral' and 'positive', it was found that nearly three-quarters (64 out of a total of 87) of the comments were 'negative', and less than 10 per cent (7 out of 87) were 'positive'. Most complaints were made about economic management and bureaucracy (23), public services (9), and the technical development of society (9) (Hollander, 1972: 46).

This in itself, however, should not lead one to over-react and to underestimate the cohesion and solidarity of Soviet society. A study of child-rearing in the Soviet Union emphasises the cooperativeness and collective discipline of the children. As Bronfenbrenner has put it:

What impressed this observer, like others before him, about Soviet youngsters, especially those attending schools of the new type [i.e. boarding schools], was their 'good behaviour'. In their external actions, they are well-mannered, attentive and industrious. In informal conversations, they reveal a strong motivation to learn, a readiness to serve their society, and – in general – ironically enough for a culture committed to a materialistic philosophy, what can only be described as an idealistic attitude toward life. In keeping with this general orientation, relationships with parents, teachers, and upbringers are those of respectful and affectionate friendship. The discipline of the collective is accepted and regarded as justified, even when severe as judged by Western standards. On the basis not only of personal observations and reports from Soviet educators, but also from entries in the minutes of the Pioneer and Komsomol meetings which I had an opportunity to examine, it is apparent that instances of aggressiveness, violation of rules, or other antisocial behavior are genuinely rare. (Bronfenbrenner, 1971: 77)

Bronfenbrenner, on the basis of a comparative study, points out that Soviet children are 'much less willing to engage in anti-social behaviour than their age-mates in three western countries (the United States, England and West Germany)'. There is greater congruity between the attitudes of children and adults, indicative of a consistent socialisation process. The peer group in the USSR supports behaviour of the adult members of society and exerts pressure on deviants to conform. We noted above that 'divergent' views are not given prominence in the Soviet press, or, if they are, are put only in an unfavourable light. This in itself has the effect of minimising knowledge of alternative belief systems and ways of behaviour and helps to maintain what Bronfenbrenner notes as conformity to a 'more homogeneous set of standards' (*ibid*, 81). This does not mean, however, that Soviet citizens are indoctrinated like robots. Bronfenbrenner notes that since 1968 official policy has encouraged the development of the individual personality and that 'both within and outside the family, there is a shift away from features which foster dependency and conformity towards new configurations more conducive to the emergence of individuality and independence' (*ibid*, 89).

These findings are corroborated by Hollander's study of the mass media. One survey found that fewer people turned to 'official' opinion leaders on questions of politics – 6·4 per cent referred to agitators, 36 per cent to Party secretaries, but 51·2 per cent 'relied on fellow workers or friends' (Hollander, 1972: 168). Some Soviet citizens in many respects are sceptical about the messages of the media; they 'read between the lines' and seek other sources of information – foreign radio and *samizdat* (*ibid*).

A Yugoslav study of public opinion (Barton *et al.*, 1973) throws some light on popular attitudes and on the ways in which attitudes are formed. (The results are included here because of the absence of such data from the USSR.) Public opinion surveys have asked people in Yugoslavia about their attitudes to various attributes of Yugoslav life. The proportion expressing 'satisfaction' to certain things is as follows:

Attribute surveyed	*Percentage expressing satisfaction*
Position of Yugoslavia in the world today	95
Honesty and conduct of the people	60
The level of family income	43
The lengthening of the period of work necessary to get a pension	18

These data are evidence of a positive attitude to Yugoslavia as a social order and of a critical attitude towards some features of its internal arrangements: only 43 per cent and 18 per cent of respondents had a favourable attitude to their level of income and to the fact that they had to work longer before they had a pension. The research also showed that those most critical of political conditions in Yugoslavia were those who most regularly read daily newspapers. Barton correctly concludes from this that newspaper readers, being the better educated and of higher social position, are the most critical section of the population and are capable of independently interpreting the media (Barton *et al.*, 1973 : 273). The investigators asked other elite groups to estimate public opinion on these topics: legislators and administrators were over-optimistic about the views of the public (i.e. they felt that attitudes were more favourable than they were), whereas intellectuals were much more pessimistic about public opinion, except on the pensions issue where they consistently underestimated the public's commitment (*ibid*, 276–9). This is probably a general characteristic of intellectuals who themselves are more critical of social arrangements. Hence in general one might 'tone down' intellectuals' reports concerning public opinion.

While Soviet research has not systematically studied the political culture, there are many data concerning general attitudes. A Soviet study of three Russian collective farms in the mid-1960s gives one some insight into the orientations to politics of collective farmers. It was found that a small minority of farmers did not like working on the farms: this ranged from 6 to 20 per cent in the three farms (*Kollektiv*, 1970: 149). More interesting than the relatively small amount of measured dissatisfaction are the reasons given for dissatisfaction. The most common reason on all three farms was 'poor leadership'; only on one farm did 'quarrelling' figure significantly. To 'poor leadership' were attributed a number of different ills: incorrect division of work, violation of the principles governing payment for work, 'bad administration' and lack of attention to the interests of the collective farmers (*ibid*, 150). The writer points out that, at one general meeting, the collective farmers criticised one of the foremen and asserted that he was 'aloof from the masses' and that he 'did not take heed of the opinion of the collective farmers'. For these reasons, it was considered that discipline was poor in the brigade. Hence one can see that these collective farmers had expectations of a 'participatory' kind and that successful man-management was evaluated in terms of the wellbeing of the collective farmer. The recommendations for the improvement of affairs included not only greater attention to political and educational work to create a more 'collective' consciousness but also a call for further democratisation of the affairs of the collective farm to involve more collective farmers in self-management (*ibid*, 153).

This call for democratisation brings out the fact that the Soviet authorities encourage different forms of participation in political and social institutions. Minagawa (1975 : 52) has pointed out that participation in forms of direct and indirect ritual at the Supreme Soviet level may have important psychological effects on ordinary citizens. The commissioners of the supreme soviets of the individual republics 'establish a dialogue between the regime and the masses by visiting localities for preliminary investigations and by holding on-the-spot meetings' (*ibid*, 58). The total number of people formally taking part in politics is very large. To the local soviets, for example, in 1971 over 2 million deputies were elected (*Pravda*, 20 June 1971) – roughly 1 deputy per 110 of the total population. As elections take place once every two years and turnover is high, several million citizens must have had some experience of participation in civic affairs. In addition, of course, literally millions of other activists and agitators participate in the elections and in voluntary work in the soviets. In 1946 Inkeles estimated that 3 million agitators participated in the election campaign, and in 1965 Hollander cites data showing a ratio of 1 agitator per 23–26 people (Hollander, 1972 : 154). This activity is paralleled by forms of participation in countless voluntary commissions or people's control groups which are organised under the Party. The activities of commissions range from inspecting the quality of work in factories to helping to maintain order in public places. Matthews (1972 : 232–3) has assembled data from Soviet surveys on this topic, and these show average participation rates of about 40 per cent of the persons sampled. In evaluating these forms of participation, one cannot claim that they give authority over the legitimate political bodies. But it is misleading to ignore such activity because (as Matthews puts it) : 'In practice, we know that all Soviet public organisations, regardless of their size or nature, are ultimately subservient to the central leadership' (*ibid*, 230). The point which needs to be laboured here is that the emotional and political involvement of the masses is secured by the political system. The process of inclusion itself helps to create feelings of social and political solidarity; such activity is a form of audience participation.

Attitudes to the future are important indexes of social morale, and we are fortunate in having a question about this in a survey of students at an institute of higher education in Moscow. Of 130 students interviewed, over half of those who answered the question (62) had an 'optimistic' view of the future; another quarter were 'optimistic but had a certain amount of doubt'; 10 per cent were fairly optimistic. Eleven per cent were 'not very optimistic but not pessimistic either', and only 2 per cent were 'not very optimistic'. The students were asked about their evaluation of life : 11 per cent thought life 'should be greatly improved'; 29 per cent said it 'should be improved'. The largest group of respondents (47 per cent) answered that 'it is good enough though some things need improving'. Only 5 per cent thought life was 'good enough'. (Source: *samizdat* survey.) These responses would indicate that although many students are aware of inadequacies in their lives, they are nevertheless optimistic about improvements within the parameters of Soviet society.

Study of the political culture has indicated certain areas of support among the population for the political elites and has shown some forms of congruity between the attitudes of people and the values of the political elite. One of the major defects of a 'conflict' approach is that it seriously underestimates the identification of the citizens of these countries with the political system which they see as carrying out many desirable policies. Compared to the poverty and inequality which existed before the communist regimes achieved power, there is undoubtedly greater social welfare. Social consensus rests on national pride and achievement,* on the widespread distribution of social services, on the elimination of unemployment and illiteracy, on many things taken for granted in western welfare societies. It also rests on political indoctrination and social control. In this context the state, including both repressive and ideological apparatuses, operates to inculcate, maintain and enforce conformity. In so doing it stabilises a particular pattern of social, political and economic inequality. Study of supports helps to explain why, despite disturbances or convulsions in some East European societies (Hungary, Eastern Germany and Poland), for the main part the type of society we are considering is characterised by internal stability and an absence of overt popular revolt. So much is this so that state-socialist societies have appeared to some to be, to use Bauman's phrase, 'revolution proof' (Bauman, 1971).

However, there are various levels at which opposition and dissent may be articulated. First, there is the level of 'systemic contradiction': this is concerned with severe structural incompatibility, which may be manifested in open revolt. Second, there are forms of institutional conflict; these may be between various administrative, cultural or political institutions, the goals or activities of which may not be congruent. Third, there are conflicts of lesser scope between occupational and status groups. Fourth, there is the phenomenon of deviance, which is a more general rejection of a society's central or dominant values, though it may not be overtly political in the sense of being manifestly opposed to any objectively defined group – it may, for example, take the form of drunkenness. While these different

*Victories in international sports provide an important index of national self-esteem; see Riordan, 1969.

vels of conflict may overlap, they need not necessarily do so. Also, hile there may be varying degrees of dissent and political alienation at these various levels, such conflicts must be related to the kind of consensus characterising the society as a whole.

Systemic Contradictions: the Intelligentsia as an 'Ascendant' Class

Parkin (1972) has advanced one of the most subtle arguments for the presence of class conflict in state-socialist society. (See also Parry, 1966, for a similar view.) Briefly, Parkin is concerned to show that a particular type of 'stratification order' engenders 'system contradictions' which 'become significant for the problem of social transformation' (1972: 46). State-socialist society, argues Parkin, is weakly integrated. Malintegration results from a lack of uniformity in the elite structure, and from lack of integration between various systems. The 'key antagonisms' are between the political and administrative apparatus of the state which gives 'effective legal guardianship of socialised property' and those groups (the intelligentsia) whose 'social power . . . inheres in its command of the skills, knowledge and general attributes which are held to be of central importance for the development of productive and scientific forces in modern society' (Parkin, 50). In a Marxist sense, argues Parkin, this latter group is an 'ascendant class', it is the 'social embodiment of those scientific, economic and creative forces . . . indispensable to the quest for modernity and social progress'. It comes into conflict with the 'legal and political order buttressing the command system which has become a "fetter" on the further development of productive forces'. The ruling class (the Party and state apparatuses) is separate from the ascendant class, and therefore the stratification order is one of 'disequilibrium' (*ibid*, 52). Parkin then identifies two classes which are in conflict: the bureaucratic class and the intelligentsia (the ascendant class).

The cleavage between these two groups, says Parkin, is manifested in many ways. First, the bases of recruitment to the bureaucracy and to the intelligentsia are socially differentiated. 'The typical member of the party apparatus . . . will be of peasant stock having no formal education beyond the elementary level. The typical member of the white collar elite will probably be of urban, middle class background, and of course a university graduate.' Second, there are functional differences between the two groups. The bureaucrats, who include directors of 'industrial firms', are dependent for 'their position and privileges on the centralised command system'. This group, asserts Parkin, has an 'obvious stake in the preservation of the existing order'. Members of the Party and administration have skills which are useful only in a command system and could not be transferred to a more dynamic market system, as advocated by such writers as Liberman or Sik. The intelligentsia, however, it not likely to be made obsolete by such changes. Third, the intelligentsia is able to compare its position with that of its Western European counterparts. In this comparison, it sees its own subordination to a 'morally, socially and culturally inferior political class'. The intelligentsia, especially in Eastern Europe, has traditionally been a 'standard bearer of national consciousness' and therefore its role is to preserve a 'sense of nationhood and cultural unity' in the face of Soviet domination in Eastern Europe (*ibid*, 56). Fourth, the existence of a clearly defined Party-state bureaucracy has the effect of unifying and focusing the interests of the intelligentsia in state-socialist societies.

The view adopted here is that there is no distinctive 'contradiction' of a 'systemic' kind between the political and administrative bureaucracy on the one hand and the cultural, scientific and economic 'ascendant class' on the other. The integration of these systems is, if anything, greater in state-socialist society than it is in capitalist society. Let us consider Parkin's points. It appears to me that he is unclear as to what constitutes the ascendant class and in what way there is a 'systemic contradiction'. What he talks about is the conflict between the political and administrative apparatus and what appears to be a social category, the intelligentsia. But we do not know exactly what constitutes the state apparatus. Institutions such as the Writers' Union and the Academy of Sciences, which include the leading members of Parkin's ascendant class, are part of the state bureaucracy in a general sense; their members have a very high participation in the leading Party. Over 50 per cent of Candidates and Doctors of Science are Communist Party members (Matthews, 1972: 220). Representatives from these institutions and associations of intellectuals sit on the Central Committee. As White (1974) has pointed out, the Academy of Sciences is linked to the State Planning Agencies and to the State Committee for Science and Technology; higher educational institutions, of course, are subordinate to a government ministry. A complication for Parkin's thesis is that the members of his 'ascendant class' are organised into various bureaucracies which form part of his ruling class. Any *Marxist* definition of the state would have to include such bureaucracies as part of the state apparatus (see Poulanztas, 1973). This means that there cannot be a major cleavage between the ruling class and this social group. (There may be conflicts between certain 'deviant' intellectuals and the ruling groups, and there may also be conflict between parts of the apparatus : but this is not Parkin's argument.) Also, the political and administrative apparatus is staffed with 'intellectuals' in the broad sense in which the term is used. The command posts of the contemporary Party in the Soviet Union and other East European states are saturated with men who have had higher education; they certainly are not characterised by having had 'no formal education beyond the elementary level' (*ibid*, 54). So much is this the case that John Hazard has even referred to the 'quiet revolution' by which intellectuals have replaced the lower class *apparatchiks* in the Party: 'From a position of suspicious specialist, the educated man moved to the position of a model Communist to be emulated by all' (Hazard, 1964 : 32).

In the 1971 Central Committee, more than 90 per cent of its members had more than secondary education (Donaldson, 1972), and at the crucial provincial levels of the Party's organisation over 97 per cent of Party secretaries have had higher education (KPSS, 1973: 25). White has correctly refuted Parkin's view that the 'skills and attributes of the political bureaucracy are useful mainly for the maintenance of the apparatus which is its own creation' and that the group lacks the skills 'intrinsically necessary to an industrial society' (White, 1974 : 44–5). He points out that, on the contrary, members of the political bureaucracy have considerable managerial and technical experience.

At the same time, 'intellectuals' have an extremely high rate of membership of the Party. As far as explicit Party membership is anything to go by, the Soviet intelligentsia is more fully integrated into the political order than its equivalent in capitalist countries. For instance, 42 per cent of engineers, 25 per cent of teachers, 22 per cent of physicians (Rigby, 1968 : 433–9) and 63 per cent of writers* are Party members. Figures for Czechoslovakia show that, in 1968, 70–80 per cent of 'leading economic officials' were Party members. The percentage of Party members among officials of social organisations was 80–90 per cent; among leading officials of central institutions, 85–90 per cent; among officials in culture and education, 70 per cent; among male elementary and secondary school teachers, 50–55 per cent; among university teaching staff, 60 per cent; among technicians in agriculture and industry, 30–40 per cent; among workers in research and development, 40–45 per cent; and among doctors, 25–35 per cent (data cited by Kusin, 1972 : 66). Of course, many of these members have no strong ideological commitment to the Party, and their motivation for joining may be instrumental. But the fact must not be lost sight of that membership itself helps to 'incorporate' them and to identify them with the Party and its values. Intellectuals may influence the process of government directly through the channels of Party and state (see, for example, Churchward, 112–

*'Writers' being members of the Writers' Union. *Literaturnaya gazeta*, 30 June 1971.

16) and indirectly through exerting pressure on the apparatus (*ibid*, 116–23). There seems to be no evidence to substantiate any of Parkin's general points – at least as far as the 'lead society' of the Soviet Union is concerned. Giddens's (1973 : 249) assertion that there is a growing 'schism' between 'Party *members*, increasingly drawn . . . from the intelligentsia, and the Party elite, who are full-time officials' also cannot be substantiated. It should be emphasised that there may be localised conflicts reflecting the social distinction Giddens makes, but this does not entail any major cleavage or schism. The institutional arrangements under state socialism involve the relatively effective incorporation of the intelligentsia into the institutions of the state.

Parkin leaves himself open to these criticisms because he does not define, except in a very general way, the groups which form the 'ascendant class'. By analogy, one assumes that as the 'bureaucratic class' includes the middle personnel of Party secretaries and factory managers, then the 'intelligentsia' includes such groups as teachers, doctors and engineers. To add precision to the debate it is necessary to define what is meant by the term 'intelligentsia', to define the apparatus of the state and to distinguish between different elements and strata within these categories.

In my view, the Soviet intelligentsia is not a *class* apart from and independent of the working class. J. Szczepanski has defined the intelligentsia as 'a collection of various occupational categories employed in (the spheres of) cultural creativity, the organization of work and communal life, as well as in the execution of work requiring theoretical knowledge' (cited by Kolankiewicz, 1973 : 46). This definition brings out the fact that the intelligentsia is not a unitary group but is composed of various 'higher level' occupational groupings. The major divisions are threefold : first, the political intelligentsia formed of men whose calling is political and who have received tertiary education usually in the general education system and often through the system of Party schools. Second, there is the technical intelligentsia the focus of which is the natural sciences and which is largely, though not wholly, apolitical. Third, there is the humanistic intelligentsia which is composed of the creative strata in the arts and social sciences; their professional concern is with man as an individual or a social being. A small part of this group is in opposition to some of the major values and practices of the government. There is no evidence to suggest any form of major incompatibility between intellectuals who are Party *members*, and Party intellectuals who are administrators.

In capitalist societies, groups of the intelligentsia may be relatively independent of the ruling bourgeois class, they may be self-employed and sell their services to all classes; their activity may to some extent be governed by professional ethical considerations. As Bell (1974) has pointed out, such groups may oppose the values of 'optimalisation' and 'rationalisation' held by the economic and political elites. But in state-socialist society, professional groups have no autonomous values derived from their calling and no independent sources of income. (There are some exceptions to this, such as doctors and dentists having private patients or writers and musicians who may receive considerable fees from their sales or services.) The Soviet intelligentsia has a role which is clearly determined by the culture in which its members live. As Churchward puts it: 'The basic role of the Soviet intelligentsia is to provide high-level specialists for all branches of human endeavour, including government and administration' (1973: 90). Such specialists find their professional activity to be highly congruent with the demands made on them by the Soviet political order. Their education closely links Soviet values to professional activity. There is no basis for a 'systemic contradiction' between the intelligentsia (as an ascendant class) and the ruling class, in the shape of the controllers of the political and administrative apparatus of the state. The intelligentsia has to be clearly situated in the context of the state apparatus.

The socialist state apparatus is more than the institutional structures of the Party and the government. Althusser (1971: 121ff.) in another context has suggested that one should consider the ways in which institutions *function*, and he includes both the apparatuses of repression (police and army) and ideological institutions (educational, family, legal, trade union). These latter institutions ensure the reproduction of the relations of production. In capitalist societies such institutions possess a relative autonomy but nevertheless function to socialise individuals into a belief system congruent with the interests of the dominant ideology. In state-socialist societies there is also a 'relative autonomy' of these institutions. However, the particular conditions of revolution and rapid modernisation mean that the repressive and ideological apparatuses are more fully and manifestly intermeshed: the values of the dominant Party are explicitly incorporated in other institutions making up the ideological state apparatus, and there is obviously no distinction between public and private apparatuses. Althusser points out that the educational apparatus is 'dominant' in advanced capitalist societies; in state-socialist societies analogously the *Party ideological* apparatus is supreme. But it is not on its own, and one must bear in mind that other institutions – educational, scientific, communications, legal – form a plurality of apparatuses (Althusser, 137).

It is between these apparatuses that many political conflicts in

state-socialist society are to be found. There are also confr[
between 'fractions' of the intelligentsia (anti-Lysenko scien[
Solzhenitsyn writers) and the ruling state apparatus and als[
groups with deviant values (religions) and the state apparaius. _
such clashes the unity of state-socialist repressive and ideological
apparatuses is clearly brought out. It is important to distinguish
between various forms of dissent and opposition. 'Dissent' may be
articulated with the aim of making the system function more
effectively and efficiently, while opposition rests on an alternative
value and belief system seeking to make major alterations to the
system. Both opposition and dissent are considered to be part of the
phenomenon of deviant behaviour.

The Manual Working Class as an Opposition

While Parkin has put the Marxist mantle of the ascendant class on to
the intelligentsia, Giddens has tossed it to the manual working class.
Western capitalist society, says Giddens, seeks to create a boundary
between economy and polity and the existence of a well-organised
trade-union movement tends to direct the working class towards
economistic demands. In state-socialist societies, however, the
structural arrangements (the inclusion of the trade-union movement
in the state apparatus and the absence of free collective bargaining)
entail there being 'no possibility of an orientation towards economism
on the part of manual or lower-manual workers' (Giddens, 1973:
250). Giddens goes on to suggest that 'A "technocratic" legitimation
of decentralisation at the level of enterprise management, which is
likely to be most amenable to the continuance of the existing opposition to dominance of the Party in political and economic life, will
tend to stimulate a resurgence of demands for the extension of
workers' management – and thus to produce a "counter-communism",
based upon ideas of localised cooperatives and genuine worker
participation in the exercise of authority in industry.' Giddens suggests that the different forms of authority in capitalist and state-
socialist industry result in different kinds of social stability. 'In spite
of the prevalence of overt manifestations of conflict which necessarily
characterise this type of industrial order [i.e. Western capitalism], it
can be argued that it is in fact inherently more stable than that which
exists in state-socialist societies, which is subject to the occasional,
but much more deep-rooted eruption of worker antagonism involving
an orientation to control' (268–9).

Giddens's argument has some serious flaws. He notes that 'The
occurrence of serious confrontations between such dissident groupings and the higher echelons of the Party organisation is probably
least likely to take place in the Soviet Union itself' (1973: 251). This

is because 'the dominance of the *apparat*' is more strongly established in the USSR than in other state-socialist societies. But the logic of Giddens's argument is that the stronger the dominance of the *apparat*, the greater the fusion of polity and economy, and therefore the greater the likelihood of the kinds of 'deep-seated eruptions' he refers to. Studies of industrial management in the Soviet Union have found no evidence to support this thesis. White can only summon up mention of some unspecified 'working class opposition' in Novocherkassk in 1962 (White, 1974 : 51), and the fact that the price of meat is held down by a budgetary subsidy (*ibid*) is no more evidence of working-class opposition than is the practice of successive British governments of keeping down the price of bread or council house rents.

White, in contrast to Giddens, points out the extent to which the Soviet working class is politically socialised. He notes that in 1972 nearly a quarter of a million people were enrolled in universities of Marxism-Leninism, that 'most Soviet citizens "basically do not question the legitimacy of the regime and most of its political messages"' (Hollander (1972) cited by White: 53). Political recruitment from the working class provides the Party leadership, notes White, 'with a political resource of some significance'. We have seen that the non-manual working class is incorporated into the political order; so too is the manual. In the USSR, membership of the Party by manual workers is less than their share of the population, but it is nevertheless considerable – 40·7 per cent in 1973 (*KPSS*, 1973 : 15). As shown in Table 2, the annual rate of increase of manual workers in Party membership has been at a higher rate than that of any other group since 1957. In 1972, 57·3 per cent of persons admitted to the Party were workers (*ibid*, 13). We must also bear in mind that the social origin of most of the non-manuals was probably manual. Opportunities for upward social mobility are great and will be discussed in more detail below (chapter 7).

The political convulsions in Eastern Europe show little evidence of the rise of a general manual-working-class consciousness. There is no evidence to suggest that calls for workers' management rather than 'economistic demands' have been made. Much evidence is to the contrary. Let us consider as an example the riots on the Polish Baltic coast which occurred in 1970–1. These events are the most explicit manifestation of manual worker unrest in Eastern Europe in recent times.[*]

It is not denied that the manual working class is a distinct *social* category compared to non-manual workers (see below, pp. 181–4), but

[*]On the working class in Czechoslovakia in 1968, see Kusin, 1972: chapter 1, especially pp. 15–17.

Table 2

Social composition of CPSU, 1957–1973

	USSR population %	CPSU membership				Av'ge annual rate of increase	
	1968	1957 (000s)	1964 (000s)	1971 (000s)	1973 (000s)	1957–64 (%)	1964–71 (%)
Manual workers[a]	54	2,398 (32·0%)	4,111 (37·3%)	5,796 (40·1%)	6,038 (40·7%)	10·2	5·9
Collective farmers	22	1,296 (17·3%)	1,818 (16·5%)	2,182 (15·1%)	2,170 (14·7%)	5·8	2·9
Non-manual workers	24	3,799 (50·7%)	5,092 (46·2%)	6,475 (44·8%)	6,613 (44·6%)	4·9	3·9
Total	100	7,493	11,022	14,455	14,821	6·7	4·5

Sources: Hammer, 1971: 19. *KPSS*, 1973: 15.
[a] Including state farm agricultural manual workers.

it is not a unitary class-conscious social entity. It has sharp internal divisions: in Poland miners form a labour aristocracy in terms of real income, peasant immigrants fill the more lowly paid unskilled jobs, and women in textiles are also lowly paid. The demands of the Gdansk insurgents were both economistic and political. The political demands were not for workers' management or 'localised cooperatives' but for more effective participation in trade unions and for more *efficient* management (Lane and Kolankiewicz, 1973: 312). Differentiation of political and economistic claims is possible under state socialism: not only are institutions such as trade unions and workers' councils concerned with the immediate economic issues, but the workers are able to relate government policies to living standards. The greater institutional linkage of unions, Party and industrial administration need not lead to greater political instability as Giddens suggests. In Gdansk, 'the discontent was a result of "the worsening economic situation, serious neglect in social policy, stagnation of real wages, shortage of supplies and the rising cost of living". The "predominantly workers' demonstrations" had as "a basis of protest, . . . dissatisfaction with the material situation and bad social conditions" ' (*Nowe Drogi* (undated issue, early 1971), cited by Lane and Kolankiewicz: 313). These demands were directly expressed against the central political elites, because the latter had become indifferent to the manual workers' interests. The bodies which should have defended their interests were unable to do so – partly for local but mainly for administrative reasons (which will be discussed below, chapter 5). It is also true that manual workers resented the 'unjust distribution of premiums and bonuses' which were enjoyed by the non-manual workers (see Lane and Kolankiewicz, 314). In Gdansk this feeling of deprivation relative to the non-manual strata also coincided with other grievances. (*Relative* because the average earnings of manual workers in the shipyards was well above the national average: 3,041 zl. compared with 2,384 zl.; *ibid.*)

The fact that there is no open 'trade union bargaining' should not be interpreted to mean that 'economism' is absent: workers' economic demands are put at a factory level and are articulated centrally by Party, union and even ministerial institutions. Hence, while it must be conceded that forms of conflict exist between manual and non-manual workers, as well as between manuals and the political elites, they do not seem to the present writer to be as great as those existing under capitalism. They do not explain the upheavals in Gdansk, which must be analysed in terms of the (poor) timing of economic policy, and neglect by the central authorities of local grievances (i.e. bureaucratic incompetence). This breakdown in communication is evidenced by the fact that many Party activists played a leading role in the protests (40 per cent of the workers' elected delegates to meet Gierek in Gdansk were Party members; *ibid*, 316). Giddens is correct to point to internal Party tensions, but exaggerates demands for workers' control. The utilisation of a Marxist class-conflict typology does not seem to be appropriate to analyse the internal convulsions of state-socialist society.

Forms of Dissent and Deviance

Here I think it appropriate to consider 'political opposition' as part of the general phenomenon of deviant behaviour. By 'deviant behaviour' we mean 'behaviour which violates institutionalised expectations – that is, expectations which are shared and recognised as legitimate within a social system' (Cohen, 1959 : 462). This includes a much wider range of activity than political dissent and opposition. The definition of socially 'deviant' behaviour begs some questions : it assumes that there is a common hierarchy of values shared by the population which is both culturally transmitted and structurally induced. In state-socialist societies it is quite clear that the political elite defines the values of the society; it defines deviance as departures from the politically conditioned expected rules of conduct. It must be made clear that 'deviance' is not considered by the present writer in any moral way. If one does not accept the rules as legitimate, then deviance from them is not morally reprehensible. From the point of view of the analysis of society, however, it is important to locate and to explain why particular groups deviate from the system of values as defined by the ruling elites or found in the official charter.

The view taken here is that deviance may be analysed in terms of social disorganisation and personal disorentation, and it may also have its origin in a belief system which may antedate that of the political elites. Deviance, then, is not simply a form of political opposition and it may have a sociological and psychological basis. Deviance such as alcoholism may result from the incapacity of new structural units to fulfil needs previously satisfied. Also, institutions or role structures themselves may not be well integrated with the values of the political elites and may articulate demands at variance with the official values; in extreme cases there may be overt hostility to 'the system'.

We do not accept the view that there is a *single universally accepted* value system. Rather we see an 'official' value system articulated by the political elites forming a central value system but juxtaposed with, and mediated by, traditional and other values. The Communist Party attempts to impose an overall system of goal-oriented values in its doctrine of Marxism-Leninism but cannot do so because of the resistances located in the structure of the social system.

Social control is exercised actively through the structures of the state to inculcate certain values and implement certain goals. Writers on state-socialist societies often overlook the existence of informal social control which operates through primary groups and which socialises people to traditional norms. In addition, and emphasised by Thomas and Znaniecki,* is the control exercised by associations which impose on individuals particular sectional values.

Here we shall discuss a select number of cases of deviance. These are not meant to represent the whole range of 'deviance' in Soviet society, but they reflect tendencies and trends of the kind of dissent found in industrial society. Very little information is available about deviance in state-socialist societies themselves and no comprehensive crime statistics are published. The issues selected here are ones which have been researched in the West, and are exclusively drawn from the Soviet Union. I shall consider social deviance (juvenile delinquency, alcoholism) and then turn to the more explicitly 'political' topics of demands for various kinds of civil rights, as well as national and religious rights.

Juvenile Delinquency and Alcoholism

The best if not the only work on juvenile delinquency in the USSR is by Connor (1970, 1972) who has utilised quantitative data drawn from local reports. From these we are able to draw up a picture of the kinds of offences committed together with the social background of the deviant.

The most frequent offence for which juveniles are apprehended is theft. In one Moscow district 38 per cent of the cases handled by the Commission on Juvenile Affairs in the early 1960s were for stealing; in Archangel *oblast* 'concealed theft' accounted for 32 per cent, 'open stealing' 12·7 per cent and 'assault with intent to rob' 7·2 per cent of all juvenile offences (in 1963; Connor, 1970: 285). 'Malicious mischief and hooliganism' accounted for 26 per cent of the cases in Moscow and about 10 per cent in Archangel; sex offences were 3 per cent and 8·7 per cent respectively. An intervening variable is drunkenness: in one corrective labour institute for juveniles it was found that 89 per cent of the inmates committed their offences when drunk. It has been reported in *Izvestiya* (27 July 1965) that 85 per cent of cases of malicious hooliganism, 60 per cent of first degree murder, and 95 per cent of minor hooliganism are committed in a

---

*Thomas and Znaniecki characterise 'the prevalent condition of our civilisation . . . as that of a plurality of rival complexes of schemes each regulating in a definite traditional way certain activities and each contending with others for supremacy within a given group' (*The Polish Peasant in Europe and America*, cited by Lemert, 1972: 34).

state of drunkenness. While we must treat these statistics somewhat circumspectly, the pattern of juvenile crime would seem to be centred on theft with very few acts of interpersonal violence – murder was less than 1 per cent of the offences in Archangel. As in western societies, girls are less prone to crime than boys: in Archangel between 1961 and 1963 they came to less than 3 per cent of the total; and from a third to a half of all girls were involved in offences concerning sex (Connor, 1970: 286).

Most detected juvenile crime is urban: in Sverdlovsk, 73 per cent of the delinquents came from manual workers' families, 23 per cent from non-manual and 4 per cent from peasant stock (Connor, 1970: 288). The delinquents appear to be of lower educational attainment and to be children of parents with 'significantly lower' education than average (Connor, 1972: 90). Children who are unsuccessful educationally seem to be more prone to crime: those who have left school and are at work are 2·5 times more likely to be charged with offences than are trade school students and 13 times more likely than adolescents in ordinary schools (Connor, 1972: 91); 'drop-outs' form a large proportion of the known delinquents. Family background appears to be an important variable. Of juveniles in Yaroslavl convicted in the late 1950s, 68 per cent had only one parent, though in 1966 one study in Belorussia showed that 77·3 per cent of delinquents came from complete families (Connor, 1972: 87–8).

This brief account of juvenile delinquency suggests that the pattern of juvenile crime in the USSR is 'not very dissimilar to delinquency in other industrial societies' (Connor, 1970: 294). It is an urban phenomenon and the delinquents are recruited predominantly from the manual working class – especially prone are youths from broken families and those with poor educational records. But there seems to be little evidence to suggest that a lower class culture reinforces a deviant sub-culture and even less to suggest that there is a political threat to the stability of the political system.

More concrete evidence of the persistence of a sub-culture may be gleaned from the study of drunkenness. Again, the quantitative data are sparse and unreliable. The prevalence of anti-drinking campaigns, official condemnation of heavy drinking and high taxes on alcoholic drinks, the restrictions on sales of liquor, public pronouncements about the high correlation between crime and drunkenness and its detrimental effects on production bring home the importance of the problem as seen by the political elites in the USSR. There can be no doubt that heavy drinking is deplored by the political elites who have tried through propaganda and law enforcement to prevent it. These official pronouncements, however, are mediated, as pointed out earlier, by institutional practice and traditional mores. Institutions have vested interests in the liquor trade: sales are a source of revenue to local soviets, and clubs and restaurants sometimes circumvent the spirit and even the letter of the law.

The existence of a sub-culture in which the practices of imbibing alcoholic drink and inebriation are accepted would seem to be widespread. Drinking is a traditional Russian pastime characterised by being the prerogative of men and based on the consumption of vodka. Traditionally, vodka was regarded as beneficial to health and a source of warmth. Despite the considerable attempts made by the authorities to prevent heavy drinking and alcoholism, it is still considered a social problem. As indicated above, drunkenness is associated with crime and many persons who are psychologically ill are heavy drinkers. At the lower levels of the social system drunkenness is socially accepted and factory managers and the police often do not enforce sanctions against drunken persons. Here, then, is a clear example of the lack of congruence between the aims of the political elites and popular activity. Alcoholism can probably be explained by cultural transmission, the socialisation of children into accepting the norms of drinking, wedded to the tension which society creates and does not solve. Rapid industrialisation and urbanisation are obvious causes of social dislocation – large numbers of men picked up and treated at sobering-up stations are unskilled (Connor, 1972: 44) and therefore likely to be urban immigrants from the countryside. As Connor points out, the drabness of Soviet life, the overcrowding and the lack of other leisure facilities are also contributory factors.

Drunkenness in the Soviet Union, then, may not be only symptomatic of the maladjustment of the individual to town life. Rapid urbanisation and the consequent movement of men from village to town does lead to a breakdown of traditional forms of socialisation and of primary group socialisation. This may create a need to 'drown one's sorrows'. But excessive drinking of alcohol is also learned behaviour brought from the countryside; it is part of the Russian's concept of the 'good life' and serves a social as well as an individual need. The fact that heavy drinking is an institutionalised part of Soviet culture explains why the pressure of the political elites to reduce dependence on alcohol has been successfully resisted.

Let us now turn to consider more explicitly political forms of dissent. These may be grouped under the following headings: campaigns for individual rights, nationalistic movements and those of religious affiliation.

The Movement for Individual Rights

By the term 'individual rights' we mean claims by individuals or groups to be left to pursue certain kinds of activity independently of surveillance or control by the state. Demands for such rights have been sympathetically viewed by western liberal democrats and by many socialists. They do, however, include a wide range of different claims, some of which are pro-capitalist, even, to use Ticktin's expression, 'Slav Fascist' (Ticktin, 1973a : 9). Though the most typical viewpoint is liberal-democratic, yet another influential group seeks greater individual rights within the parameters of the Soviet political system. The configuration of various kinds of dissent has been described by Bociurkiw (1970), Katz (1971), Reddaway (1972), and Tökes (1974). Study of such dissent is important because it indicates the kinds of demand which are not fulfilled in the Soviet system and reflects many of the underlying social tensions.

In the latter part of the 1960s numerous protests occurred and many petitions were addressed to the leaders of the Soviet state.* They shared in common a demand for the right to criticise the government publicly and for law-enforcement agencies to ensure fairness to the accused. Tökes has studied 538 samizdat documents issued between 1968 and 1970. The various demands in terms of percentages were for : political democracy, 25·5 per cent; nationality rights, 22·7 per cent; human rights-socialist legality, 17·6 per cent; developmental rationality (economic problems etc.), 13·6 per cent; religious autonomy, 7·6 per cent; quality of life, 6·6 per cent; artistic controls, 6·4 per cent (Tökes, 1974 : 16). Many demonstrations were held in public places. These were brave protests against the infringement of democratic rights and the illegality of the trial of various writers such as Sinyavski and Daniel (Hayward, 1967: 233–99). Many of the appeals to the Soviet government or Party leaders emphasise the rights of persons to 'one of the most basic of human rights – the right to hold independent opinions and to communicate them by any lawful means' (*Petition to UN Commission . . .* , 1969). But such a demand in itself is meaningless if the particulars of the 'independent opinions' are not defined. Demands for 'free elections' may involve advocacy of deep-seated changes in the nature of the regime itself. Grigorenko, one of the leading political dissidents, regarded elections in the following light : 'The elections are a mere farce, necessary to those in power so that they can demonstrate to the outside world that the entire nation stands behind them' (Grigorenko, 1969).

One of the most moderate critical viewpoints is that of Academician Andrei Sakharov who takes a 'convergence' standpoint. The

*Yesenin-Volpin (1973) defines six forms taken by the civil rights movement: petitions with demands for the observance of legality, public meetings and demonstrations, literary activity, dissemination of literature, activity of lawyers, appeals to courts.

Soviet Union, he says, has 'demonstrated the vitality of the socialist cause, which has done a great deal for the people materially, culturally and socially and, like no other system, has glorified the moral significance of labor' (1968 : 73). But western capitalism, he believes, is not leading to the 'absolute impoverishment' of the working class and is not likely to collapse. 'Both capitalism and socialism are capable of long-term development, borrowing positive elements from each other and actually coming closer to each other in a number of essential aspects.' In 1974 he returned to this theme and emphasised the important role of this borrowing: 'It is precisely in convergence that I see the only way to the salvation of mankind' (Sakharov, 1974).

Like Khrushchev, Sakharov regards the prevention of world war and nuclear conflict as the foremost political task of modern governments. Cooperation between the capitalist and socialist states is advocated to work out 'a broad programme of struggle against world hunger' (1968 : 86). Changes in the Soviet Union would be very much in the direction of movement to a western-type democratic system. Like other Soviet dissident theorists, Sakharov proposes the ending of 'irresponsible and irrational censorship', the abrogation of 'all anti-constitutional laws and decrees violating human rights', amnesty for political prisoners, the complete 'exposure of Stalin', and further extension of the economic reforms. (We may note that many of these claims are ambiguous: what is 'irrational censorship', whose (and which) 'human rights' have been violated?)

These rather compromising views have been challenged in a document prepared by 'numerous representatives of the technical intelligentsia of the Estonian SSR', who criticise Sakharov's dependence on 'scientific-technical means', on the 'goodwill of the leaders of our society' and on the 'common sense of the people', and argue that the causes of the problems of modern times lie in the 'spiritual, the political, the organic' (translation in Reddaway, 1969 : 94). By 'spiritual' cause, they refer to the 'removal of Christianity as a basic ideological force', which has not been replaced by the 'new materialist ideology'. The moral recovery of the Soviet people from Stalinism depends on their finding a new 'moral-philosophical teaching'. These writers see the political situation as being in an 'unstable' and 'precarious' balance which may lead to the establishment of neo-Stalinist rule. Political freedom, it is argued, is the only antidote to neo-Stalinism and they call for 'the rights of minority groups to opposition to be established by law', the revitalising of the Supreme Soviet, and the introduction of voting within the context of a multi-party system. Again they oppose the 'concept of class privilege' and call for the nationalities problem to be justly settled. In international affairs, this group is critical of its own society's doctrine of militant, offensive communism and calls for the renouncing of the 'senseless accumulation of territory' (*ibid*, 96). Its own programmatic statements, however, do not constitute a comprehensive policy. They include 'positive rapproachment' in international affairs, laws guaranteeing political freedoms, complete release of political prisoners, and an undefined form of 'radical economic reconstruction'.

The protests on particular issues have been aggregated into a general liberal-democratic criticism of the political order of the Soviet Union. The 'Memorandum of Democrats to the Supreme Soviet of the USSR on the Illegal Seizure of Power by the Leadership of the CPSU and its Anti-Constitutional Activity' ('*Memorandum . . .*', 1972) sets out not only a number of essential reforms of Soviet society but also a critique of the ruling Party. The memorandum asserts that the Communist Party took power away from the Provisional Government and introduced its own political organisation *over* all state and social organisations. The political 'monopoly' of the leadership of the present CPSU is illegal as authority is constitutionally vested in the soviets. The Party does not promote democracy or further the interests of the people; rather it gives to the citizens of the USSR 'material and spiritual poverty, lack of rights, arbitrariness and exploitation' ('*Memorandum . . .*', 1972: 41). The political demands of this group are the elimination of the leadership of the CPSU in the government of the country; the transfer of all power to the Supreme Soviet; the proper functioning of the legal organs, the court system and government apparatus 'in conformity with constitutional standards'; the introduction of 'democratic freedoms', 'general democratic elections', and the working out of a new constitution (*ibid*, 118–19).

The 'democratic movement' described above seeks to change Soviet society legally, by working from within the legal limits laid down by the Constitution. But the democrats lack any sociological analysis of their own society. It would appear that they are not opposed to the collective ownership of property and they remain silent about other major aspects of the Soviet system (education and social welfare). Their orientation is not overtly revolutionary, but seeks as a first step accommodation within the 1936 Constitution.

Solzhenitsyn is the epitome of another type of 'opposition' in the Soviet Union. It seems clear that Solzhenitsyn does not lead and has not actually led any political group or movement. His real or supposed danger to the regime lies in the nature of his views and in his literary ability to articulate such views forcefully. In his 'Letter to the Soviet Leaders' (written in September 1973, published in the *Sunday Times* on 3 March 1974) Solzhenitsyn provides us with a summary of his views on Soviet society. He makes it clear that he is not a socialist; he rejects and opposes Marxism, though in fact he is concerned with the ideology of *Soviet* Marxism-Leninism. He singles out two major 'failures' of the Soviet Union's* policy: opposing world imperialism, and supporting communist movements abroad. These faults stem from '*exact adherence to the precept of Marxism-Leninism*'. Russians, says Solzhenitsyn, have been and are being asked to 'die in an *ideological* war – And mainly for a dead ideology!' He rejects Marxism as being a 'primitive, superficial economic theory. . . . It was mistaken when it forecast that the proletariat would be endlessly oppressed and would never achieve anything in a bourgeois democracy. . . . It missed the point when it asserted that the prosperity of the European countries depended on their colonies. . . . It was mistaken through and through in its prediction that socialism could only ever come to power by an armed uprising. . . . And the picture of how the whole world would rapidly be overtaken by revolutions and how states would soon wither away was sheer delusion, sheer ignorance of human nature. . . . Marxism is not only not accurate, not only not a science, has not only failed to predict a *single event* in terms of figures, quantities, time scale or locations. . . .' Solzhenitsyn rejects the whole ideology of Marxism-Leninism as it is understood in the USSR. Such an ideology is 'intolerable', '*nothing constructive rests on it*, it is a sham, cardboard, theatrical prop – take it away and nothing will collapse, nothing will even wobble'.

What, then, does Solzhenitsyn seek to put in the place of (Soviet) Marxism-Leninism? He has no programme but rather asserts a set of values. He is a Russian patriot: '. . . it is the fate of the Russian and Ukrainian peoples that preoccupies me above all. . . .' He is a Christian: 'I myself see Christianity today as the only living spiritual force capable of undertaking the spiritual healing of Russia.' He seeks to reassert traditional values: 'A civilisation greedy for "perpetual progress" has now choked and is on its last legs.' Solzhenitsyn is opposed to more than the rule of the Communist Party: he rejects the doctrine of progress originating in the Enlightenment – 'The whirlwind of progressive ideology swept in on us from the West . . . has tormented our soul quite enough. . . .' He is against the large-scale urban-industrial order, against rapid economic growth. 'The urban life which by now as much as half our population is doomed to live, is utterly unnatural. . . . An economy of non-giantism with small-scale, though highly developed, technology, will not only allow for but will necessitate the new building of towns in the old style.' Solzhenitsyn, then, is a traditionalist, a nationalist, and is opposed to Marxism and modern large-scale industrialism.

*Strictly speaking, Solzhenitsyn is mainly concerned with Russia and the Ukraine.

At the other end of the scale are dissidents who attempt to utilise Marxism-Leninism to justify their opposition to the regime. They deplore 'official' Marxism-Leninism (Stalinism) and seek a return to fundamental values. This tendency took as its model the 'socialism with a human face' associated with Dubcek and the Czech reformers of 1968. Such views are associated with writers like B. V. Talantov who provides something of a Marxist analysis of present-day Soviet society. Like theorists of totalitarianism, he argues that the Soviet political order is a 'total, unlimited and uncontrolled dictatorship of the CPSU' (Talantov, 35). The relationship between the political elite and the 'non-party toilers' who make up the 'oppressed class of the production of material wealth' is exploitative. After 1929 the Party changed from being a political party as such to 'a directing and ruling class of state bureaucrats'. It is now a ruling class and has a class consciousness. One of the weaknesses of class analysis of the USSR is that it does not demarcate the basis of the Party's class power. Talantov, however, locates the substance of class power in the system of the *nomenklatura* (see above, p. 78) and also in the special skills of administration and management which are controlled by the Party's own educational system. The Party maintains the stability of the system (and itself as a ruling class) by preserving its control of the *nomenklatura*; this, says Talantov, serves like property under capitalism and secures the position of the members of the ruling class by ensuring the 'hereditary transfer of rights to descendants'. These rights have no juridical foundation and are furthered by education, connections and 'protection'. While Talantov recognises the antagonism betwen Party and non-Party members, his chief demands are in support of the democratic movement: the struggle for the liquidation of censorship, for freedom of speech and for the press, and for freedom of conscience. He deplores the new elite of privileged persons and the transformation of the Communist Party into an organisation defending inequality rather than battling against it. The Talantov group looks to support from progressives within the Party. But some writers also envisage a 'bor'ba nizov' (struggle from below) and if other means fail, call for the formation of a new party (G. Alekseev, 1969: 61).

The general political criticisms of the Soviet political order, described above, all share a demand for greater pluralism in the political system; they assert individual rights against Party rights. Two other important currents of dissent share this liberal-democratic orientation, but stress and aggregate their demands around the rights of nationalities and religious groups.

Nationalities

The Soviet Union is composed of twenty-three major nationalities.* In Soviet theory, with the march of the Soviet Union to communism, these nations are considered to be merging into one *Soviet* nation. Groups of some of these nationalities in the 1960s began to oppose Soviet policy and to assert their own national rights. This form of deviance may again be considered to be a conflict between traditional national values and those of the Communist elites, though national claims are legitimated in Marxist-Leninist terms. Among the Ukrainians there seem to have been particularly militant groups. Bociurkiw (1970: 84) reports that between 1959 and 1962, several groups (Ukrainian Workers' and Peasants' Union, Ukrainian National Committee, United Party for the Liberation of the Ukraine) demanded secession from the USSR. These were snuffed out by the Secret Police and it is asserted that many of their members were imprisoned and that some were shot.

Not only the Civil Rights activists but also many of the 'nationalists' plead for their cause on the basis of the Soviet Constitution and Leninist norms. A petition to the Prosecutor of the Ukrainian Republic by a citizen of Odessa called on him to indict the Ukrainian Minister of Higher and Secondary Education. It was alleged that the Minister had violated the Ukrainian Criminal Code in respect of its clauses on national and racial equality (Article 66) and 'Leninist principles of opportunity for higher education' (Articles 66 and 167); for failure to implement the resolutions of the Twentieth Congress of the CPSU on the liquidation of the cult of personality (Article 66); and for disorganising the 'educational process in the system of secondary and incomplete secondary education' (Article 167) (Chornovil, 1968: 170).

The following petition (Chornovil, 1968: 205–7) to the Chairman of the Council of Nationalities of the Supreme Soviet of the USSR contains many of the demands made by various nationalist groups. It should be noted that these demands are 'reformist' and require change within the context of the Soviet system rather than any major structural change.

1. To stop every kind of national discrimination against Jews.
2. To re-establish the statehood of the Crimean Tartars and of the Volga Germans.
3. To return their immovable property to the repatriated families of people unjustly deported.

---

*i.e. having over a million members in 1970, the largest being Russians (129 million), Ukranians (41 million), Belorussians and Uzbeks (each 9 million), Tartars (6 million), and Kazakhs (5 million). In addition, there are some 100 small nationalities with populations of less than half a million.

4. To repatriate the people of the Baltic Region, Western Ukraine, Belorussia, and Moldavia who were unjustly deported to Siberia.
5. To investigate the disappearance of the Latvian army personnel.
6. To proclaim a broad amnesty for all victims of the Stalin personality cult.
7. To release the women martyrs Kateryna Zarytsika, Halyna Didyk, and Odarka Husyak.
8. To examine the discriminatory attitude towards the Ukrainian population of the Kuban, Bilhorod, and Starodub areas and to apply measures to eliminate this attitude.
9. To end all forms of educational discrimination against nationalities in the Ukraine, Belorussia, Moldavia and other republics.
10. To condemn the practice of deporting the inhabitants of the national republics to Siberia and of populating their lands with Russians.
11. To re-examine the system of passport restrictions and to condemn passport discrimination which contradicts the Universal Declaration and undermines the friendship of peoples.
12. To revise the boundaries of the national republics for the purpose of establishing exact ethnographic boundaries.
13. To organise a broad discussion in the press of all the problems raised here.

The case of the Ukrainian nationalists has been put forward clandestinely by two writers in the Soviet Union, Dziuba (1968) and Chornovil (1967). Dziuba argues that the Ukraine's territorial unity and sovereignty have been undermined by population movement (immigration of Russians, emigration of Ukrainians) and by the subordination of various institutions (particularly industrial) to Moscow. The cultural identity of the Ukrainians, he says, is being lost because of the lack of sufficient national education in its schools. Similar points have been detailed in an open letter to the deputies of the Soviets of the Ukrainian Republic by Anton Koval (1970: 130–3). Koval points out that of thirty-three industrial ministries operating in the Ukrainian Republic only six are under the Republic's jurisdiction. He calls for their subordination to the Ukraine and also seeks the introduction of self-government in economic enterprises. In the sphere of government, Koval advocates the adoption of a new constitution giving greater powers to the republics, democratising elections (with the nomination of more than one candidate), ensuring the existence of various political parties. Numerous other policies are advocated – the abolition of censorship, freeing of political prisoners, greater self-government in universities, dissolution of the secret police. In cultural affairs, there is a call for the Ukrainianisation of all educational institutions, for the elimination of practices discriminating against 'the cultural heritage of the Ukrainian people' and for an end to the prosecution of 'leading figures of Ukrainian culture'.

The Jews are a minority who figure prominently in 'dissident' movements. Some see themselves as representatives of Jewish groups wishing to assert their rights in the USSR, others agitate for emigration, and yet a third group plays a part in the general movement for civil rights. The first two groups particularly complain of anti-Semitism, discrimination against Jews in employment and education and the destruction of Jewish religious and cultural movements (Bociurkiw, 1970: 90–1). The movement for emigration is strongest and most widespread among Jews originating in territories which were incorporated into the USSR after the Second World War (e.g. Eastern Poland) and among the Oriental Jews (Katz, 1971: 21). It seems likely that the Jews in the Democratic Movement are Jews from Soviet Slav lands who seek equality of treatment as citizens with other Russian Soviet subjects, and greater inclusion into Soviet society. Ross's survey of Soviet Jewish emigrants to Israel (noted above, p. 88) shows that 65 per cent thought it not possible to be a good Jew and a good communist; and 55 per cent likewise thought it impossible to be both a good Jew and a good citizen (Ross, 1974: 113). For this group disillusionment was greatest about the possibility of influencing policy – 92 per cent thought it impossible for the Soviet citizen to have any impact; 88 per cent thought that the rules in the USSR were not equally applied; and more than 83 per cent were opposed to the Soviet regime (*ibid*).

Religious Movements

While Khrushchev had a reputation for 'liberalisation' in the arts, he was responsible for a policy of repression against the churches. This policy brought to a head demands by the religious movements which have continued to the 1970s. Defence of religious rights has a similar rationale to that of the democratic movement described above. The legality of the government's action in closing churches and harassing worshippers is questioned: it is argued that Soviet law guarantees separation of church and state and that the churches have rights under the Soviet Constitution. As with other forms of protest, religious leaders 'loyal' to the regime have been and are denounced by the dissidents who have their own pressure groups. This is particularly the case among some members of the Russian Orthodox Church and among the Evangelical Christian-Baptists. Members of other religious groups which have protested about Soviet religious policy include some Catholics in Lithuania and some priests of the (illegal) Ukrainian Uniate Church. There are also a number of sects (Jehovah's Witnesses and True Orthodox Christians) that are officially proscribed and therefore lead an illegal existence.

Michael Bourdeaux (1970) has collected and described documents which illustrate the persecution of the Orthodox Church. A petition by two Orthodox priests deplored the activities of the 'leaders and plenipotentiaries' of the Council for Affairs of the Russian Orthodox Church, who have 'transformed it *into a clearly discriminatory* organisation, the entire activities of which are directed at a systematic violation of the laws on the separation of the church from the state and a systematic obstruction of the performance of religious rites, which represents a criminal offence under Articles 194–2 and 194–3 of the Criminal Code of the RSFSR' (cited by Bociurkiw, 1970: 93). The priests, in addition to condemning the illegal activities of the Council, called on the government to 'restore socialist legality' and to restore to the Church the places of worship closed under Khrushchev. These demands, it should be noted, were couched within the framework of Soviet legality and they recognised that the interests of the church in civil affairs 'coincided with the interests of a free state under the rule of law'.

Though direct links between religious dissent and political dissent are few because the religious people do not want to be accused by the authorities of using the church for political ends, some Christians have been more overtly political and have justified their criticism of the Soviet government by reference to Christian ethics. Commenting on the persecution of dissenters, a Pskov clergyman wrote as follows:

> A Christian is bound before God to be a whole man, a free man – free to think, not to be untruthful or to act deceitfully either towards himself or towards others. To persecute a person for exercising this freedom of personal peaceful beliefs, the freedom to express the truth, is Caesar attempting to take away something that is God's. It is essentially a crime against humanity, against the free and sacred humanity bestowed upon him by God in Christ, Our Lord . . . Marchenko and other unknown representatives of the Russian intelligentsia are today suffering in the 'severe regime' conditions on behalf of that Christian principle.
>
> (*Russkaya mysl'*, 26 June 1969; cited by Bociurkiw, 95)

Many such writers argue that the Church is incompatible with Soviet power and that the latter has tried and is trying 'completely and finally to destroy' the Church (Anon, 1972: 76). The union between the Church and an anti-Christian state is 'a contradiction', as is a hypocritical kind of division of state and Church. The same writer goes on to note that the place of Christian belief has been taken by the 'heathen cult of Lenin'; the 'icon corners (*krasnye ugly*) in Russian houses are turned into the so-called "red corners" (*krasnye ugolki*)', and sometimes in houses one sees the 'place of the sacred icon occupied by "the eternal living Lenin" or by a radio receiver'. The complicity of the leaders of the Orthodox Church with the Soviet state leads the author of this piece to advocate the formation of an underground (*katakombnaya*) church (*ibid*, 87).

Religious dissent among 'unofficial' groups of Baptists (the Initsiativniki) has been less political in orientation and more concerned with preventing government interference with their own religious activities. The sect has not only utilised petitions to various bodies but has also resorted to more direct action to secure its interests (see Bourdeaux, 1968). It has refused to accept the state's right to forbid it to produce literature, to hold services without permission and to organise meetings and lessons for children. The dissident Baptists, though, have claimed that their activity is not constitutionally illegal and that they have a right to freedom of conscience, and to the separation of church and state. The reaction of the Soviet state to the Initsiativniki's activity has been to pass more stringent acts regulating it. Arrests, intimidation and deprivation of employment, fines and imprisonment were imposed on the dissidents (see 'Appeal from the Dissident Baptists', 1970). Evidence would seem to suggest, however, that the persecution has increased rather than diminished the strength of the believers (Bociurkiw, 99). But we must bear in mind the fact that the number of religious believers and dissenters remains relatively low compared to the activists and followers of the official creed of communism.

The persistence of religious belief in the Soviet Union involves an explanation in social, psychological, religious and ideological terms. Not only is religious belief a kind of 'hangover' from the previous non-socialist society, but it provides a form of adaptation to grief, failure and despair in life. The reason why the political elites have pursued a relentless policy against religion is because of its *ideology*. Organised forms of religion are vehicles for expressing 'ideological protest' and as such they must be considered, therefore, as forming a part of political dissent (see C. Lane, 1974).

Composition of the Various Opposition Movements

Katz has attempted to estimate the numbers who are involved in one way or another with 'basic civil rights and the rule of law in the USSR'. He discusses participation in *samizdat* (or illegal publications) and asserts that 'a reasonable approximation would be several hundred active members, and several thousand as sympathisers and activists. . . . The widest category of people reached by *samizdat* can conservatively be estimated in millions' (1971 : 11). The number of active members would appear to be extremely modest. Katz's category of people 'reached by *samizdat*', including those 'who hear about it from friends' or 'hear about it from foreign radio stations and foreign visitors', would appear to be an extremely amorphous one, and not one necessarily having any ideological identification with the values and beliefs of *samizdat*. More importantly, however, it is misleading to consider *samizdat* readers or even activists as forming an 'opposition', for this is ideologically as diverse and politically committed a set of people as those writing for, or reading, such western papers as *Private Eye*, the *New York Review of Books*, and the *New Statesman*.

Chornovil (1968 : 80–1) has given a profile of persons convicted in 1966 for anti-Soviet nationalistic propaganda and agitation. In his view, those convicted are aged between 28 and 30 years, had a peasant or working-class background, had been successful at school, and had gained entry to a university where, even if their speciality was technical, they had taken an active interest in native (particularly Ukrainian) language and culture. Amalrik (1970), himself a leading activist in *samizdat* activity, analysed the social background of signatories (738) to petitions protesting about the Galanskov-Ginzburg trials. The largest single social group was men in academic work (45 per cent), followed by 'people engaged in the arts' (22 per cent), engineers and technical specialists (13 per cent), other non-manual workers (teachers, doctors, lawyers) (9 per cent), and students (5 per cent). In all 94 per cent of the sample were non-manual of one type or another. Only 6 per cent were workers, and there were no peasant signatories (Amalrik, 1970 : 15–16). There seems to be little doubt that the intelligentsia is the major group participating in the Democratic Movement; there are few manual workers and a negligible number of peasants (Katz, 1971 : 12). The movement seems to have reached a peak during the trials of the mid-1960s. The number of petitions has declined in the early 1970s, many of the leaders have been arrested and exiled or have emigrated and the movement seems to have faded out.

On religious groupings the available data are again uneven. A western estimate is that 58 million people are 'practising religion' in the USSR (Reddaway, 1968 : 27). But this figure includes Muslims. However, we have estimates both from the legal organisations themselves and from the research of Soviet sociologists. The director of the Institute for Scientific Atheism claims that 15 per cent of the urban and 25 per cent of the rural population are religious believers. The largest church membership is that of the Russian Orthodox Church, having 30 million churchgoers in 1961 (see C. Lane, 1974 : 2–3). The Baptists claim a membership of some half a million; the Pentacostalists, Jehovah's Witnesses and Mennonites each about 40,000; and the Adventists some 25,000. The Orthodox Church has the broadest social composition, having members among both peasants and intelligentsia. Its active membership, however, is not only declining but is 'predominantly old, female, poorly-educated and unqualified and rural' (*ibid*). The only significant participation by manual workers in any illegal activity appears to be among the breakaway Baptists' groups, but information here is sketchy. The sects have a much higher degree of religious commitment and – at least as far as study of the Baptists shows – their membership is younger, more urban-industrial and better-educated than that of the Orthodox Church.

Dissent and Soviet Society

While the data at our disposal on dissent are not by any means complete, we are able to come to a number of general conclusions. First, the demands of the various dissidents must be seen as being composed of separate and specific objections to various arrangements of the Soviet order. As a whole, they cannot be considered as providing a profound theoretical critique of, or viable practical alternative to, Soviet communism. The evidence would not appear to support Katz's view that 'the dissent movement is a powerful catalyst for change in the USSR' (1971 : 29). But it is likely to secure limited rights for certain groups (such as the Tartars, or Baptists) and important changes in procedures (say in organisation of the press or the Courts) rather than result in any major change as required for a revolt or revolution. It is in no way comparable to the Bolshevik movement in Russia before 1917 (see Katz, 28–9). Rather than being 'a movement', dissent is nucleated : it ranges from criticisms of large-scale industrialism (Solzhenitsyn) to demands for proper observance of Soviet laws (petitions on trials of writers). Most of the claims could be met within the framework of Soviet society : and Solzhenitsyn has addressed his appeals to the leaders of the Soviet state. The second general point that may be made is that dissent is voiced by the intelligentsia – particularly by the upper professional groups. There would appear to be very little, if any, general support by the masses – either workers or peasants – for the proposals here considered. As Bauman has expressed it : there has been no 'holy alliance of the intellectuals, who think, and the masses, who feel and suffer' (1971 : 49). Thirdly, the forms of manifest political dissent studied must be considered as *relatively small* and exclusive movements. The large masses of the population remain untouched by it and reject its values. Allegiance to the values of Marxism-Leninism and to the Communist Party has grown. Religious dissent must be seen in the light of the decline of religion and the general secularisation of life, as in other industrialised countries.

There can be no doubt from the various sources cited above that the political authorities repress in various ways movements which are opposed to the arrangements of state socialism or to its ideology. Why does this repression and control take place? The various theories of class or elite dominance which were discussed above all have in common an explanation which regards repression as originating from the preservation of the interests of the ruling class or elite. If, as I have argued, such theories are mistaken in application to the structure of power of state-socialist society, what alternatives have we to put in their place? It has been argued above that state-socialist societies are primarily mobilisation and development regimes. To understand the actions of the political authorities in their suppression of deviance, Durkheim's analysis of social structure appears useful.

Durkheim pointed out that societies undergoing industrialisation faced the problem of ensuring solidarity; differentiation, he said, meant the obsolescence of mechanical forms of solidarity, and new forms of social integration became necessary. In state-socialist society, 'official' Marxism-Leninism is an ideology which acts as a social cement. It defines those things that are 'sacred': the October Revolution, Lenin, the Party, Communism; it also has other values which it shares with western societies – the belief in progress, in industrialisation, centralisation and the nation state. To attack such values and beliefs is to attack the political elites, because these elites help shape ideology. But it is more than that: it weakens the integrity of the social order and its forms of social integration, and it encourages disorganisation. We saw that Solzhenitsyn is not a very serious political challenge to the regime in the sense that he had no party, no political organisation. From the political elite's point of view he represents a more general threat to social stability.

In the West, particularly England, social development has occurred slowly over centuries; the 'disruptive' elements are less of a problem to the maintenance of the political order because the values of the system are widespread, more deeply engrained. The legitimation of private property, of the market in politics and the economy is very deep-seated, especially in the older industrialised systems. *Individual* rights to private property are like cement which keeps the whole fabric of the society together. Physical repression is perhaps less important than ideological control. Alternative value orientations are well integrated or incorporated through trade unions and parliamentary-type political parties. Under these circumstances the individual is considered to be the primary· unit and society is seen as the emanation of the individual's interests : in other words, in liberal-democratic theory, the individual takes precedence over society. In collectivist Bolshevik social theory (Soviet Marxism-Leninism) the relationship between man and society is reversed. Society is the dominant unit : the individual has no interest independently of society. Claims for the assertion of individual rights are claims against society; they are demands for a particular kind of community. The Soviet Union and other state-socialist societies have had to carry out industrial development in the face of resistance from the carriers of traditional values; the political elites have had to establish their legitimacy after revolution and/or war. They have had to shape traditional orientations to their dominance and therefore feel more insecure when faced with dissension and opposition. The question of 'civil rights' cannot be posed in the abstract : the implementation of some rights for some people restricts other rights for other people. Hence one must define which rights for which people. The Soviet political elites have defined the major goals of Soviet policy to construct communism (regarded here as a state-sponsored form of modernisation) : rights of individuals and groups which are held by the elites to hinder the attainment of these goals have been suppressed (Yesenin-Volpin, 1973). The Procurator at the trial of Grigorenko put this clearly when she said : 'Article 125 of the Constitution of the USSR grants democratic rights to Soviet citizens, but we cannot tolerate the utilization of these rights to the detriment of our communist construction' (cited by Bociurkiw, 1970 : 81). Forms of *anomie* characterise Soviet society : many of the officially prescribed goals conflict with each other and they also have no institutionalised means for implementation. Hence demands are put outside the official political system by 'true' Marxist-Leninists for the implementation of certain courses of action.

While there certainly is dissension in state-socialist society, 'opposition' is not characterised by 'systemic contradiction' or class struggle. More typical and more important, in my view, are the forms of dissent defined above. Some have their origins in traditional belief systems and are reinforced by individual disorientation resulting from urbanisation and from the absence of support from the local community. In addition, there are grievances felt by individuals or groups when their interests (legitimate or otherwise) or expectations are infringed. These different forms of dissent overlap. As Yesenin-Volpin (1973 : 7) has noted, '[opposition-minded] liberals have turned away to religious or mystical quests for a better morality, or to decadence, or simply to private life'.

It cannot be denied that repression of certain activities is a characteristic of the modern state. Harsh treatment of deviants by the political authorities, however, may paradoxically help to perpetuate dissent. Sociologists of deviance point out that society's reaction to deviance has an important effect on the nature of the deviance itself. In many cases the political elites can define sanctions and may segregate the deviants. If societal support is given to the elite's sanctions the deviant may be stigmatised and he may have no alternative but to organise his own life and define his identity around the facts of deviance (see Lemert, 1972: 63). Consequently the deviant may become more alienated from, and hostile to, his society. The lawmakers and law-enforcers may thus magnify the social (and political) costs of deviance; 'social control' and repression may institutionalise it. The exclusion of Solzhenitsyn from the Soviet Union and the use of administrative methods against certain categories of dissenter may be mistaken even from the regime's own point of view, for such action may strengthen secondary deviance.

5
The Political Elites

In the last chapter we considered those who disagreed with the goals of Soviet Marxism-Leninism and we dealt with conflict between the socialist state and the groups which dissent from some of its central values and practices. Here we shall consider those individuals and groups who subscribe to the goals of state-socialist society and to the values of Marxism-Leninism. At the same time, however, there may be disagreements about means (or norms) concerning the implementation of these goals, and the various institutions of the state (police, Party, economic ministries) may develop particular interests.

The socialist state is not a unitary body. Althusser in another context has suggested that the *repressive* state apparatus might be distinguished from the *ideological* state apparatus (1971 : 136). The former consists of the government, the armed forces and the police, and the latter is made up of various apparatuses – ideological, legal, political (parties, unions), communication and culture. In state-socialist society, the distinction between public and private domains is irrelevant, and Althusser is certainly correct in pointing to the *plurality* of apparatuses. While it is true that they all 'function' in conformity with the interests of the dominant political elite, they all have a certain autonomy and, while subscribing to the dominant ideology of Marxism-Leninism, there may also be important differences of interest between them.

The socialist state helps to further the interests of the working class by its ownership of the means of production. It is composed of several different institutions and groups. Just as the character of individual capitalist states may differ, depending on the composition and history of their ruling classes and the acceptance of their legitimacy by the people, so too do the specific features of the state vary between individual socialist countries. The configuration of conflict between groups varies between individual societies and over time for each society. The major institutional conflicts are between the Party, the government apparatus and the police and military forces. As in capitalist societies, such conflicts may occur and be resolved without altering the fundamental class nature of the society expressed by ownership relations. In particular, this means that the form of state ownership of the means of production is safeguarded, though groups within the state apparatus may wish to alter the constellation of forces. The various groups forming the socialist state may also have different political, economic and social priorities. Here we shall illustrate how the saliency of various interests differs between socialist states. As our knowledge of the nature of interchanges between the interests making up the socialist state is limited, we may first outline the representation of interests at its inner councils (the Central Committee and the Politbureau). Differences in the density of representation are indexes of the influence wielded by various fractions of the ruling groups and these may be considered over different time periods following a revolution.

Political Leadership

State-socialist societies have all moved from a revolutionary situation to a post-revolutionary one. The leadership which is appropriate to a revolution may be found inadequate during a period following it when different qualities may be necessary. It is often asserted that while communist revolutions are led by intellectuals, in the industrialisation process which follows it the leadership moves to a 'managerial' intelligentsia who are more competent in organising industrial development and its associated social changes (Kautsky, 1968: 165). Bauman (1971, 42) has put this another way when he refers to the 'withdrawal of status' from professional revolutionaries after they have outlived their purpose and when they are socially undermined by men with technological skills. In such circumstances there often arises a conflict between the 'idealist' or political veterans and the 'modernisers', and it is sometimes hypothesised that pursuit of a policy of industrial change involves a victory for the latter. Problems of administration figure largely in the post-revolutionary period and the formation of a socialist state gives rise to elites with some allegiance to institutions outside the Party. How then is the transition made? Does the inclusion of interests outside the revolutionary Party in the socialist government lead to its 'degeneration' – to a loss of socialist ideals?

One important factor affecting the position of the ruling Party after seizing power is its strength before the revolution. Obviously a Communist Party such as the Russian or Chinese which commanded considerable support and was in the forefront of a powerful revolutionary movement would be able to call on many more people with congruent socialist beliefs when in power than would a Party such as the Hungarian or the East German which had a small base. In the latter case one might expect socialist activists to be more easily 'swamped' when faced with the problem of manning the command posts of a modern society. Other aspects of the recruitment of political leaders also affect the political outcomes of post-revolutionary governments. One might expect the orientations to certain political problems to vary according to whether a political leader came from a minority ethnic group, whether he had a career in the Party or in the state bureaucracy, or whether he had a higher education or Party education or only elementary education.

Study of the Party central committee in various countries will help to illustrate the differences in the political systems of the countries concerned. The Central Committee (CC) is an important inter-mediary between top decision-makers (the Politbureau) and the political groups in the society. Membership of the CC gives access to its specialised committees and to the Politbureau. It is a larger group than the Politbureau, and one may reasonably infer that changes in the representation of groups at this level reflect their changing importance for the management of the country. Also, the kind of political policy adopted may be a reflection of the con-figuration of interests present in the leadership. Here we shall con-sider the case of Soviet Russia and then study four East European countries (Bulgaria, Czechoslovakia, Poland and Hungary) and China.

The case of the Soviet Union is in many ways distinct from the other countries mentioned above: in addition to its cultural setting, the Soviet Union has had a much longer continuous history of Com-munist Party rule than any other society. Therefore, it is appropriate to consider the Soviet leadership in three time-spans: that following the October Revolution of 1917, that of the Stalin period and that of the post-Stalin period.

The Soviet Union

The consolidation of the Revolution and the rise to power of Stalin has been generally regarded as illustrating a profound change in the nature of Communist Party leadership. In the initial stage of revolu-tion the leaders have been seen as 'masters of persuasion'; they are intellectuals and skilled political propagandists. Lasswell *et al.* have depicted the leadership as being made up of men of urban birth and bourgeois background who have attended university and have joined the Party when adult (Lasswell, 1952: 33). With the consolida-tion of the Revolution, however, administrative and police skills become more important and necessary for the survival of the new order. New men with a different outlook enter the stage; they have been considered as 'specialists in coercion'. They are men of rural birth and peasant background, they have primary or secondary education, they join the Party early in life and their chief activity is organisational and political Party work (*ibid*, 33; for full biographical details see Schueller, 1951). After the revolution has been consolidated and a certain level of modernisation has been reached there is yet a third type of leadership. This is characterised by men who are highly educated, technically trained and organisationally based. But before considering in more detail the institutional position of men in the Politbureau let us turn to the wider leadership network of the Central Committee and lower Party organs.

In the immediate post-revolutionary years the Central Committee of the Soviet Party was relatively stable in its personnel. Rigby (1971b) has shown that full members of the Central Committee were largely re-elected from one congress to the next: figures comparing the membership of consecutive congresses from 1918 to 1930 were 67 per cent, 90 per cent, 79 per cent, 84 per cent, 89 per cent, 93 per per cent, 83 per cent and 83 per cent (1971b: 14). These figures indicate that there was a permanent core of men at the centre of the Central Committee; in addition, of course, new men were being added as the size of the CC grew. The period from 1936 to 1938 saw a purge of this core: only 23 per cent of the Central Committee elected by the XVII Congress (1934) survived to 1939 (XVIII Congress). As Levytsky has suggested, the 'new political elite' of these years was made up of men with a bureaucratic outlook rather than the idealistic 'independent thinking' men previously attracted to the Bolshevik Party (Levytsky, 1969: 19). This process was one of intense political violence which has been emphasised in Solzhenitsyn's *Gulag Archipelago*. Levytsky has analysed the causes of death of members of the Central Committee from 1912 to 1969: of 145 full members, 62 were liquidated or died in imprisonment (plus one executed by the British in Baku), 3 were murdered, 3 committed suicide and 2 were killed in action (Levytsky, 1969: 21).

T. H. Rigby has examined the middle and lower levels of the Party organisation between 1917 and 1922. These include the delegates to Party conferences and members of provincial and district committees. Rigby points to three sources from which the political elite was recruited: persons who had been Bolsheviks before the Revolution, revolutionaries who joined up with the Bolsheviks, and others who became active in politics only after the Revolution. As one would expect, immediately after the Revolution the first group was dominant but 'their dilution by members of the other two groups, and particularly the last, set in very quickly, so that within four or five years of the establishment of the new regime the revolutionaries were heavily outnumbered by "new men" on all but the topmost levels of the elite' (1971a: 422). Taking the Party Congresses as an index, the percentage of men joining the Party *before* 1917 was: Sixth Congress (1917), 97 per cent; Eighth Congress (1919), 77 per cent; Ninth Congress (1920), 49 per cent; Tenth Congress (1921), 36 per cent, Eleventh Congress (1922), 48 per cent. Turning to the provincial elites, defined as members of provincial (*gubkom*) and district (*uezd*) committees, we see that in the former the proportion of those joining the Party after 1917 rose from 22·9 per cent (in 1919) to 44·0 per cent (1922); in district committees the comparable figures were 54·8 per cent and 70·5 per cent. By 1921, a very large proportion of the leadership of the provincial Party organisations were 'new men': 70 per cent of all 'major *gubernia* (provincial) level officials' had joined the Party after 1917, as had 27 per cent of their secretaries; in 1921, 24 per cent of Party members holding official posts at the provincial level and 16 per cent at district level had previously been members of other parties. In 1920, the proportions of former members of other political parties at the provincial level were as follows: Party officials, 24·4 per cent; Soviet officials 26·4 per cent; trade union officials, 32·5 per cent; military officials 17·4 per cent (*ibid*, 422). Thus we can see that within a very short time after the political revolution in 1917, at the lower levels of the political elite, the Bolsheviks were becoming dependent on new Party members and on men whose allegiance had been to other parties. The relatively short period of the Party's existence and its underground character meant that when it took power it become dependent on men who had little, if any, revolutionary experience. This is hardly surprising when we recall that at the beginning of 1917 there were estimated to be only 23,600 Party members, a number which had risen to 200,000 in August of that year. The comparison may be made with China where the Party had had a much longer period during which it prepared for full-scale rule and had a much larger membership on which it could draw.

The increase in membership was also paralleled by changes in the education and social composition of the elites. Congress delegates with higher education fell from 32 per cent in 1917 to 13 per cent in 1922; conversely, those with less than secondary education rose from 45 per cent to 64 per cent between the same dates (Rigby, 1971a: 429). The number of delegates who were manual workers (or of manual origin) rose from 42 per cent in 1917 to 49 per cent in 1922. No peasants were present at the Sixth Congress (1917) and the number rose to only 7 per cent in 1922. At the lower levels of the elite, leading provincial officials in 1920 were largely either manual workers or office workers by social origin; peasants and professionals ('intelligentsia') formed a small part, as shown in Table 3 (Rigby, 1971a: 431).

Table 3

Social composition of leading provincial officials, 1920 (%)

	Manual workers	Peasants	Office workers	Intelli-gentsia	Not known	Total
Party	36·2	6·9	35·1	12·5	9·3	100
Soviets	36·0	6·7	39·1	12·8	5·4	100
Trade unions	41·9	2·0	43·9	6·5	5·7	100
Military	25·0	3·8	46·9	9·9	14·4	100

The large numbers of 'office workers', particularly in the army, is noteworthy as is also the small proportion of peasants. However, the recruitment of peasants increased both in the Party (from 8 per cent in 1917 to 28 per cent in 1921) and at the provincial committee level (to 28 per cent by 1922). These figures bring out the fact that the Soviet Party did not have roots in the rural areas, but drew support from the urban classes – particularly manual and non-manual workers.

The post-Stalin central committees were renewed more rapidly than those of the early Stalin era. Between 1952 and 1956, 66 per cent of the full members were re-elected and the figure fell to 52 per cent between 1956 and 1961 even though these committees witnessed a large increase in membership (numbers were 125 in 1952; 133, 1956; 175, 1961) (Rigby, 1971b: 14). This is an indication that Khrushchev was creating a new inner core, though he did not resort to the coercive measures of the Stalin period. The changes which were taking place after Stalin's death have been studied by Fleron (1970) and Gehlen and McBride (1968).

Fleron analyses the changes in representation in the Central Committee between 1952 and 1965 in terms of 'recruited' and 'co-opted' officials. By 'recruited' Fleron means officials who 'entered the political elites at very early stages in their careers and who thus had little opportunity to form close ties with a professional-vocational group'; 'co-opted' officials, on the other hand, were those who 'entered the political elite in mid or late career and who had probably established very close professional-vocational ties outside the political elite' (Fleron, 1970: 123). In this instance, *political elite* refers to the holding of a position in the Party, government, Young Comunist League (YCL) or trade unions. The *Party elite* is a part of the political elite made up of those with positions in the Party or the YCL. Between 1952 and 1961, the proportion of co-opted officials in the Central Committee increased: this was so both for the Party elite and for the political elite. In 1952, 24·6 per cent (14) of the political elite were co-opted, whereas in 1961 the figure was 50·3 per cent (75) (Fleron, 125). During this period there had been a decline in the number of professional and particularly Party officials in the Central Committee and an increase in the number of men who had other careers and had been co-opted to the ruling elites. The significance of these changes probably lies in the fact that Khrushchev was diversifying the leadership by bringing in men with careers outside the political institutions. By the process of co-option he was strengthening their links with the political bureaucracies. This policy of widening the composition of the Central Committee has continued under Brezhnev and Kosygin (see Donaldson, 1972: 395). In this way key occupational and functional groups may be incorporated into the political elites, thus ensuring both their representation and their loyalty. The fact that in 1956 only 28·6 per cent, and in 1971, 26·4 per cent of the full CC were also in the central government apparatus should not lead one to minimise its importance. As will be immediately apparent from Fig. 3, in 1963 the leading government ministers were very strongly represented in the Central Committee. In 1952, however, the representation of the political apparatuses came to only 50 per cent of the total – central Party, 16·7 per cent; regional Party, 19·4 per cent; central government, 8·3 per cent; and regional government, 5·6 per cent (Fleron, 113). Hence while the representation of various interests took place in the Central Committee, the political organs strengthened their hold on the Politbureau (see below, p. 130) and this made for firm political control of the system by professional politicians: in 1971, the single largest group of CC full members (45·1 per cent) were from the Party apparatus (Donaldson, 1973: 394).

The most recent major change is toward the technician manager. This may be seen from the education and occupation of the members of the Central Committee in 1966. Of its 184 full members, 65·2 per cent had received technical education, 9·3 per cent had had university education, 8·1 per cent had completed military academy, 4·4 per cent had finished Party school only; a mere 2·2 per cent had received only secondary education (Gehlin and McBride, 106). Following this education, 84 per cent of the full members had actually practised their profession – only 16 per cent had been occupied after graduating in other (mainly Party) work. After such training and work experience 54·9 per cent of these men were subsequently engaged (after 1953) in the Party apparatus, 18·4 per cent were employed in the state bureaucracy as 'high level bureaucrats' in the heavy, light and agricultural industries, another 6·5 per cent were in the cultural, welfare, planning and security ministries; the next two highest groups were the military (7·6 per cent) and trade union officials (3·3 per cent)

Figure 3. USSR Council of Ministers: overlap with Party posts, 1963

PRESIDIUM

Chairman
*

First Deputy Chairman   First Deputy Chairman   First Deputy Chairman
*   *   *

Deputy Chairman   Deputy Chairman   Deputy Chairman   Deputy Chairman
*   *   *   *

Deputy Chairman   Deputy Chairman
*   *

Cema Questions   Current Questions   Costs Questions   Transportation Coordination
*   [-]   [-]   [-]

COMMISSIONS OF THE PRESIDIUM

SERVICE UNIT
Administration of Affairs
(Housekeeping Functions)
Chairman

SUPREME COUNCIL OF NATIONAL ECONOMY
Chairman
*

Deputy Chairman   Deputy Chairman
*   †

MINISTRIES ALL-UNION
Foreign Trade
*

Railways   Sea Fleet
*   †

Council of National   State Planning
Economy (Sovnarkhoz)   Commission (Gosplan)
                            *

State Committee¹   State Committee
for Construction   for Coordination of
(Gosstroy)   Scientific Research
*   Work
                           *

UNION-REPUBLICAN

Agriculture   Finance
                *

Communications
†

Culture   Foreign Affairs
*   *

Health
*

Defense   Higher & Specialised
*   Secondary Education
                *

Other Ministries
(without Portfolio)
(Total 3)
*

STATE COMMITTEES
Cinematography   Labor and Wage Matters
†   *

Cultural Relations   Radio Broadcasting
with Foreign Countries   and Television
                            *

Foreign Economic   Procurements
Relations   †
†

OTHER COMMITTEES,
ADMINISTRATIONS, ETC.

Committee of   Committee of
Party-State Control   State Security
*   †

Central Statistical   Board of
Administration   State Bank
‡

Ex-Officio Members
(Total 15)
6*
6†
3 [-]

(Chairmen of Republic Councils of Ministers)

KEY

Full Member   Candidate Member   Member
*Central Committee   †Central Committee   ‡Central Auditing Commission   [-] Not known
CPSU   CPSU   CPSU

Source adapted from: United States Senate, Committee on Government Operations (88th Congress, 1st Session), *Staffing Procedures and Problems in the Soviet Union* (Washington: Government Printing Office, 1963), p. 17.

¹ There are nine other state committees and three state production committees with no representation on the Central Committee.

(*ibid*, 109). These figures illustrate the trend toward the technically qualified manager, who becomes dominant in the political elite.

The recent tendency is for the newer and younger members of the Central Committee to be recruited from the Party apparatus. Donaldson (1972: 396) has shown that of full members of the CC in 1971, 24·3 per cent had had careers in the Party whereas nearly twice this number (41·1 per cent) had pursued a career in the state apparatus. Of the younger men born between 1920 and 1937, however, 60 per cent were in the Party apparatus, whereas only 4·4 per cent were in the state apparatus. It seems probable that impetus for change within the political elite is likely to come from the men with Party careers rather than the older men with long experience in government administration.

These developments may also be seen in the composition of the Politbureau. Rigby has shown that the full members of Stalin's Politbureau were predominantly drawn from the government apparatus. In 1951, out of a total of eleven men, ten were government functionaries: they included the Chairman of the Council of Ministers (Stalin) and nine Deputy Chairmen; only one man (Khrushchev) was exclusively from the Party apparatus (Rigby, 1972: 6). By 1971, however, not only had the number of full members increased to a total of fifteen, but the number of men with posts in the Council of Ministers had fallen to three: Kosygin (its Chairman) and two First Deputy Chairmen; in addition there were the Chairman of the Council of Ministers of the Ukraine and the Chairman of the Committee for People's Control. The number of leading Party functionaries had increased considerably. In the 1951 Politbureau, four men had Party posts: in addition to Khrushchev, mentioned above, three held joint posts – Stalin, as General Secretary; Malenkov, a minister and a secretary of the Central Committee; and Andreev, Chairman of the Party Control Commission in addition to his government jobs. By 1971, however, there were six secretaries of the CPSU Central Committee (including Brezhnev, the General Secretary), the First Secretary of the Moscow City Committee of the CPSU and the First Secretary of the Central Committee of the Communist Party of Kazakhstan (Rigby, 1972: 6–7). In addition, the Chairman of the Presidium of the Supreme Soviet and the Chairman of the Central Committee of the Federal Trade Union Council were now included.

Rigby also compares the administrative life experience of the men in the two Politbureaus. As a rough guide he considers different areas of work activity and has calculated the proportions of the Politbureau who have had experience in that field. The 1971 Politbureau had men who had been in a much wider variety of posts than had the

1951 body. They had much greater participation in Party organisations than government ones. In the former (1971), all the members of the Politbureau at one time or another had held a post of some kind in the Party; whereas in the latter, one-fifth had never held a Party post at all. A third of the former had been in the Apparatus of the Central Committee whereas only 9 per cent had done so in the 1951 Politbureau. The position in respect of the government institutions was reversed: in Stalin's Politbureau everyone had held a government post and 91 per cent held one in the Council of Ministers; in Brezhnev's Politbureau, a quarter had never held a government post and less than half (47 per cent) had experience in the Council of Ministers. In 1971 there were proportionally more men having had posts in the Young Communist League (*Komsomol*), in management (67 per cent compared to 18 per cent) and manual work. Those who had or still held police posts had fallen from 27 per cent to 7 per cent (Rigby, 1972: 17).

The educational profile of the Politbureau was also transformed between the two dates here considered. In 1971 it was dominated by men with higher technical education – ten out of fifteen, compared with only two out of eleven in 1951. (Two-thirds of the 1971 Politbureau possessed diplomas in one or another kind of technology.) Half (six) of the members of the 1951 Politbureau had received an elementary education, one had had a secondary technical and two had incomplete higher technical (Rigby, 1972: 11). It might be noted here that the tendency of the Politbureau to recruit men of university education was also true of the four East European countries to which we shall turn below. Between the dates of 1949 and 1967, the percentage of members with university education rose from 33 to 55 in Poland, from 0 to 39 in Hungary, 19 to 36 in Czechoslovakia; in Bulgaria, however, it fell from 33 to 25. (The comparative figures for the USSR were 39 per cent and 60 per cent; Farrell, 1970: 96.)

Poland, Hungary, Czechoslovakia and Bulgaria

Let us now turn to consider four countries of Eastern Europe which in many ways were explicitly set up after the Second World War on the Soviet pattern. Before dealing in any detail with the political leadership characteristics of these four countries, it is necessary to sketch briefly some of the salient factors concerning the history of their respective communist parties. (For more detailed histories see Griffith, 1965.) Common to all these countries is the fact that they were in the path of the advancing Soviet Red Army, and the Soviet Union played an important part in shaping their character after the expulsion of the Nazis. Despite the fact that Hungary and Bulgaria had been Axis powers, the evolution of all of these states followed a common political pattern which might be generalised as follows. First, there was a period of coalition between communists and other groups; second, a transitory stage of coalition but one in which the communists were dominant in government; and third, a period of communist *de facto* monopoly of power.

Of the socialist countries of Eastern Europe, Albania and Bulgaria have been the least affected by manifest internal dissent. In the transition from capitalist to state-socialist society, the path of Bulgaria has been smoother than that of the other three East European societies to be considered here. Its population is nationally homogeneous – in 1970, over 85 per cent of the population was Bulgarian. The Bulgarian Communist Party was relatively popular before 1944 and its history goes back to before the First World War. It had successfully contested elections in the inter-war period, though in 1944 the Party had only 25,000 members. At the election of 1945, the Fatherland Front won 364 seats out of 465 and the communists held 277 – a majority. In 1948, when the dictatorship of the proletariat was proclaimed it became dominant and Soviet and Stalinist policies were applied strictly and consistently. As Beck points out : 'Bulgaria was the first country to establish a new constitution patterned on the Soviet constitution. It was among the first to adopt a five-year plan. Industry was nationalised all at once rather than in stages. The economic New Course, which elsewhere soon spilled over into attacks upon existing regimes, was contained in Bulgaria. Even de-Stalinization was treated lightly' (Beck, 1973 : 93). The Party has a solid core of workers and peasants : in 1958, workers constituted 36·1 per cent of Party members, and non-manuals 21·7 per cent; by 1970 the comparative figures were 38·2 per cent and 25·6 per cent (Staar, 1971: 37). We can agree with Beck that, compared to Poland, Hungary and Czechoslovakia, Bulgaria had fewer changes at the 'structural and policy levels'.

Before the Second World War in Poland, the bulk of the urban workers supported the Socialist Party (PPS) and the Communists never had as wide support as in Bulgaria. The Party's history was characterised by internal splits; it had been made illegal under the Pilsudski regime and was dissolved by the Comintern in 1938. After the war, the Party was reformed and called the Polish Workers' Party, then merged with the Socialist Party (PPS) to form the Polish United Workers Party (PUWP). The incorporation of the PPS into the PUWP gave it a minority share of top positions and effectively left power in the hands of the Communists. The amalgamation gave the new Party a membership of some 1¼ million. Other minor parties (the United Peasant Party and the Democratic Party) kept their separate existence, though of course they had to work within the framework of the new republic. These parties contest elections against the PUWP – which maintains a majority of the seats: in 1965 the PUWP won 255 seats out of 460 and polled 55·5 per cent of the votes (Staar, 1971: 133). Since 1957, non-manual workers have formed a large proportion of Party members: 38·8 per cent in 1957 and 42·5 per cent in 1970. As in Russia after the October Revolution, in Poland the nationalisation of industry took place gradually, and even in the 1970s some handicraft workshops and retail trade remain under private ownership. In agriculture in 1946 and 1947 a land reform divided previously large estates among the peasants, thereby neutralising the opposition of the peasants to the communist government. Between 1949 and 1956, measures for the collectivisation of agriculture were taken; these, however, achieved at their height the collectivisation of only 8·6 per cent of the cultivated area. After 1956, collectivisation was made voluntary and in 1962 covered only 1·2 per cent of the cultivated area. Hence such a large area of private enterprise in agriculture is a distinguishing feature of People's Poland and, with the relatively strong Catholic Church, provides a source of non-communist values.

The Communists in Hungary were also weak and before the Second World War had a smaller base even than the Communists in Poland. After the downfall of the soviet republic of Bela Kun, the leaders left Hungary, and between the wars Party activity was extremely weak, for the Party was illegal and Marxists had to work within the Socialist Party (Seton-Watson, 1956: 39). Many of them returned from the USSR after the Second World War to lead the Communist Party under which the Soviet occupying forces formed part of a coalition government. In the elections held in 1945 the Communists polled only some 17 per cent of the votes. But Party membership rose from 2,000 in 1944 to 1·4 million in 1949, with many of the new members coming from the Social Democrats. Even with this small base, the Party (now called the Hungarian Workers' Party after unification with the Social Democrats) became the ruling power. In the 1960s the Party had a membership of some half a million who were predominantly manual workers: only 9·1 per cent of the members were non-manuals in 1962, though this figure rose to 38 per cent in 1970. Two countries, Poland and Hungary, both experienced severe political upheavals in the wake of Khrushchev's de-Stalinisation and both had changes of government in 1956. The most violent revolt against Communist power took place in Hungary and was suppressed by Soviet troops.

Unlike the Hungarian Party, the Czech before the Second World War was one of the strongest communist parties in Europe. It had flourished before 1939 in the most democratic of East European governments under Masaryk and Benes. After the war, in 1945, the Party had 27,000 members, a figure which rose to over a million in 1946. At the general election of that year the Communists polled 38 per cent of the votes, securing 113 out of 300 seats, and emerged as the largest parliamentary party – though the social-democratic parties secured nearly two-thirds of the votes (Taborsky, 1961: 234). In 1948 the Communists carried out a coup and seized power. Like Yugoslavia, but unlike Poland, Hungary and Bulgaria, a distinguishing social phenomenon of Czechoslovakia is its mixed national composition: in 1970, 64·9 per cent of the population was Czech and 29·1 per cent Slovak. In the 1960s manual workers made up about a third of the Party members (33·4 per cent and 30·2 per cent in 1962 and 1966) and non-manuals accounted for 28·6 per cent and 30·5 per cent respectively. Of the four Eastern European countries here considered, Czechoslovakia showed relatively little political change following the fall of Stalin and liberalisation elsewhere, and there were no parallels to the uprisings in Hungary and the convulsions in Poland. In 1968, the replacement of Novotny by Dubcek through an internal democratic process heralded the introduction of quite a novel form of communism, though cut short by the intervention of Warsaw Pact armies in August 1968 (see chapter 6, below).

These very brief sketches illustrate the considerable divergencies between the strength of the Communists in the four countries. Now we may examine the leadership profiles which may help to explain the various political outcomes and may also illuminate general trends in the societies concerned. On the basis of Beck's data we may anticipate the discussion below and generalise as follows. First, as in the Soviet Union, we shall note a general trend away from a 'revolutionary' leadership towards a more professional one, and an increase over time in the representation of officials in the leadership. Second, following the seizure of power, there is a general tendency in all four countries for the central committee to expand to include previous non-Party (e.g. social-democratic) and other mass organisations (e.g. the anti-fascist front). Once established with this wide base, the third stage begins, which involves the inclusion of specialists with technical and managerial skills. The inclusion of these various groups differs in intensity and scope in the four countries studied and the political stability of the various countries would appear to be linked both to the history of public support and to the stability of the leadership profile.

Beck compares four sets of central committees in these four East European countries from 1948 to 1966. He shows that, on average for the four countries, the categories of 'revolutionary activist' both before and during the war fell off sharply with the passage of time.

Members of 'mass organisations' (trade unions, national front, anti-fascist, partisan) were drawn into the central committees in large numbers in the first, second and third sets of committees, but fell off during the fourth. While those with 'revolutionary experience' declined, men with positions in the Party apparatus increased their representation over time, and this was especially so for 'local first secretaries' who were promoted to the central committee. They increased on average from 1 per cent in the first set to 13 per cent in the fourth set; central level functionaries increased in number likewise from 19 per cent to 33 per cent. Those with Party education increased over the time period of the second/third and third/fourth sets of central committees; members having had party education in the USSR, however, suffered a continual decline. The representation of the 'government hierarchy' shows no clear unilinear trend. Members of the central government (excluding members of the Council of Ministers) increased from the first to third set, but declined between the third and fourth set of central committees. The numbers of regional government officials declined between the first and second and between the third and fourth set, but showed a large increase between the second and third. One other clear tendency is apparent from the statistics: men with a technical and educational career increased their representation over time in all the central committees studied. Those with a career in journalism declined between the first and second, and between the second and third, but increased between the third and fourth. Military men increased between the first and second, but their participation increasingly fell off after this. These empirical data would confirm the hypothesis that 'Communist development is characterised by increased bureaucratisation of the system over time; that is if bureaucratisation is reflected in an increased value placed on experiences in the Party as a functionary, [and in] government and mass organisations' (Beck, 1973: 127). The process of leadership recruitment involves building a central committee made up initially of men with political roots in the Party, followed by the co-option of men who have experienced other careers.

What, then, are the differences between the four countries? Beck distinguishes between three different types of leadership profile. The first is what is termed the 'revolutionary activist' composite, and this is the mark of the Bulgarian leadership. In examining leadership attributes in the four countries it was found that they varied least with the passage of time in Bulgaria. In 1948, the Bulgarian central committee had a membership with far greater experience of Communist Party life than did any central committee of the other three countries: for instance, 30 per cent had received Party education in the Soviet Union, compared to the average (including Bulgaria) of 13·5 per cent; 53 per cent had been in Communist Youth organisations compared to the average of 24 per cent (Beck, 1973: 94–5); membership in national front and partisan activities was similarly high. By 1962, the Bulgarian central committee increased the number of its members with university training and with careers in management and technical jobs. Beck points out, however, that this category is lower in Bulgaria than in the other three countries. By 1966 the Bulgarian central committee had slightly increased the number of men under forty and of those with specialist education, but the leadership was still overwhelmingly drawn from those who had 'begun with extensive experience in revolutionary activities, Party-associated activities and government activities. These experiences increased as the leadership also acquired stronger roots in mass organisations' (*ibid*, 103). None of the other countries started with such a strong Party base nor did they stabilise it as much as did the Bulgarian.

The profile of the leadership of Czechoslovakia was least like that of Bulgaria. Given the importance of the Communist Party in pre-communist Czechoslovakia, one would have expected considerable experience of Party and government work among the leadership of the first central committee founded in 1949. Czechoslovakia, however, was found to be not much above the average on this score and 'did not approach the general strength of these attributes in Bulgaria' (Beck, 1973: 119). The composition of the third central committee (1962) brings out the fact that the Czechoslovak Party was seriously falling behind the other countries in promoting men from lower Party organisations. For instance, on average 35 per cent of the members of the four central committees at this time had been or were members of CP youth organisations: in Bulgaria it was 61 per cent, but in Czechoslovakia only 21 per cent. The status of local first secretaries was represented on average by 9·5 per cent of the members of all central committees: for Czechoslovakia it was 6·2 per cent and for Bulgaria 14·2 per cent. With the representation of 'central-level functionary', 'high-ranking central-level functionary', and 'candidate member', Czechoslovakia fell far below the average of the four committees. Where Czechoslovakia did score highly was on the representation of CP regional functionaries and regional first secretaries. This obviously reflects the Czech and Slovak national interests. If the Bulgarian central committee continued to have a large proportion of its members with revolutionary experience, the Czech Party was at the other end of the scale. The average rate of participation of members in the Party for the four countries during the Second World War was 53 per cent; in Czechoslovakia it was

36 per cent – and in Bulgaria 71 per cent. The average proportion of CP members active before the Second World War was 34 per cent; in Czechoslovakia it was 23 per cent and in Bulgaria 50 per cent. The representation of men in residence in the USSR before the seizure of power was also very low: 14 per cent compared to the average of 19 per cent and the Bulgarian proportion of 26 per cent

The Czech central committee was not incorporating representation of important political interests to the same extent as in other countries. The representation of youth on the central committee was as follows: CP youth organisation members 14·95 per cent in Czechoslovakia in 1968 compared to 29·77 per cent on average of four comparable central committees (Bulgaria 59·42 per cent); CP youth organisation official (below central level) 6·7 per cent, compared to 11·45 per cent on average (Bulgaria 23·19 per cent); CP youth organisation official 4·12 per cent, compared to 11·11 per cent on average (Bulgaria 17·39) (Beck, 1973: 89, 94, 95, 120). On the other hand, there was a more than proportional increase in members with an educational and technical career, while men with a military and journalist career were declining absolutely and relatively. Of course, one cannot infer from this that the political outcome of the situation was due simply to the leadership profile. Rather, it is more reasonable to assume that in terms of the pressures exerted on it and generated by it, the leadership was not the best to maintain stability.

The profile of leadership in Poland and Hungary is different from that of Bulgaria and Czechoslovakia. Poland, compared to Bulgaria, is typified by considerable changes in the types of men included in the four central committees. In the first central committee (1948), there were comparatively few men who were in the Party hierarchy. In Bulgaria, for instance, local Party functionaries were 27·66 per cent of the total, compared to 12·68 per cent in Poland; the comparative figures for regional functionaries were 44·68 per cent and 22·54 per cent; for central-level functionaries 36·17 per cent (Bulgaria) and 12·68 per cent (Poland); for high-ranking central-level CP functionaries 21·28 per cent and 15·49 per cent; for candidate members of the central committee 6·38 per cent and 1·41 per cent. There were a few cases where Party participation was higher in Poland than in Bulgaria: men with experience of local first secretary came to 2·83 per cent, but the figure was 0 in Bulgaria; regional first secretary was 12·68 per cent in Poland and 6·38 per cent in Bulgaria. The Polish political elite had not the same kind of institutional career in the Party; fewer had had experience in the Party youth organisations and experience in revolutionary activity. On the other hand, 32·39 per cent had been members of the Social-Democratic Party and 23·94 per cent had been officials in that Party: in Bulgaria the proportions were 23·40 per cent and 8·51 per cent. The Polish party elite might be regarded initially as being less firmly committed to communist ideology than the Bulgarian party elite. After 1948, there was a movement towards a more 'Party-centred' elite; here, however, there was a greater emphasis placed on the recruitment of central rather than regional or local Party officials. The average membership of the second set of CCs by central-level functionaries was 21·05 per cent – 23·38 per cent for Poland in 1954; by high-ranking Party central-level functionaries the average was 18·75 per cent – Poland, 37·66 per cent. The tendency became more dominant in the comparison of the third set of committees: for the three categories of central functionaries, Poland had much higher rankings than the other countries. Both before and after the Polish October in 1956, the political elite was heavily biased in membership towards central rather than local political institutions and may therefore have lost touch with the grass-roots.

By 1968, the representation of regional Party officials had increased slightly, but still central party officials were in the ascendancy. One other important change in Poland was the advance of men with managerial-technical careers. In fact, of the four types of non-Party career, this was the only one which experienced a constant increase over the four committees. Members of the central committee having had a managerial technical career came to only 2·82 per cent in 1948, 5·19 per cent in 1954, 12·99 per cent in 1959, and 15·38 per cent in 1968 (Beck, 104). While we should not infer that the personnel making up the leadership may alone explain the instability of Polish political life, it is undoubtedly the case that the leadership appeared, in Beck's words, to be somewhat 'insular' and 'isolated'.

The Hungarian Communist Party was also characterised by great inconstancy of leadership following the passage of time. The political background of the members of the central committee was most similar to that of Poland. Considering those members of the 1948 central committee which met immediately prior to the fusion of the Social Democrats with the Communists, 23·33 per cent were Social Democrats and 15 per cent had been officials in that Party; the figures for Poland were 25·35 per cent and 16·90 per cent; for Czechoslovakia they were 7·29 per cent for both categories and for Bulgaria 4·29 per cent for both categories (Beck, 115). The number of men with revolutionary experience was also low in Hungary. Those who had been active as CP members before the Second World War made up only 33·3 per cent of the Hungarian Central Committee in 1948 – compared to an average of 50 per cent for the four countries combined; similarly 35 per cent had been revolutionary activists during the War compared to an average of 56·9 per cent. The proportion in the 1948 Hungarian central committee with Party positions was also the smallest of the four countries. The figures (percentages) for various Party statuses, with the average of the four central committees shown in brackets, are as follows: local functionary 3·33 (12·7), local first secretary 0 (1·46), regionary functionary 13·33 (31·39), regional first secretary 0 (9·49), central-level functionary 13·33 (18·98), high-ranking central functionary 11·67 (13·5), candidate member of central committee 0 (2·19). Hungary also had the lowest ranking in 1948 for men with careers in the military (3·33 per cent), journalism (15·9 per cent), and education (3·33 per cent), and came only above Poland in the ranking of men with managerial-technical careers (3·33 per cent) (Beck, 116). The relative position described above persisted to the second central committee in 1954 and characterised the leadership during the revolutionary upheavals of 1956. The weak social foundations of the Party were reflected in the structure of political leadership which could not contain the revolt of 1956 without the help of Russian troops.

The Hungarian central committee which met in 1962 had a very different composition from the two earlier ones. The number of activists increased both relatively and absolutely. The representation of men with experience in Communist youth organisations rose. Perhaps most significant of all is the changed representation of Party statuses: the figures for 1954 and 1962 are as follows (Beck, 1973: 114).

	1954	*1962*
Local functionary	12·99	25·0
Local first secretary	1·30	10·0
Regional functionary	10·39	38·75
Regional first secretary	0	22·5
Central-level functionary	19·48	41·25
High-ranking Central-level functionary	7·79	30·0
Candidate member of Central Committee	9·09	25·0

There were also increases in the representation of men with experience in government and mass organisation. By 1962, the profile of the central committee of the Hungarian Party was similar to that of the Bulgarian Party of 1948.

China
The People's Republic of China offers an interesting contrast to the East European countries we have studied. The Party, like the Russian, came to power independently, after fighting a protracted civil war. China was one of the very poorest of countries in terms of

economic wealth, and the peasantry played an important part in the seizure of power and in providing support for the Party. The form of development carried out does not appear to have followed the East European pattern of 'managerial socialism', and socialist idealism (at least ostensibly) has carried forward into the period of industrialisation (see below, chapter 6). It is pertinent, therefore, to inquire whether the political elites have had a different character.

Derek J. Waller has examined Chinese political elites during the Kiangsi Soviet* period and the Eighth Central Committee of the Party which met in 1956 (Waller, 1973) and the Ninth of 1969 (Waller, 1973a). This research, though not exactly comparable with that of Beck, provides a useful contrast between the composition of the central committee of the Chinese Party and that of the four East European central committees. The Central Executive Council (CEC) was the supreme executive body of the Chinese Soviet Republic. The first CEC elected by the First National Congress in 1931 was composed of delegates almost exclusively from the area under Communist control; to the Second Congress, however, were elected men from other areas of China under Nationalist control, and it was slightly more representative (676 came from the Soviet areas compared to 17 from outside) (Waller, 1973: 157). These two CECs combined give a good profile of the Communist political elite during this period. The Eighth Congress (1956) was the first to be held after the Communists had established their power on the mainland. The Ninth Congress (1969) took place after the Great Proletarian Cultural Revolution which began in 1965.

Waller has found biographical data on about a quarter of the members of the CEC. As is usual in such cases, the small amount of information available is probably due, in addition to genuine gaps in the sources, to reticence to disclose middle or upper-class social origins. Even so, the predominant background of the leadership characteristic of the CEC is that of rural landlords and officials: 49·2 per cent of the sample were from this group, 20·3 per cent were of the peasantry, 10·2 per cent were workers, 8·5 per cent were merchants and capitalists, 3·4 per cent military, 3·4 per cent professional, leaving a residue of 5 per cent. The educational level of a sample of 81 was high: the largest group (30·9 per cent) had had formal university education, the next highest (22·2 per cent) had been educated in Higher Party schools, 12·3 per cent had received Higher Party school and other higher education, 11·1 per cent secondary education, 6·2

---

*The Chinese Soviet Republic (usually known at the Kiangsi Soviet) was declared under the chairmanship of Mao Tse-Tung in 1931. It was based on control of the Kiangsi–Hunan region by the communists and lasted until 1934 when the communists were driven out by the Kuomintang.

per cent military, 4·9 per cent primary and 3·7 per cent higher technical education; only 8·6 per cent had had no formal education at all. As to the careers of leaders before they joined the Party, of a sample of 76 of whom the previous occupation was known, 30·3 per cent had been in the professions of teaching, journalism or law, 26·3 per cent had been students, 14·5 per cent had been in the army, 6·6 per cent were peasants, 18·4 per cent had been workers, and 3·9 per cent were professional revolutionaries. Many others, however, as Waller points out, had had no careers at all but had joined the Party as a career by becoming revolutionaries. The occupation of the CEC personnel in the Soviet areas was closely connected to political activity: 37·7 per cent were in the Party apparatus, 33·0 per cent were occupied in military or police work, 21·7 per cent were engaged with political work in the army and 7·5 per cent were in education and youth work (Waller, 1973: 164–5). As in Russia before 1917, the Chinese Communists were disproportionately drawn from the higher social groups.

The continuous revolutionary activity and the existence of the Kiangsi Soviet prior to the setting up of the People's Republic of China sharply sets off the Communist Party of China from the other communist parties of Eastern Europe, including the Soviet Union, discussed above. Furthermore, there was considerable continuity of membership through to the post-revolutionary elite. Of 97 men in the Eighth Central Committee in 1956, 82 (84·5 per cent) had participated in guerrilla warfare during the period of the Kiangsi Soviet (Houn, cited by Waller: 167). Of the 44 full members of the central committee elected in 1945, 35 (about 80 per cent) were former members of the CEC, as were 8 of the 10 men on the Politbureau at this time. In 1956, of the full members of the Eighth Central Committee elected at the Party Congress, 42 (43·3 per cent) were former CEC members as were 15 of the 17 full members of the Politbureau.

Thus the political composition of the post-revolutionary political elite shows considerable similarity to that of the Kiangsi Soviet. This is remarkable considering that from 1949 onwards the Chinese Communist Party was facing the problems connected with rapid economic and social change and administration. We have seen that the Soviet and Eastern European leaderships showed signs of constant renewal with the admission of many young men, even over a relatively short period of time. This was not the case in China. Comparing the age structure of the two elites, we see that 66·4 per cent of the Kiangsi elite were born before 1905, as were 51·2 per cent of the Eighth Central Committee (1956); those over thirty-six years of age accounted for only 15 per cent of the total in 1931, whereas *all* the Eighth CC were over thirty-six years and more than half were over fifty-two years of age (Waller, 1973 : 171). The picture in the latter CC is one of an ageing and almost 'permanent' CC. Similarly, in considering the date of entry to the Party, we see that the dominant group was that which entered the Party between 1924 and 1927 – two-thirds of the 1956 CC were of this Party generation.

It is important to consider the types of new men who entered the elite – though these were a relatively small proportion of the total. Waller points out that the distinguishing characteristic of these men was the fact of their *similarity* with the traditional leaders (*ibid*, 173). Unlike the other political elites we have studied above, the Chinese Communists did *not* introduce into the elite younger better-educated men with careers in management, industry or education. As Waller puts it : 'There is no evidence to show that replenishment was used to give elite representation to cadres who joined the Party in later periods, and with the majority of the elite dating their affiliation with the Party from its earliest days of revolutionary struggle, there was also very little evidence of adaptation to the demands of the post-revolutionary society' (Waller, 1973 : 182). There is no evidence of a decline in the representation of the military and police, nor was the scientific-intellectual category rising. Of the new men in the CC in 1956 only two features appeared different from those of the incumbents : first, the newcomers were more likely to be associated with the Party than with the state; second, there was an increase in the representation of mass organisations.

Hence China up to 1956 was still led by revolutionaries who had not relinquished power to managerial modernisers. Selection seemed to have been geared to maintaining the homogeneity of the elite rather than bringing forward younger men with different kinds of industrial and administrative experience. It might be hypothesised that the reliance on political rather than managerial means to achieve modernisation may at least partly be explained by the stability and homogeneity of China's leadership.

The Cultural Revolution led to considerable changes on the central committee. The number of full members rose from 79 in 1965 to 170 in 1969. Waller's investigations show that, despite the changes in membership, there were few changes in the composition of the elite in terms of 'sex, race and province of origin' (Waller, 1973a : 7). The proportion of women rose from 5 per cent to 8 per cent, the proportion of non-Han members rose from 2·5 per cent to 3·5 per cent. The central–south China region (including Hunan) made up 47 per cent of the known provinces of central committee members. Some important changes, however, took place in the age composition and previous career of the incumbents. Though the average age (of known members) for both committees was 63 years, there was an influx of younger men: in the 1969 elite, 17 per cent (of the men with known ages) were fifty-five years or less compared with only 6 per cent of the 1965 CC. At the same time, however, the number of men over seventy actually increased from 12 per cent to 15 per cent. One should perhaps emphasise the fact that the majority (58 per cent) of the central committee were men who had joined the Party before 1928 – having been in the Party over forty years in 1969. Waller points out that the *oldest* group in the central committee in 1965 (those born in the nineteenth century) were politically upwardly mobile during the Cultural Revolution. Those who were purged were the men who had been first elected to the central committee in 1956. In terms of the occupational and institutional composition of the CC, the major change during the Cultural Revolution has been the increase in the representation of the military. The share of men with military careers rose from 17 per cent in the 1965 CC to 44 per cent in the 1969 Committee; the proportion of men with a career in the state apparatus fell from 35 per cent to 18 per cent and those in the Party apparatus dropped from 29 per cent to 10 per cent. Another important change was the inclusion of a large group (21 per cent of the total of known careers) of ordinary worker-peasants. The total number of economic experts, scientists and academics fell from 18 per cent in 1965 to only 7 per cent in 1969.

The picture we have of the Chinese Party's central committee is one of the continuing dominance of the old political elite; despite an increase of younger men in 1969, the over-sixties even strengthened their position. Unlike the other communist parties studied above, the Chinese political elite does not appear to have co-opted members of the managerial and technical elites. Men with such skills in the Party and the state bureaucracy have been purged from the political elite and their places have been taken by men from the army and by ordinary workers and peasants. Political integration and control have a greater importance than economic and management imperatives. This is probably due to the very low level of economic development of People's China. Her problems are largely those of political mobilisation and the creation of different forms of motivation rather than of the integration of an industrialised urban society. We shall return to this point later (pp. 163-4).

Comparison of People's China and Czechoslovakia brings out two divergent trends in the development of state-socialist society. The first advocates a more rapid and political movement from pre-capitalist formations to socialist ones. Supporters of such policies believe that some higher forms of socialism may be introduced without going through the capitalist relations of production, and they advocate grass-roots participation in decision-making and the minimisation of material incentives in industrial production and of differentials in consumption. They believe that methods used under capitalism are not appropriate for the introduction of socialism.

The second group, while aspiring to such communistic social relations, adopts a more gradualist and pragmatic policy. This latter group feels that they have to compromise their communist ideals and accept at least for a short period the kind of relationships and practices which are part of the capitalist or traditional mode of production. Writers such as Richard Lowenthal (1970) see this cleavage as one between 'utopia' and 'modernity' and pose the problem facing Communist leaders as one of having to choose between the goal of developing the forces of production and that of achieving a classless society. Supporters of the Chinese Cultural Revolution are regarded as examples of the 'utopian' school and the 'democratic reformers' of Czechoslovakia as representatives of the 'modernisers'. As we have seen above, the development of the material base also gives rise to new groups of administrators, executives and technicians. These groups push for sectional autonomy for various production activities: they seek greater wage differentials and they justify the latter claim in terms of the 'rationality' of material incentives; but this outlook later may act to institutionalise their privileges. These differences in policy may be reflected in inter-generational conflict between, on the one hand, the younger technical/administrative personnel and, on the other, the older and more ideologically oriented Party members.

In analysing this incipient conflict in state-socialist societies one must bear in mind the historical trajectory through which each society passes. Rather than comparing their policies cross-nationally at one point in time, it makes more sense to compare the evolution of policy at different times following the revolution. Another important factor is the actual level of development of the means of production in various societies: countries such as the Soviet Union and Czechoslovakia which have developed industrial structures and large urban and industrial populations face different problems from societies such as China which are economically very backward and are composed of rural peasant populations. Some recent developments in these two countries will be used in the next chapter to illustrate the different paths which may be taken in the evolution of state socialism. In addition, we shall consider the case of Yugoslavia which in many ways is different from either and is distinguished by reliance on 'market' mechanisms and by the aspiration for a high degree of direct workers' participation and control.

6

Counterpoints to the Soviet Model

*Decentralisation and Workers' Control in Yugoslavia**

*Decentralisation and Workers' Control in Yugoslavia**
Many of the criticisms of the Soviet Union's type of state socialism
have been voiced, though in a muted form, by the Yugoslav socialists.
Tito and his followers during the Second World War and the initial
period of building socialism in Yugoslavia, had been staunch supporters of Stalin and enthusiastic copiers of Soviet institutions. As
Zaninovich has put it: 'The regard held by Yugoslav communist
leaders for Stalin and the Soviet system was only slightly less than
religious adulation and spiritual reverence. . . . As a result, the
Yugoslav communist state became the model satellite in its commitment to the ideals of Marxist industrial society . . .' (Zaninovich,
1968: 46–7). Following the split with the Soviet Union in 1948, the
Yugoslavs not only developed their own independent patterns of
trade and foreign affairs but also articulated an ideology of socialism
different in many respects from that of the Soviet Union. (As Ross
Johnson has pointed out, the ideological position did not change
suddenly in 1948, but had its roots in previous history. Johnson, 1972:
5.) What the Yugoslavs share with Soviet Marxists, and which distinguishes them from western social democrats, is allegiance to the
theories of Marx and Lenin: in particular to the notion of class
struggle, to the inevitable triumph of communism and to the Party
as 'the ideological vanguard and organizer' (*Programme* . . ., 1959:
xiv) of the workers' movement. But socialism as it developed in the
Soviet Union, and particularly under Stalin, is criticised because of
its over-centralisation and bureaucratic control. 'Our own experience,
and that of other socialist countries, has shown that when the management of the economy is exclusively in the hands of the State

*I am grateful to Mr F. Singleton of Bradford University for advice on
sources.

machinery, the inevitable result is a growing tendency towards greater centralisation of power and closer amalgamation of State and Party machinery; they grow stronger and strive to divorce themselves from society and [to] impose their power upon it' (*Programme* . . ., 21).

Before considering this theoretical position in more detail it is necessary to sketch in some of the salient features of Yugoslav society. Like Czechoslovakia, Yugoslavia is a multi-national state: the major nationalities are Serbs (41·8 per cent in 1970), Croatians (23 per cent), Slovenes (9·2 per cent), and Macedonians (5·6 per cent). These national differences are accompanied by separate religions – the Orthodox Church being associated with the Serbs and the Catholic with the Croatians and Slovenes. There are also over a million Muslims (about 5 per cent of the population). Croatia and Slovenia are more highly developed and richer than the other areas of the country (Slovenia had a GNP per head of 378,000 old dinars in 1962, Croatia 232,000, Montenegro 142,000, Serbia 187,000, Macedonia 134,000; Bicanic, 1973: 76). Tito had proclaimed the existence of his own government as early as 1943, and, unlike other communists to come to power in Eastern Europe, had led a successful guerrilla campaign against the Germans. He was supported by the West during the war and, as a national resistance leader, had considerable support within Yugoslavia itself. The Communist Party of Yugoslavia had a membership of 12,000 in 1941, 140,000 in 1945, and nearly half a million in 1948; by 1970, the League of Communists of Yugoslavia had a membership of over 1,100,000 (Staar, 1971: 203).

The Yugoslav socialists recognised the inherently socialistic nature of the Soviet Union and, rather than dwelling on the causes of the distortions of Soviet socialism, they have endeavoured to formulate polices to overcome the deficiencies of the Soviet model as devised under Stalin. In the first place, the Yugoslav socialists take a different attitude to the development of socialism on a global scale than did the Soviet Union, at least under Stalin. They have emphasised that there are roads to socialism other than the Soviet road. Yugoslavia was able, it was argued, to build socialism without being subservient to the Soviet Union; and certainly the CPSU should have no authority over other fraternal parties. 'To proclaim the path and form of socialist development in any single country as being the only correct path and form is nothing but a dogma obstructing the process of the socialist transformation of the world' (*Programme* . . ., 48). In the advanced capitalist countries, argue the Yugoslavs, the forces of socialism are much stronger than they were before the Second World War, and social-democratic parties and trade unions have an important part to play in achieving socialism. In this situation, therefore, Communist parties should cooperate with social-democratic parties.

With regard to internal policy, the Yugoslavs made more radical departures from the Soviet model. The major changes are in the concept of the state and the role of the Party under socialism, and concerning the nature of socialist property. The Programme of the League of Yugoslav Communists recognises the importance in the *initial* period of building socialism of 'a high degree of concentration of political power in the administrative apparatus' (*Programme . . .,* 79) and of the Communist Party's playing a decisive part in the management of the machinery of government. With the consolidation of socialist power, however, the continuation of 'revolutionary-administrative means' of control is not justified. 'Therefore, as soon as there is no longer any objective social need for the state to play such a role, the Communists and all conscious socialist forces, as the driving force and fulcrum of progressive development, must increase their political activity with a view to creating and developing forms of democracy enabling the working class and the working people generally to take charge directly of the management of an expanding area of social affairs in the economy and in other spheres' (*Programme . . .,* 80). The precise forms of these changes involve the direct participation of the workers in management, the dominant role of the government apparatus is replaced by devolution to local councils, and Party hegemony gives way to cooperation with other political bodies.

The Yugoslav Communists take seriously the notion that the state should begin to 'wither away' with the progress of socialism. 'As the socialist democratic system develops, the role of the state administration begins to diminish in the direct management of the economy, in the field of cultural and educational activities, the health service and social policy, etc. The functions connected with the administration of these activities are increasingly transferred to various social self-governing bodies, which are independent or linked up into a suitable democratic organisational machinery' (*Programme . . .,* 87). The Yugoslav system of government is based on decentralisation where more powers are given to local councils and the central government becomes a kind of 'social regulator'. The directing role of the Party was to be minimised and to be replaced in the long run by 'forms of direct socialist democracy', and the Party would gradually wither away (Hoffman and Neal, 1962: 167). Though the intention is not for the Communists 'to renounce their leading role in society', the aim is to achieve their 'leading role less and less through *their own power* and more and more by means of the direct power of the *working people* who operate the socially-owned means of production and by means of the most variegated forms of social self-government' (*Programme . . .*, 91). Party secretaries and other functionaries were required to relinquish their leading positions in government institutions, and the League of Communists of Yugoslavia would no longer be 'the immediate operational guide and directive-giver neither in economic nor in government and social life' (Zaninovich, 84).

Workers' control of the economic enterprise was held to advance socialism to a higher level. It was considered that the Soviet type of centralised ministerial control led to bureaucracy and to alienation among the workers. 'State ownership' of the means of production on the Soviet pattern has been rejected as an end-state of socialism: Yugoslav socialists look to social property which is controlled by those who 'participate *directly* in the processes of social self-administration and enterprise production' (Zaninovich, 144). Control and management (with certain restraints) of enterprises are vested in a workers' council elected by all members of the enterprise. This in turn elects a managing board and director (Zaninovich, 79–80. For changes in the 1960s, see Moore, 1970). 'The new social position of the producers under conditions of socialist construction, and their changed relationship towards production, results both from the fact that the producers have changed from wage earners into the direct managers of production and distribution and from the fact that through such management they are able to fulfil the personal requirements of everyday life, namely, higher earnings, and a higher personal and general standard' (*Programme . . .*, 100–1).

We have discussed in outline the major propositions in the Yugoslav model of socialism. The main differences from that of the Soviet Union are a more compromising policy towards political opponents – both to social democrats and to the capitalist West – the weakening of Party and state hegemony, and the introduction of political devolution in the form of popularly elected local bodies and of workers' control of the enterprise. The Yugoslavs adopt a critical and friendly relationship to the USSR.

Before we examine workers' control in more detail, we may note some of the criticisms which have been made of the Yugoslav theory. Firstly, it has been argued that its foreign policy has made Yugoslavia dependent on western capitalism and has weakened the strength of the international communist movement and likewise that it has 'exposed the Yugoslav people to the danger of losing the revolutionary gains achieved through a heroic struggle' (*Statement of International Communist Movement* (1960), cited by Renmin Ribao,

26 September 1963). Secondly, the continuation of a mixed economy involving private enterprise in both town and village has led to Chinese criticisms that private capitalism continues in Yugoslavia. Thirdly, the effects of concentrating power in the enterprise and replacing central administrative means by reliance on 'market' relationships has led to the *de facto* rise of a 'bureaucrat-comprador bourgeoisie'. Workers' self-government, it is argued by opponents, is a syndicalist/anarchist notion, which has been repudiated by Marxist-Leninists. In fact, critics such as the Maoists assert that the workers' councils are merely a formal apparatus – 'a kind of voting machine'. Fourthly, it is suggested that the socialist planned economy has been undermined: unified economic planning has been abandoned; the introduction of 'profit' as the criterion of enterprise success results in the needs of society being ignored, as under capitalism; the relations between enterprises are based on competition and are therefore not socialist.

Many of these criticisms, of course, are similar to those made of various tendencies within the Soviet Union. A major difference in Yugoslavia from the Soviet model, however, is the introduction of workers' councils. These are institutions crucial to Yugoslav socialism. As Blumberg has put it: 'More than any other institution, [the workers' council] symbolises the avowed intention of the Yugoslav Communists to disperse the power of the centralised state, and to create in its place a society of loosely connected, self-governing organisations' (Blumberg, 1968: 196).

Workers' councils must be discussed both in terms of their internal structure and in relation to the political structure in which they operate. Obviously the kind of 'self-government' which is possible in an economic enterprise is limited by the source and cost of capital: it is possible for workers to 'control' the flow of production in an enterprise with its property being owned by private banks, and this situation is distinct from one in which finance and type of product are controlled by an administrative board. Hence in the discussion of workers' councils and workers' control one must specify control of what, by whom and in whose interests.

Marxist-Leninists have always in principle been opposed to workers' control in a syndicalist sense. It is true that Lenin advocated 'workers' control', but what Lenin envisaged was far from the Yugoslav concept of 'workers' self-government'. At the time of the Provisional Government (February–October 1917) Lenin and the Bolsheviks supported workers' control of industry. Workers' organisations were necessary to hold the management 'in check' and workers' control then was a form of opposition to the (bourgeois) government (see Kaplan, 1968: 57). Support for workers' control and the factory committees should be seen as a tactical position which the Bolsheviks adopted to ensure support for the revolutionary cause. After the seizure of power by the Bolsheviks, central control of the economy under the Party had to be assured, and the control of individual economic enterprises under workers' committees was at variance with this policy. 'We must at the very outset state that workers' control is not socialism. Workers' control . . . does not mean the immediate socialisation of the factories and shops and much less the transfer of enterprises into the hands of individual groups' (Lozovsky (1918), cited by Kaplan: 127). Workers' control, it was foreseen, could easily have turned production units into the individual or private property of the workers in them. Lenin and the Bolsheviks conceived of state ownership and Party control of industry, and workers' management was inimical to this view. At least during the period of the dictatorship of the proletariat Lenin conceived of state ownership.

> Any direct or indirect legalisation of the possession of their own production by the workers of individual factories or individual professions or of their right to weaken or impede the decrees of the state power is the greatest distortion of the basic principles of Soviet power and the complete renunciation of socialism. (Lenin, *On Democracy and the Socialist Character of Soviet Power.* Cited in Renmin Ribao, 1963: 18.)

One of the principal reasons for this opposition is to be found in the Marxist criticism of syndicalism. To give workers in a factory exclusive rights over the property and the produce of that factory is to put them in the same position as capitalists. It encourages a bourgeois property-owning mentality and it replaces the capitalist owner with the enterprise's workers who may function as owners. As Lozovsky pointed out in 1918: 'Merely because there will be a thousand instead of ten factory owners in an enterprise, it still does not become socialistic' (cited in Kaplan, 1968: 126).

Blumberg has pointed out that 'workers' control' is a Guild Socialist and not a Marxist concept (Blumberg, 1968: 188, 193).* The Yugoslav argument is that nationalisation of the means of production is a necessary but not a sufficient condition for socialism. Nationalisation giving rise to state ownership and control of econo-

---

*There are two English Fabian tracts on workers' control in Yugoslavia: Singleton and Topham, 1963, and Moore, 1970.

mic enterprises leads to the worker being estranged or alienated from his produce; it also leads to gross inequalities of power. Hence workers' control is a way of equalising political participation. Workers' control means that 'the producers themselves must govern [the means of production] thereby bringing about democratic and Socialist relations in production' (*Congress of Workers' Councils of Yugoslavia*, cited by Blumberg, 1968: 190). How, then, are these values given practical institutional form? Firstly, we must discuss the relationships between enterprises and other institutions, and secondly, we shall turn to consider the internal structures of the economic enterprise.

As implied above, workers' management and the institution of workers' councils were not introduced from the beginning of the socialist political order. They evolved with the passage of time. Bicanic has divided this process of evolution into three main stages: centralised planning (1947–51), decentralisation (1952–64) and poly-centrism or market socialism (since 1965) (Bicanic, 1973: 41). The first period was one of central planning of the Soviet type with enterprises receiving up to 90 per cent of their investment from the state; the management of the individual enterprise (and its work-force) had little effective control of its own activity. The phase beginning in 1952 introduced a different economic system: the government and economic apparatuses were separated, self-management of enterprises was introduced giving enterprises the right to make certain decisions about the scope of production. They paid 40–50 per cent of their income to the government. From 1965 the scope of self-management was extended and the enterprise was allowed far greater independence; the market became a more important mechanism governing relations between enterprises.

The economic reform of 1965 strengthened workers' self-management. Until this time only 46 per cent of enterprise net income was available for internal distribution for wages and other funds; the remainder had to be paid to the government. After 1965, 70 per cent of revenue was left to accrue to the enterprise (Bicanic, 1973: 213). Enterprises were also allowed to distribute their income between various forms of expenditure (e.g. wages, welfare, investment) as they thought fit. The administrative determination of prices was replaced by market relations: in theory, prices reflected relative scarcities, and this in turn influenced the rate of capital formation in various parts of the economy. The banking system also became much more independent, and investment and commercial banks may be founded on the basis of savings from enterprises. The executive committees of the banks make decisions on proposals submitted to them and the founders of banks receive dividends from the banks' income. As Hanzekovic has pointed out, 'The Bank and Credit Act of 1965 was the first to come into contradiction with the principle that income can only be received as a result of work performed. For the first time it was made possible for income to be received as a result of investment' in Bicanic, 1973: 223). Since 1967 it has been possible for foreign capitalists to invest in Yugoslavia, subject to a limit of 49 per cent of any enterprise's assets and to certain restriction on the remittance of profits abroad.

It can be seen that central planning in Yugoslavia has been very much weakened at the expense of enterprise and commercial autonomy. The central government determines (as is the case in mixed economies of the British type): money supply, the exchange rate of the dinar, external tariffs, taxes, investment policy. Economic policy has resulted in problems similar to those found in western capitalist societies. Wages and salaries paid by enterprises have risen. Inflation has been rampant: the level of prices doubled between 1970 and 1974. Unemployment has increased from 290,000 in 1971 to 410,000 in 1974 (OECD, 7). There has been a large exodus of nearly a million workers to Western Europe and conflicts between management and workers have sometimes led to strikes (Singleton and Saksida, n.d.: 5). The country continues to have balance of payments deficits, and its underdeveloped areas have continued to lag behind the industrialised areas. Market relations between enterprises have led to the formation of monopolies through the 'collusion of several workers councils' – Singleton and Saksida give an example of the synthetic fibres industry forcing the government to make a discriminatory tariff against imported goods which was followed by an increase of their prices by 40 per cent (*ibid*). Though the state administration has been weakened *vis-à-vis* the enterprise, the banking system, which is responsible for the allocation of finance, may be an equally formidable opponent providing unity to the system (Samardzija and Klein, 1971: 158).

Workers' self-management gives the right to those employed in an enterprise to participate in its management (ILO, 1962: 3). Technically, legal ownership of the enterprise remains with the government though workers have the right to use and enjoy the property; workers' management or self-management gives to the workers in an enterprise certain rights over the income and investment policy of the undertaking. It was introduced in Yugoslavia in 1950. Until 1963, self-management applied to economic enterprises; after that date it included all forms of employment (educational, commercial, social services). The earlier period was one of 'workers' 'self-management' and the latter, one of 'social self-management'.

In the 1950s, the workers' councils were representative bodies, rather than organs of direct democracy. A single workers' council was elected by the workers in various departments of a factory (Moore, 1970: 13). In the period defined above as that of de-centralisation (1952–64) there were many limitations on the activities of the councils. The government levied taxes and determined the levels of wages and prices; the council had responsibility for the distribution of surplus earnings. The factory manager was appointed by a commission composed of representatives of the workers' council and the local government commune, and such managers were res-ponsible to the commune, not the workers' council. The manager was clearly in control of the enterprise, as the law gave him the right to 'make contracts and allocate working assets . . . to make decisions relating to the termination of the employment of workers'. The manager was also required to carry out the 'orders and instruc-tions of the appropriate state organs' (cited by Singleton, 1970: 2–3). A move towards 'direct democracy' took place in 1961 when sub-groups of between 40 and 50 persons within factories had their own councils, subordinate to the main council, and had some power over appointments, the distribution of income and labour discipline. Since 1965 all enterprises have been required to have councils in all their various branches or departments, and in small enterprises with less than 30 workers affairs are managed directly. Workers elected to the councils may serve for a maximum of two two-yearly periods. The workers' council is the sovereign body in the enterprises. It is 'charged with the responsibility for the management of the social property of the enterprise, the planning of production, the setting of targets, the fixing of wage rates, prices and the determination of investment policy. It has all the rights of using the property of the enterprise, but cannot sell it' (Singleton and Saksida, 4). The workers' council elects a managing board (not necessarily composed of members of the workers' councils). The factory manager is also a member of the board and he is selected by the joint commission mentioned above, but is responsible to the workers' council. The workers' council may dismiss the manager, who may override a decision of the council only if it is contrary to law.

Let us now turn to examine the role of workers in the decision-making process. One might expect that the frequent change of representatives on the workers' council would result in their lacking the experience to be a serious counter to the manager and his senior technical staff, who are responsible for administration. A study examining the opinions of different social groups within the enterprise found different views about who was influential. Respondents were asked to rank the influence on decision-making in the factory of top management, staff, and workers' councils. (The data are for five factories in Slovenia: cited by Singleton and Saksida, n.d.: Table 4.) Of the top management all (100 per cent) thought that the top management and staff had a strong influence and 43 per cent thought that the workers' councils also had a strong influence. Of the manual workers, 31 per cent thought that top management had a strong influence and the figures for staff and workers' councils were 44 per cent and 35 per cent. Of the members of the workers' councils themselves, 63 per cent believed that staff had a strong influence and 37 per cent thought that the top management and workers' council did (Singleton and Saksida, n.d.: Table 4). Studies which have examined the participation of various groups also show that the workers' council is not the effective source of power in the enterprise. As Benson (1974: 257) has concluded, 'No research findings have yet come up with the conclusion that the introduction of workers' self-management in the economy has resulted in a democratic distribution of influence within the enterprise.' A study of twenty Yugoslav enterprises showed that position in the organisational hierarchy was closely correlated to participation in the affairs of the enterprise. The most important groups in rank order were: higher management, non-supervisory staff, higher plant supervisors (cited by Warner, 1972: 195). Another study of the influence of socio-economic groups on the work and decisions of the workers' councils in three Zagreb factories showed the following order: top management, staff specialists, heads of economic units, party and trade union officials, supervisory staff, white collar, highly skilled and skilled workers, semi- and unskilled workers (cited in Benson, 258). The important role of the director is substantiated by Kolaja's study of two factories (Kolaja, 1965): 'in both factories the workers' council was under the director who also was a prominent member of the League's organisation' (*ibid*, 67); the suggestions of the manager and management 'were practically always accepted by the workers' council' (*ibid*, 69). Kolaja also points out that other organisations in the factory (the League, the union, youth organisation) are subordinate to a hierarchy outside the factory, whereas the workers' council is an autonomous organisation.

The importance of the Party as an institution which provides unity to the system has not been considered in much detail in the western literature on workers' councils. Party influence, albeit indirect, over the direction of the councils must be very significant. One study of seventy factories has shown, for example, that nearly 70 per cent of the managerial personnel were officials of the Party and trade union organisation and more than a third were in the key post of Party secretary (Benson, 1974: 267).

Strauss and Rosenstein (1970) suggest that management looks to workers' councils, not for advice on production but as a means of estimating 'the *impact* of management policy upon workers. . . . Managers in both Yugoslavia and Sweden find council meetings useful as "sounding boards" in which they can try out worker reactions before introducing changes. (Roughly the same function can be played by union representatives in "working harmony" situations in the United States)' (1970: 207). The positive effects of the workings of workers' control are to provide a mechanism for the discussion of problems and an institution for resolving them. As Kolaja has pointed out, the existence of the councils has helped to keep open channels between the workers and the management, and in this respect 'it could be said that its effect [has been] beneficial' (Kolaja, 1965: 70). Paradoxically, however, both Kolaja and Strauss and Rosenstein indicate that the councils have been used as instruments of management. The council member represents the workers, but as he becomes involved in management decisions it is likely that 'he will become alienated from his constituents' (Strauss and Rosenstein, 208). Participation through workers' councils may strengthen management; 'in Yugoslavia it has helped indoctrinate peasant workers with industrial discipline and has also helped identify and train potential managerial talent' (Strauss and Rosenstein, 1970: 212). Participants on workers' councils are drawn more than proportionately from the ranks of skilled and highly skilled workers; women, young workers and the unskilled are under-represented (Riddell, 1968: 66). Kolaja's findings suggest: 'the fact that the council or its managing board worked in close co-operation with management precluded its becoming a genuine workers' body' (Kolaja, 1965: 72). It did, however, give the workers a sense of identification with the enterprise – an identification that Kolaja found missing in Poland. 'For the Polish workers, management and all the other higher personnel were perceived as a diffuse and generalised category, labelled "they". . . . In the two Yugoslav factories, and especially in Factory B, complaints and hostile remarks tended to be concrete and tangible, referring to specific issues that did not lend themselves as easily to scapegoating. In the Yugoslav case there was definitely more give and take between management and labour' (*ibid*, 73). Workers' management may be considered as a device which gives some real participation and a *sense* of participation to workers in an industrial enterprise, but rather than being a source of decision-making, it functions to integrate the workers into an industrial system.

The Great Proletarian Cultural Revolution in People's China

We have seen earlier that the Soviet Union has profoundly influenced the course of events in China : during the early period of Communist rule the Chinese copied extensively from Soviet practice, but in later years, and especially while Russia was under Khrushchev, the Chinese have become more critical. Indeed, much of the policy adopted by Mao may be interpreted as an attempt to avoid what is considered to be the 'degeneration' of societies in the Soviet camp. In recent years the Chinese leadership has tried to develop quite different forms of administration, of incentives to encourage work, of participation in decision-making.

To understand the implications of the Cultural Revolution in China it is necessary to be acquainted with some fundamental features of the development of China and to note some of the major differences compared with the USSR. China in 1949 was quite a different kind of society to Russia in 1917. Russia was a European power : she had a Christian religion and centuries of intellectual and cultural intercourse with Western Europe. From the time of Peter the Great (1672–1725) Russia had been copying European technology and had been in close contact with its culture. By the time of the October Revolution, an advanced capitalist type of industrial system had been implanted. China, on the other hand, had been a relatively closed continent. Industrial development, even by 1949, was no match for the progress made under the Tsars and agricultural technique was akin to that of medieval Europe. China was one of the poorest countries in the world. She has a high population density with only about half an acre of cultivatable land per head (estimate for 1953: Hughes and Luard, 1971: 7). Before the Communists came to power there was only a rudimentary rail transport system, no large-scale public works had been undertaken, industrial employment was on a small scale. The major centre of heavy industry was located in Manchuria: 'by far the greater part of the country carried on, as for the last 2,000 years, an early iron-age economy' (*ibid*, 16). Even by 1969, the annual average per capita gross national product was only £40 – twelve times smaller than in the USSR in that year. China had been ravaged by civil war and invasion for a period of some twenty years. In Russia, not only had the political revolution been a relatively short affair but the political base of the Bolsheviks had been in the cities, and the working class played an important part in the Revolution, whereas in China the cities fell last of all to a peasant-based guerrilla army. In Soviet Russia the early revolutionary phase was more rapid and engendered more class conflict than in China. The 'commanding heights' of the economy were nationalised by June 1918 and public ownership of medium industry was completed by

1920. In China the process was much more gradual. The Chinese communists were the leaders of a struggle for national liberation and they were able to count on the support of many of the entrepreneurs and managerial executives. As mentioned above (p. 24), *private* ownership of the means of production was guaranteed by the 1954 Constitution. The national bourgeoisie not only forms part of 'the people' but also part of its 'democratic dictatorship' which is 'based on the alliance of the working class, the peasantry and the urban petty bourgeoisie' (Mao, 1949: 421). Between 1949 and 1952, only the businesses of capitalists ardently supporting the Kuomintang were nationalised. Entrepreneurs having small concerns were recognised as having useful skills and the Communists sought their support for the People's Republic. Gradually, they believed, such men would be assimilated into socialist industry. It was not until 1956 when remaining private firms became 'private-state' enterprises effectively owned by the government that 99 per cent of the total output (in value terms) was under state control although the owners received compensation in the form of interest payments.

The control and organisation of agriculture had parallels in the Soviet Union. First came a land reform which destroyed the gentry and gave the land to the peasantry, who worked it as private plots. Second, collectivisation occurred which weakened the rich peasants and was a precondition for large-scale agricultural production. While the reasons for collectivisation cannot be considered here in any detail, there can be no doubt that it was forced on the Stalinist leadership in Russia by the difficulty of maintaining political control of the countryside and by the increasing difficulty of procuring grain from the peasantry. A reliable and cheap supply of grain from the countryside was regarded as being essential to the success of the industrialisation drive. The effects of collectivisation, however, were more negative in Russia than in China: a considerable part of the peasantry was alienated from the Soviet order by the seizure of land, machinery and stock and in the short run there was a run-down of capital. Events took a similar course in China. At first a policy of gradual and voluntary collectivisation was envisaged: the Common Programme had stated that 'the People's government . . . shall guide the peasants step by step to organise various forms of mutual aid, labour and production cooperation according to the principle of free choice and mutual benefits' (cited by Hughes and Luard, 1961: 148). In 1953 three stages in the goal to the Soviet type of collective farm were envisaged: 'temporary mutual-aid groups, permanent mutual-aid groups and semi-socialist agricultural producers' cooperatives' (*ibid*, 149). The yield of grain was so low in 1954 and hoarding of grain by peasants so widespread, that the government decided on a rapid process of collectivisation. By 1956, 83 per cent of all peasant households had joined 'advanced cooperatives'. Collectivisation in China had important goals besides the narrowly economic. As Gray (1974) has suggested, collectivisation enabled China's greatest re-source (labour power) to be used rationally in intensive cultivation; not only was the size of farming unit enlarged, but community de-velopment projects could also be organised.

Unlike Russia after 1917, the Chinese communists had a model of a state-managed industry which they were able to copy (Schurmann, 1971: 239–50). During the First Five Year Plan the slogan was: 'Learn from the Soviet Union'. The development of heavy industry was a major aim, and the Soviet Union set up many industrial plants. Industrial organisation of the state sector was centralised, and the style of management was hierarchical, encouraging neither Party nor workers' control. Efficiency was seen to lie in unity of command and strong labour discipline. As in the Soviet Union, monetary incentives were used to ensure the proper motivation to work. Egalitarianism was opposed and wage differentials were used for 'the economic purpose of keeping the worker on his toes, and getting the maximum labour out of him' (Gluckstein, 1957: 225). Labour was graded ac-cording to level of skills and type of industry in a similar way to that of the Soviet Union. The basic principle was: 'to each according to his work'. As in the Soviet Union, the role of trade unions was to promote labour efficiency, to implement economic plans and to administer social security services. In the period 1953–7, besides a gradation of pay scales for different categories of labour, piece-work was also introduced and norms were assigned to each job, some 20 per cent of pay coming from bonus or piece work (Hoffmann, 1964: 84).

From the end of 1954 policy changed, the Party reasserted its primacy and the 'vertical rule' of the ministries was opposed (Schur-mann, 267). In management, greater political expertise came to be preferred to technical skills. The Eighth Party Congress in 1956 repudiated the Soviet one-man management principle and in its place it was resolved that management should come under the control of the Party committee. In 1958, the policy of the Great Leap Forward envisaged very high targets and at this time labour-intensive work-shops were introduced in the countryside. From an economic point of view, the formation of such units had some advantages. They were able to utilise a low amount of capital input, which was sensible in a country with abundant labour reserves; the gestation period of the investment was short and returns were rapid (Wheelwright and McFarlane, 1973: 46).

The agricultural communes were forms of agrarian socialism; they were administrative, social and productive organisations. On the positive side they allowed for 'the direct transformation of labour reserves into physical capital' (*ibid*, 54). Lowenthal argues that such policies 'clearly reflected the proneness of the higher Party cadres to relapse into the utopianism of their civil war days as soon as the decision to put politics in command freed them from the restraining influences of economic specialists. . . . The provincial Party committees increasingly ignored the central planning experts and accounting authorities and by-passed the experienced industrial managers in their area, relying instead on inexpert party men appointed as deputy managers to carry out the committees' demands in a spirit of guerrilla autonomy and provincial autarchy' (Lowenthal, 1970: 64). But such a point of view ignores the important social-psychological consequences of the policies pursued. One of the major problems facing China was to transform the psychological and social attitudes of the population. Maoist policy tried to foster responsibility and entrepreneurial ability (foresight and willingness to take risks) among the population (Gray, 1974: 39). Development is dependent not only upon central decision-making and bureaucratic forms of communication: it also requires participation by the masses. In discussing workers' participation in China, Harper makes the point that physical labour has been 'culturally disparaged' in China and that workers' councils can function as a source of recruitment of managerial personnel having practical line experience (Harper, 1971: 112).

Economic policy moved away from the use of material incentives to a greater emphasis on ideological imperatives and 'greater reliance was placed on the revolutionary fervor of the masses' (Hoffman, 1964: 93). Material incentives, it was said, had led to 'the growth of individualism, egoism, and the equal-treatment ideology among the masses' (Liu Shao-Chi'i, cited in Hoffmann, 94). In the sphere of incentives to work, putting 'politics in command' meant 'first of all [the] awakening of enthusiasm', and the emphasis was on emulation campaigns intended to develop 'collectivist attitudes and behaviour'. Honorific rather than material rewards became dominant.

In the villages, the development of communes was an attempt to change the fundamental attitudes to work and traditional systems of work. Attempts were made to form production brigades which could handle water works and build small-scale industries (Schurmann, 467). In the communes, supplies in kind accounted for some 70 per cent of members' income, and this policy was regarded as a movement towards communism. There can be no doubt that following the introduction of the communes there was an economic crisis, In addition to organisational problems in the communes the Chinese leadership also faced the effects of the sudden withdrawal of Soviet aid.

In 1961, targets were cut, the communes were reorganised and managers were given more authority. Material incentives were also re-introduced; piece-rates again found a place in industry: 'wage-grade systems, bonuses, and other payments were modified in 1961 and 1962 in line with the notion of more pay for more work' (Hoffmann, 1964: 96). In the communes, supplies in kind were reduced to 30 per cent of total income. Profitability as a stimulus to production and the operation of the market was given a more important role. The period 1961–4 saw less reliance on administrative and 'political' means and was similar in character to the New Economic Policy introduced in Soviet Russia in 1921. (For a brief summary see Wheelwright and McFarlane, chapter 3.) This failure of the commune movement, it is generally said, discredited the applicability of revolutionary traditions to economic management.

Lowenthal argues that the Party apparatus (and particularly its members of the postwar generation) supported a managerial and technocratic position (*ibid*, 65). The older generation of Communist leaders looked to the army and to youth as a basis of support. These two groups have provided the basis for an attack on the established executives of state and Party which occurred during the Cultural Revolution. There seems to be no doubt that the Maoist policy of encouraging socialist forms of social relations was not carried out by many government institutions and was opposed by many of the Party and government executives.

In 1964 a 'socialist education' campaign took place which was seen as part of the ideological struggle against the bourgeois outlook associated with Soviet communism. The aim here, as in the Cultural Revolution proper, which was inauguarated in 1966, was to indoctrinate youth with a militant revolutionary consciousness. The Great Proletarian Cultural Revolution was explicitly regarded by Mao as a continuation of the socialist revolution. Schram defines its two general aims as 'to change the structure of power in society, and to carry out an irreversible transformation in the patterns of thought and behaviour of the Chinese people' (Schram, 1973: 85) These goals implied that ideological and political campaigns against hostile groups, such as intellectuals or bureaucrats, were necessary to overcome any tendency to drift away from socialism. At an ideological level, Maoists stress the dialectic of 'one divides into two', which emphasises the continuation of division and contradiction under socialism. In contrast, the Soviet dialectic of socialism – 'two fuse into one' – was labelled revisionist and it was held that this principle 'is deliberately designed to satisfy the needs of modern revisionists and to help them in their propaganda in favour of peace between classes, class collaboration and the reconciliation of contradictions' (*Peking Information*, 21 September 1964, cited by Wheelwright and McFarlane, 91).

Mao and his followers also take a less compromising view of the need to introduce 'bourgeois' forms of incentives and styles of behaviour. Hence material incentives and wide wage differentials are opposed. There is still a recognition, however, of the need for 'proper' incentives. In fact considerable differentials exist between various grades of workers. Howe has collected data which show intra-enterprise differentials in factories in different provinces between 1948 and 1972 (Howe, 1973: 36). His figures show an overall ratio (highest to lowest) of 5:1 in 1948, 5:1 in 1956, 7:1 in 1957 and 7:1 in 1972 (*ibid*, 40). Considering wages and salaries in the government service, Howe points out that differentials fell from 31:1 in 1955 to 20:1 in 1958. 'There are references in Red Guard literature to further compressions of the bureaucratic income structure in 1959, 1960 and 1963. In the Cultural Revolution, the whole structure of governmental and staff occupations seems to have been under pressure and at least partially abolished. But the latest reports suggest that, by the autumn 1972, the old system had been revived in modified form' (*ibid*, 41).

The adoption of certain aspects of communist society should also, according to some of Mao's supporters, be commenced at an early period during the socialist stage. Hence forms of the higher stage of communism may be introduced during the building of socialism. Changes in social relations, it is thought, can be effected during the transition to communism relatively independently of the level of productive forces. Hence educational and other cultural institutions may help to create the correct moral climate and to shape the character of Communist man. Earlier, when discussing the USSR, we made the distinction between the socialist relations of production and the bourgeois relations of distribution. Maoists oppose this kind of division under socialism and advocate the introduction of socialist forms in both production and distribution. This is the process of the development of continuous revolution in the transition from socialism to communism, rather than from capitalism to socialism. The introduction of communes, of 'political' management in industry, of wage equalisation, were all viewed by the Chinese leaders as steps in the transition to communism. Mao's outlook is to emphasise that individual motivations of men are of great importance to the fulfilment of revolution. It is insufficient for a socialist revolution to succeed in the sphere of ownership of the means of production. A revolution must occur in men's minds. In socialist society a collectivist mentality should rule over the individualistic. The old ideas embodied in orientations socialised through generations do not automatically go away. In Mao's view 'direct action' is required to drive out the old attitudes and to inculcate new ones. The Cultural Revolution, then, was directed by the supporters of Mao (the Red Guards) against all persons in authority who safeguarded the old ways: and especially against those in the Party and government administration and those in education concerned with the transmission of culture.

In industry the Cultural Revolution led to the destruction of the system of hierarchical management, and in its place were put Revolutionary Committees which were reported to have abolished 'the last vestiges of bureaucratic management' and to be 'reverting to extreme forms of democratisation' (Howe, 1973: 147). From 1969, however, a movement back to a more formal bureaucratic structure occurred and the *People's Daily* emphasised the importance of discipline and of technique. 'Rational rules and systems' had to be restored.

In the field of education important changes occurred. The educational system set up after 1949 was largely modelled on that of the Soviet Union, and while this was a great improvement on the existing system it had many shortcomings. The schools were largely concentrated in the urban areas, and the rural areas were very underprivileged. Much of the education provided was of less value to the needs of China than to more economically advanced countries such as the Soviet Union. In medical schools, for instance, much attention was paid to neuro-surgery while problems of mass public health were ignored (Gardner and Idema, 1973: 259). Much of the advanced education was long in duration and expensive and, as the skills learned met a restricted demand, it was wasteful of resources. The political role of the education system, it was held, was not to inculcate proper socialist attitudes: 'Far from wishing to "serve the people", many students became elitist, contemptuous of the masses and ignorant of their needs' (*ibid*). The changes introduced after 1966 were threefold. First, an attempt was made to make education available to the masses in the countryside. Second, learning was oriented more towards vocational training. Third, greater stress was put on the inculcation of values – of serving the people rather than aspiring to join an elite; education was seen as 'a universally available prerequisite for useful participation in a modernising economy' (*ibid*, 261).

In the sphere of politics, Mao attempted a mass mobilisation of youth against the entrenched bureaucrats. The pattern of communist revolution, therefore, does not follow the Leninist-Stalinist policy of leading the revolution 'from above', but sees change being activated by the leader and stimulated by mass activity 'from below'. A decisive shift in political power seems to have occurred in 1964, when the Party began to be replaced 'by the army as the dominant force in Chinese society and the arbiter of ideological orthodoxy' (Schram, 1969: 105). The Cultural Revolution was directed against 'people within the Party who are in authority and are taking the capitalist road'. As Schram has pointed out, the challenge to the supremacy of the authority of the Party as an institution is 'in itself a change without precedent in the history of the communist movement' (*ibid*, 106). The Cultural Revolution sought to 'unleash a *revolution* to transform the Communist Party from top to bottom' (Schurmann, 507). Mao's policy was expressed in the slogan, 'To rebel is justified'. The Red Guards attacked the existing Party and government institutions. In 1967 'Revolutionary Committees' were established, composed of members of the People's Liberation Army, new revolutionary activists (Red Guards) and Party and government personnel. The attempt here was to supplant Party and government organisations.

One important objective of the Cultural Revolution was not merely to destroy the privilege of Party and government hierarchies but to make a decisive attack on accepted ideas of political and social stratification. The authority residing in the Party functionary and scientific expert were to be replaced by the authority of the masses led by Chairman Mao. The 'masses' were largely the toiling peasants. Hence a shift has taken place in Maoist thought from the Leninist notion of the Party of the working class spreading 'consciousness' among the masses, to learning from the experience of the masses. The person of Chairman Mao has also been magnified as a leader. In the 1970 draft of the Constitution, he is recognised as 'The great leader of the people of all nationalities in the entire country . . .' ('Text of the 1970 Draft . . .', 100), and all workers are required by the Constitution to 'study and apply creatively the thought of Mao Tse-Tung'. In the Constitution adopted in 1975, 'Marxism–Leninism–Mao Tse-Tung thought is the theoretical basis guiding the thinking of our nation.'

The Cultural Revolution should be seen in the context of the nature of the Chinese Revolution. The leaders of the Party did not have a mass base of proletarians as was the case in Soviet Russia. While Russia was backward and agrarian, it was much more advanced than China. In 1917, 60 per cent of Party members were manual workers. The Chinese Party had mass support in the countryside from peasants who were largely illiterate. Their traditional culture was parochial or parochial/subject and did not give them a psychological and social predisposition to economic growth and change. The Cultural Revolution then sought to bring about a transformation of the political culture. Many of the changes instituted by the Cultural Revolution were directly relevant to the small-scale, labour-intensive and generally rather primitive industry existing in China. Howe points out, for instance, that the kinds of incentive that are appropriate for workers in modern capital-intensive industry are not at all suitable for handicraft-type organisations. In the latter case, 'the development of internal incentives within a framework of less structural organisation is more likely to be efficient' (Howe, 1973: 148). The previous ruling and commercial classes continued after the seizure of power by the Communists and were more likely to be absorbed into the management of things than in Russia where the Civil War and emigration took a large toll of the previous ruling strata. Indeed, many capitalists and intellectuals supported the Revolution as a nationalist cause. To the time of the Cultural Revolution, municipal land had not been nationalised and landlords still received rent from property; many former capitalists still received rent from property; also, many taken over by the state. In other institutions, personnel from the traditional classes remained in their positions. This was also true of Russia, but here the educational system, for instance, had already been transformed under the Tsars, whereas in China the traditional scholar class remained more strongly entrenched. Mao looked to the new generation who had been educated under the communist regime to oppose traditional groups and those now in the Party apparatus. In doing so, however, he set himself both against the previous ruling elites and against the notion of Party dictatorship itself. In the place of the Party, he and his successor were named in the draft Constitution of 1970 – though the name of his successor has since been dropped. Increasingly, the cult of personality of Mao has come to dominate the scene in China.

The Cultural Revolution in China has several distinct aspects. It legitimates the rights of a faction within the political elites: this group centred around Mao is composed of the more idealistic communists. It opposes men who take a more 'administrative' view of socialism and who operate the government and Party bureaucracies. Hence there is an element of a power struggle inherent in the Cultural Revolution. The Maoist elite sought and received support from the army and from youth. The objectives of the Cultural Revolution, however, have been in keeping with the particular needs of Chinese society. They recognise the importance of the barrier to social change presented by the political culture. Political sociologists have tended to interpret political culture only in terms of the stability of capitalist liberal democracies. In socialist societies where the political rulers are intent on instigating change, the political culture – in the sense of individual orientations to political objects – acts as a brake on political transformation and forces the political order to perpetuate its non-socialist characteristics. The Cultural Revolution was a radical attempt to change these orientations. The objectives were not simply political but must be seen in the wider perspective of achieving modernity: of inculcating initiative, of introducing modern methods to an extremely backward peasant population. The very low level of technology puts a premium on harnessing labour power collectively, and to this extent the Cultural Revolution's stress on collective rather than individual effort is a rational policy to stimulate economic growth. While the Cultural Revolution appears to reject advanced technology, modern science, labour discipline, specialisation and material incentives, it is rather the case that such values are accepted but are considered to be less appropriate for China's present stage of development. The copying of the Soviet model was not apposite to Chinese conditions. The general applicability of the Cultural Revolution to other state-socialist societies would appear to be limited to societies at similar levels of economic development and with a similar political culture. The policies devised in China would be quite inappropriate to European societies. The movement, however, does bring out the fact that the political elites of socialist societies may become complacent and accept political attitudes which are traditional in character. For the consummation of a socialist revolution, especially one which begins in an economically backward society, changes in personal attitudes are necessary. The Great Proletarian Cultural Revolution was one such attempt to influence the formation of personality to change the political culture.

Socialist Pluralism: the 'Reform Movement' in Czechoslovakia

At the opposite end of the scale to the Chinese reaction against the Soviet model of socialism is that of the 'Czechoslovak reformers' of the late 1960s. The proposals for a significant change in policy in economic, political and cultural sectors in Czechoslovakia as advocated by the reformers have to be viewed against the background of the ideological and political climate of Eastern Europe at the time and against the peculiar problems facing the leaders of Czechoslovakia.

Czechoslovakia and Eastern Germany were the most industrialised states to join the Soviet bloc after the Second World War. By 1955 per capita income in both these countries was approximately 40 per cent higher than in the Soviet Union. One important characteristic of the country inherited from before the war was the significant regional variations: the Slovak areas were largely agricultural while industry was located in the Czech lands comprising Bohemia, Silesia and Moravia. Following the pattern of Soviet Russia after

1917, the Czechoslovak communists first nationalised the 'commanding heights' of the economy, then gradually extended state ownership and control over the remaining small number of enterprises. By 1953, 84 per cent of the national income originated from enterprises under state ownership, and by 1959 the collectivisation of agriculture was completed and only 16 per cent of arable land remained in private ownership. Economic policy after 1949 was to industrialise the country extensively. In pre-war Czechoslovakia, agriculture contributed 23 per cent of the national income; by 1961 this figure had fallen to 14 per cent. The comparable figures for industry and construction showed a rise from 53 per cent to 74 per cent. Again, as in the early Soviet process of industrialisation, heavy industry forged ahead and consumer goods industries developed more slowly. Taking 1948 as a base (100), by 1960 the index of producer goods had risen to 434 and that of consumer goods to 307 (Feiwel, 1968: 12).

The organisation of the economy was based on a system of central planning copied in all essential respects from the model of the Soviet Union. Its features may be briefly summarised here. In consultation with various ministries, the state planning office draws up a draft economic plan which is submitted to the top Party and state bodies for approval. The national plan defines quantitative targets for all industries which, through the ministerial system, are divided up and allocated to the various production enterprises. With given inputs in terms of materials, wage rates and so on, prescribed by the enterprise's plan, the factory is then required to meet the quantitative targets also defined for it.

This rudimentary system had been successful in the Soviet Union and had ensured a rise in production in Czechoslovakia after the Second World War. In the 1960s, however, the Czechoslovak economy experienced a severe setback. From 1960, growth rates fell. The annual rate of growth of *industrial* output was as follows: 1960, 11·9 per cent; 1961, 8·9 per cent; 1962, 6·2 per cent; *1963, – 0·6 per cent*; 1964, 4·1 per cent; 1965, 7·9 per cent (*ibid*, 13). At the same time, the Czechoslovak national income during the first five years of the 1960s was growing much more slowly than in other East European countries. The average increase of national income between 1960 and 1965 was only 1·8 per cent, compared with 5·9 per cent in Poland and 6·3 per cent in the USSR. In 1963, Czechoslovakia had a negative growth rate of 3 per cent (*ibid*, 60). These developments provide the background to the various economic reforms which were advocated with increasing force by critics of the Soviet-type model. But before considering the policies put forward by reformers, such as Ota Sik, we might sketch in the political framework in which the economic reforms were being conceived.

The general relaxation of central political controls in the Soviet Union and the greater liberalisation of intellectual life there associated with de-Stalinisation met with little response in the late 1950s in Czechoslovakia. The Party leadership under Novotny took a hard line of repression against intellectuals and others who wanted such things as a relaxation of censorship and freer contact with the West. A watershed was reached in 1960 when a new constitution proclaimed that Czechoslovakia had completed the socialist stage of development and was entering the epoch of the construction of communism. This new phase, however, did not lead to any reduction in state–Party domination; it did not entail any significant changes in economic organisation or any relaxation in the cultural sphere.

But pressures for change were building up. Within the Party, many felt that the lead given by Khrushchev, in exposing the crimes perpetrated under Stalin, should be followed in Czechoslovakia. In addition to the falling levels of production there were more deeply seated social cleavages. The advent of a communist government had not solved the internal political division which existed between Czechs and Slovaks. The centralisation of political and economic life in Prague and the domination of the Czechs in the Party led to resentment by the Slovaks who had not lost their feelings of national consciousness. Also, the intelligentsia had not been appeased by the Novotny leadership. Partly linked to the cause of Slovak rights and partly opposed to other manifestations of 'Stalinism', intellectuals began to criticise artistic and literary standards and demanded greater independence from political control (see Golan, 1971: 24–7). In the early 1960s, within the Party, demands continued for reforms on a wide range of issues – for economic decentralisation, for rectification of previous Stalinist practices, for greater autonomy for the Slovaks and for greater 'liberalisation' in culture. The articulation of these demands took place within the framework of the Party under right-wing leadership. But the effects of de-Stalinisation in other parts of Eastern Europe and the relaxation of controls in the Soviet Union undoubtedly made it impossible for the Novotny leadership to utilise coercive measures against critics of official policy; many among the leadership also saw the need for reform. While these political and economic tensions were interrelated, the most important proposals for reform were to be made in the sphere of economic management.

The proposals for substantial economic reforms were put forward in 1964 by Ota Sik, the head of the Institute of Economics in the Czechoslovak Academy of Sciences. In a report of that year, Sik recognised that deep-seated problems of economic planning existed. To solve these problems, new principles of industrial management and pricing were advocated. It became accepted that the old system of economic planning did not encourage the efficient use of materials or labour, nor did it direct investment to industries requiring modernisation; it was unable to determine the assortment and quality of consumer goods required. The reforms were predicated on two principles: first, the market was to be utilised as a mechanism to reconcile demand and supply (for both goods and labour); second, material incentives would play an important part in stimulating production. The aim of the reforms was to increase the efficiency of the economic system, and to do this great reliance was placed on economic rather than administrative stimuli. (For a brief account see Sik, 1965: 15–21; Shaffer, 1968: 50–6.)

Sik has attempted to justify theoretically the role of markets under socialism. He argues that Marxist-Leninists associate commodity production with private property and that many such thinkers (erroneously) believe that, as the building of a socialist society takes place, commodity relationships expressed through prices determined by a market would be replaced by 'direct communist distribution of goods' (1967: 21). From this viewpoint, a *socialist* economy could function quite efficiently without markets. The persistence of markets in the Soviet Union was said by Stalin to be derived from different kinds of ownership (state and collective farm). Within the state sector, there could be no need for exchange relationships between enterprises because there was only one form of ownership. Thus, rather than a market form of relationship, there arose 'direct exchange of products' (*ibid*, 25).

In Sik's view, economic relationships under socialism should not be considered solely from the viewpoint of legal attributes of ownership, but in terms of the whole range of economic relationships and processes by which 'production, distribution, exchange and consumption of all sources of production . . . (and consumption) are carried out' (Sik, 1967: 33). Such economic relationships involve, for example, a large number of possibilities concerning the 'division and combination of labour . . . of alternative means of consumption, and . . . combining aspects of production' (*ibid*, 160). Such possibilities, argues Sik, cannot be worked out from a 'single centre'. To enhance the development of the productive forces of socialist societies, market relations are necessary, and the then existing forms of central planning are considered inadequate and inefficient.

Unlike capitalist markets, however, the market under socialism does not reflect antagonistic contradictions or capitalist money-commodity relations because it prohibits 'private appropriation of the means of production'. Sik argues that under the socialist market there can be no form of 'capitalist profit-seeking interest'; for there is 'no private profit and no private person who can appropriate the income and make a profit on the exploitation of the labour of others' (*ibid*, 362). 'Socialist market relationships are a necessary form of exchanging labour activity among people, helping to overcome rapidly the contradictions that still arise within social labour; they are an essential process, by means of which . . . people appropriate production in a socialist way' (*ibid*, 353). The market under socialism, for Sik, is an instrument which 'harmonises group and social economic interest'; it helps to bring production into line with demand, and it unifies the direction of investment policy. Under socialism, the market is not dominated by the interests of one class but by 'the general interests of the whole society' (*ibid*, 355). The concrete proposals put forward in 1964 were based on these assumptions.

Decentralisation of decision-making played an important part in these proposals. Individual enterprises were to be given greater autonomy. It was intended that they could be organised so as to maximise their own 'profitability' in a financial sense. They would have to compete on the market with other enterprises and even with foreign firms. The enterprise would not be constrained by numerous centrally determined targets, but would be allowed certain 'inputs' which could be utilised to the maximum advantage on the market. Prices would then find their own level and be determined by market forces. Interests would be reflected in the market and through it rather than, as hitherto, by being controlled by the central planning authorities. The earnings of workers were to be geared directly to their individual efforts and to the income of their enterprises. Thus the state would not guarantee wages. The introduction of market principles meant that wages, too, would be dependent on the 'market position' of various groups of workers, which in turn would lead to greater wage differentiation. Whereas Czechoslovakia had had one of the most egalitarian patterns of income distribution, this was now to be changed in favour of greater differentials for managerial and executive personnel – if they were efficient. Opposition to egalitarianism and to its effects was put clearly in the Party's 1968 Action Programme as follows:

> The Party has often criticised equalitarian views, but in practice levelling has spread to an unheard of extent and this [has] become one of the impediments to an intensive development of the economy and to raising the living standard. The harmfulness of equalitarianism lies in the fact that it puts careless workers, idlers and irresponsible people to advantage as compared with the dedicated and diligent workers, the unqualified compared with

the qualified, the technically and expertly backward people as compared with the talented and those with initiative. (Ello, 1968: 20.)

However, it was not intended that there would be a return to a full-scale labour market, at least for a considerable time. Certain 'basic wage scales' and wage rates of government and other types of employees were to be fixed centrally.

After a number of experiments with the new system in 1965, some of the reforms were introduced in 1966. The state plan reduced the number of obligatory constraints from 1,200 to 67, the effect of this being to 'prescribe the specific structure of production in the individual enterprises only in bare essentials . . . most of the enterprises had no obligatory production task set' (Sokol, 1967: 8). Industrial enterprises were not given any obligatory targets for gross production, productivity of labour or the reduction of production costs. Enterprises could freely combine factors of production as they thought fit. Wages were not calculated on the basis of plan fulfilment but on the level of gross income which, in turn, depended on the efficiency of management and the level of productivity of workers.

Central planning, however, was not to be abolished completely, and in fact under the proposals was to retain an important role. The distribution of the national income between investment and consumption, between social consumption (such as social services) and personal consumption, and between major forms of capital investment, scientific research and educational needs would all remain the prerogative of the government. Financial, credit, price and wage policy would all play an important part in the state plan (Kohoutek, 1968: 127). Control would be retained over regional development and foreign trade. Prices, too, were not completely subject to market pressures. Some prices were still fixed by the centre. These included raw materials and many necessities. Other prices were 'partially fixed', which meant that limits were determined centrally within which prices could move. Defenders of Sik's proposals (Kohoutek, 131; Shaffer, 54) point out that this model is not *per se* a 'return to capitalism'. Not only is nationalisation of the means of production ensured, but the very character of the market is different, for central control over the *capital* market was retained.

The reforms advocated by Sik and which were gradually being put into effect cannot be understood independently of political developments. Their implementation meant not only that those interests concerned with central planning lost a certain amount of power, but also that the 'steering' function of the Party was at least being affected, and possibly being made secondary, by the forces of the market. This process involved a partisan debate between the more traditional communists such as Novotny supporting the Soviet form of central planning and Party hegemony, and those like Sik and Dubcek who advocated greater reliance on the market and a more pluralist political structure with a weaker Party. This division, particularly over the role of the Party in socialist society, has led to considerable division in the world communist movement and to the opposition in principle by the CPSU to the Czechoslovak 'Reform Movement'.

The principles of the economic reforms had direct parallels in the sphere of politics. Just as the individual consumer was to be given greater sovereignty in the economic market, so too demands were put forward for greater individual and group influence in the political market-place. Paradoxically, it was the conservative political elite which had provided a major theoretical component for the ideas of the reformers. It has been pointed out earlier that, after the USSR, Czechoslovakia was the first country to declare her social structure to be 'socialist'; in 1960 she entered the epoch of the transition to communist society and the state was conceived of as being composed of the whole people. Under these conditions both the USSR and Czechoslovakia were engaged in the 'purposeful building of a *qualitatively new* material and technological basis. . . . Socialist relations cannot be reduced to basic juridical relations of property, they must be regarded as an expression of the *real and many-sided* status of people who, liberated from the shackles of capitalist relations, freely labour in production, in the sphere of science and other areas, enjoying greater opportunities (and with greater incentives) to display initiative in the interests of society than are afforded by any non-socialist formation' (Mlynar, 1965: 58). Czechoslovakia, then, was essentially a unitary class society of the working class led by the Communist Party. It was characteristic of Czechoslovakia during the socialist stage that 'antagonistic classes no longer exist and the main feature of internal development is becoming the process of bringing all socialist groupings in the society together' (*Action Programme*; reprinted in Ello, 1969: 129). The Party could no longer be regarded as a ruling class party because there were no longer any other classes to dominate. On the other hand, this theory did not mean that all differentiation ceased under socialism. A political scientist, Michal Lakatos, argued that social differentiation might be determined not only by the division of labour, but might originate from such factors as size of income, role in management and ethnic, national and sex status (see Golan, 151). These social divisions might be reflected in the development of particular group interests which in certain respects might be opposed to each other and might be conceived of as non-antagonistic contradictions. During the transition to communism, the function of leadership was to coordinate the expression of group interests which became more important and posed problems for the political leadership quite different from those associated with the earlier phase of building socialism characterised by the class struggle (Mlynar, 59).

It could be asked what the role of the Party was in maintaining this harmony. The more traditional supporters of the Party argued that it should establish the principles on which society should be governed, and that therefore the interests of various social groups would be defined by the Party. Also, in 1965 it was conceded by the Party leadership that 'non-antagonistic' class interests still continued during the transitional stage (Golan, 153). This viewpoint rather weakened the force of the earlier statement and justified the dominance of the working class and the safeguarding of its interest by the Communist Party. The reformers argued, however, that the free expression of various group interests should be encouraged, as separate group interests could be legitimately articulated in a socialist society. The Party's role could no longer be hegemonic under these circumstances, and such writers tended to attack both the scope of the Party's activity and its methods of decision-making. In terms of scope, it was argued that the Party should not take over or duplicate 'the functions of state and economic organisations' (Mlynar, 61).

As to the process of politics, it was pointed out that Lenin had conceived of *democratic* centralism and that the time had come for the masses to articulate their interests. The kind of centralism characterising the development of communist parties had occurred under specific historical conditions which no longer existed. Stalin had adopted a 'one-sided' interpretation of the dictatorship of the proletariat quite inappropriate for the movement to a communist society (see Golan, 155). In April 1968, Dubcek said that the kind of democracy advocated 'cannot mean a weakening of the leading role of the Party, but only a new adaptation in the spirit of Leninism, effective, purposeful, meeting the new conditions. There is no question of impairing the influence on, and tasks towards, the socialist state, but of the best expression of the principle of democratism and the necessary centralism, so that the democratic element of the development of our society, inherent in the socialist state, might find an ever better expression' (reprinted in Ello, 1969 : 71). The time had come, it was said, to move away from the practice of command by administrative fiat towards greater participation by the masses. A greater exchange of views between Party and people was advocated to prevent the Party from becoming 'out of touch'. Mlynar emphasised that 'there must be a flow of influence *from the people generally to the state (and the Party)*' (Mlynar, 62). The Action Programme of

April 1968 repudiated the 'monopolistic concentration of power in the hands of Party bodies'. Party resolutions and directives had 'to express correctly the needs and possibilities of the whole society'. The Party was called on to satisfy the various interests making up the society, and participation of the masses in politics was advocated. 'Public opinion polls must be systematically used in preparing important decisions and the main results of the research are to be published.'

Other writers went much further than the official 'Action Programme', and many of their proposals effectively challenged the tenets of Soviet Marxism-Leninism. One writer (Strinka) thought that there should be 'institutionalized criticism' or opposition (cited by Golan, 1971: 156). Michal Lakatos, in opposing the manipulation of people by the political system, suggested that a parliamentary body should be truly representative and 'a real carrier of politics and not merely a formal representative' (Lakatos, 1966: 6). Elections should provide the possibility of a real choice, and should reflect rather than suppress social interests. Responsible forms of discussion should be encouraged, and in the Action Programme Dubcek described political parties as 'partners whose political work is based on the joint political programme of the National Front. . . . *The National Front as a whole and all its component parts must be allowed independent rights and their own responsibility for the management of our country and society*' (reprinted in Ello, 1969: 152, 153). The Party, therefore, would lose its omnipotent character and would interact with and be responsive to social interests. These views were predicated on a belief that the individual has priority over the social system, and it was an individualistic and liberal philosophy rather than a Marxist-Leninist one in which society comes before the individual. Such views implied that the Party was not able to represent the interests of all groups in society and might even ignore or be at odds with important sections of the population on certain issues.

How, then, could such an orientation be reconciled with the official doctrine of democratic centralism? Some critics argued even that the leading role of the Party as expressed in the Constitution was undemocratic and 'totalitarian' (Ludvik Vaculik, cited by Golan, 1971: 163). The citizen, it was claimed, should have a right to participate in the government, and this could not be realised if the government and its ancillary institutions such as the courts were controlled by the Party. Some of the reformers attempted to justify a Marxist humanism which they saw as antithetical to the theories of Lenin, Stalin and Mao. The same writer argued that Lenin's theory of the Party was suitable for Russia but was 'unsuitable for democratic countries in which there are no illiterate people' (cited by Golan, 1973: 133).

Most critics, however, realised that for both practical and theoretical reasons the Party had to continue 'to lead', but they wanted a less authoritarian form of leadership. The manifesto *2,000 Words* of June 1968 attacked the leadership of the Party: 'The incorrect line of the leadership changed the party from a political party and an ideological alliance into a power organisation which became very attractive also to egotists . . . cowards . . . and unprincipled people' (Vaculik, 1969: 137). But the manifesto went on to recognise that it would be 'unjust and unreasonable' to carry out 'some sort of democratic revival without the Communists or possibly against them'. Eduard Goldstucker acknowledged that 'we must work out guarantees of socialist democracy while having only one leading party' (cited in Kusin, 1972: 165). This meant that the Party would not be as dominant as hitherto but would operate within a framework that included other, non-communist parties. Vaculik's manifesto envisaged the replacement of Communist Party hegemony by an alliance between it and non-communist parties. In effect, this denied the Leninist principle of democratic centralism, and the manifesto was opposed by the Party leadership. Svoboda, for example, recognised the importance of the Party's leadership function but this was not seen to include 'the direct management of the society in individual, specific spheres' (cited by Golan, 1971: 166). This attitude was particularly important in relation to the new economic policies, and here Svoboda asserted that the Party had no administrative function, but only a political function. The cadre system also came under criticism. It was said that it was no longer necessary for the Party to maintain control over the selection of personnel. As the structure of the country was socialist, it was not necessary for class and political considerations to be tied to appointments.

Many of the criticisms made by the 'reformers' were accepted by the Dubcek Party leadership. In April 1968 the Central Committee of the Party published their 'Action Programme' (see Ello, 1969). The Party's programme included promises for the implementation of freedom of speech, press assembly and religion. The electoral law were to be reformed to give the voter a choice of candidates. The existing though inactive non-communist parties forming the National Front were to be given greater scope for activity. Party control over the parliament and government apparatus was to be weakened. The judiciary was to be made more independent. Economic reforms were promised to give enterprises greater independence, and trade with the West was to be increased. Federal status was to be conferred on Slovakia.

The government under Dubcek put many reforms into effect. Censorship was made less stringent: the media enjoyed considerable independence and in fact published a wide range of views. Novotny and six of his supporters were expelled from the Central Committee and their Party membership was suspended. An extraordinary Party Congress was called for September 1968.

These developments in Czechoslovakia were condemned by the communist leaders of the Soviet Union and other states of Eastern Europe. They became anxious about the loyalty of the Czechoslovak Party to the world communist movement in general and to the Warsaw Pact and Comecon in particular. It was objected that 'democratisation' involved a departure from socialism and a movement back to capitalism. 'It is our deep conviction that the offensive of the reactionary forces, backed by imperialism, against your party and the foundations of the socialist system in the Czechoslovak Socialist Republic threatens to push your country off the road of socialism and thus jeopardises the interests of the entire socialist system. . . . We cannot agree to have hostile forces push your country from the road of socialism and create a threat of severing Czechoslovakia from the socialist community' (Tass statement, 18 July 1968; reprinted in *Problems of Communism*, vol. XVII, no. 6, p. 16). The adoption of such liberal measures in Czechoslovakia would have made it a model for reformers in other East European states and would have led to the weakening of the Communist leadership in such countries. The absence of firm Communist Party control, together with the more western orientation of the economic and cultural reformers, created great doubts among the Soviet Union's leaders about the continuing role of Czechoslovakia in the Warsaw Pact. On 20 August 1968, the Soviet Union and other Warsaw Pact countries invaded Czechoslovakia. The leaders of the Communist Party were arrested and the country was occupied. The era of the liberal reforms was over.

The significance of the proposed reforms in Czechoslovakia lies in the ways in which social differentiation and group interests of an advanced industrial society were to be accommodated in a communist-type political system. The proposed reforms recognised the manifold groups and interests which are generated in an industrial society. The Czechoslovak political culture inherited by the communist rulers was more liberal-democratic in orientation than those of the Soviet Union, Yugoslavia and China. There were more 'democratic aspirants' and political participants. The stress in the evolving form of Czechoslovak socialism was on pluralism and widened forms of participation, and conversely on the reduction of the powers of government and Party. Such a form of socialism would have a greater appeal to the public in other industrial Western European societies with strong social-democratic political movements. But the repercussions of the Czechoslovak model on the established political leaders of the Warsaw Pact countries posed a threat to their dominance and to the essential nature of the political and social system that they controlled. A weakening of state control generally and the narrowing of the role of the Party might well have weakened the social solidarity of state-socialist society in many East European countries and it would certainly have enfeebled the military power of the Warsaw Pact. For the reformers, the integration of Czechoslovak society was to be ensured by the internalised values and norms of a humanistic socialism – analogous to the supposed liberal-democratic values of western capitalist states. There is a certain naivety about these views. Many studies of the political culture of liberal-democratic countries have shown the absence of democratic values and beliefs among the population (Converse 1964). Under capitalism, an essential integrating device is law which ensures rights to property; the sanctity of private property is itself a major component in the system of values of capitalism. Likewise under state socialism it is the political institution in the form of the Party-state which provides the cement which holds the society together. Under communism, of course, the state will wither away. But in the *transition* to communism, the state is necessary. While Dubcek and the communist leaders in Czechoslovakia probably share these sentiments, the development of the reform movement appeared to be leading to the weakening of the *principle* of Party authority, which in turn might have led to the collapse of the regime and to the assertion of other values – capitalist, managerial or technocratic. Politically, the speed of change in Czechoslovakia was too rapid. While the policies advocated were democratic and in many ways appropriate to a socialist society in a way in which the traditional practices of the Czechoslovak Communist Party were not, the handling and implementation of these policies by the Communist leaders led to distrust on the part of their allies. This distrust together with the radical implications of the model for the Soviet-type systems in other East European countries led to the invasion and to the downfall of the Dubcek leadership.

Part Three

THE SOCIAL STRUCTURE

7

Social Inequalities: Occupational and Status Groupings

In earlier chapters we discussed various forms of political conflict. Here we shall turn to examine tensions having a more social character which may not be articulated in terms of specific political demands and yet have a latent as well as a manifest political significance. What we have in mind is competition by various groups for rewards and status, and the differential access by such social strata to commodities and services. This may result in claims for the redistribution of income or of other forms of rewards by those who are under-privileged, though inequality may be legitimated by societal values and accepted by privileged and underprivileged alike as a more or less permanent feature of the social system.

State-socialist societies, like capitalist societies, are hierarchically organised; they are not equalitarian. But inequality of power, income, education or honour does not necessarily lead to conflictual relations between rich and poor, deprived and privileged, educated and ignorant, the prestigious and the outcasts. Indeed, the *acceptance* of manifest inequality is more characteristic of human society than is rejection of it. Functionalist theorists have sought to explain this acceptance of inequality in terms of the necessity of inequality to ensure the efficient and effective operation of a social order. For such theorists, those who occupy positions of power and responsibility have to be rewarded. The presence of such rewards (in the shape of income or honour) ensures that the important positions in society are filled by the most suitable and best-qualified persons; the existence of rewards also ensures that the occupants of particular roles fulfil them conscientiously.

Traditionally, Marxists have rejected these arguments in support

of the legitimation of unequal rewards. Rather than seeing inequality as 'functionally necessary', they consider it to be related to pre-socialist forms of society. Inequality does perform a positive role in the development of capitalism, but under a communist form of social organisation such forms of inequality would not be rational. Under communism the division of labour will disappear, class conflict will be absent and men will receive 'according to their need' and will work 'according to their ability'. State-socialist societies *aspire* to communism and therefore to an equalitarian form of society. But in their present arrangements all state-socialist societies manifest distinct patterns of inequality (Lane, 1971; Matthews, 1972; Lipset and Dobson, 1973). How do they justify these inequalities? Para-doxically, the argument put forward by the elites of state-socialist societies, which is now inherent in their central value systems, is essentially a functionalist one. It derives from Stalin's statement that under socialism men give according to their ability and receive according to their *work*. According to Stalin, some work contributes more to the national income than other work, and requires greater training and more skill; another fact is that some workers perform more efficiently than others. These differences in skill and effort (in input) justify differential rewards, and in practice workers are paid according to the amount of work done, the level of skill and the efficiency in applying their skill.

The differential pay rewards are well known (Matthews, 1972: 90–3; Lane, 1971: 71–9) and need not be repeated in detail here. The ratio of the maximum to average earned income in industry is approximately 15/20:1. This range applies not only to Eastern Europe, but also to China even during and after the Cultural Revolution (see discussion above p. 161 and the data cited by Lipset and Dobson, 1973: 126–7). Are there any breaks in the hierarchy in-dicating the boundaries of particular social groups? In this discus-sion we must distinguish between mere statistical categories and social categories, and between objective differences and subjective awareness of them. The major social divisions are between skilled and unskilled, manual and non-manual, and men and women.

Skilled and Unskilled; Manual and Non-Manual
As we have seen, differences in rewards based on levels of skill are legitimated by ideology: differentials in earnings are considered to be functionally necessary in the epoch of building socialism. The other divisions, however, are not so legitimated. Parkin (1971) has suggested that the 'manual/non-manual cleavage, which charac-terises the class structure of capitalist society' does not exist in state-socialist societies which are more characterised by distinctions based

on levels of skill (Parkin, 1971 : 144–9). In support of this argument, Parkin cites statistics which show that manual workers as a group receive higher incomes than clerical and administrative workers (though lower than engineering and technical staff). In Czechoslovakia the ratios in 1964 were manual workers 100, clerical and administrative staff 84.5, engineering and technical staff 130.3. Matthews points out that in the USSR in 1966 'the average wage for the industrial "employee" was about 17 per cent lower than that for the industrial "worker" ' (Matthews, 1972: 90). Parkin generalises that the 'overall reward hierarchy' under state socialism runs through four groups: professional/managerial, skilled manual, unqualified white-collar, unskilled manual (*ibid*, 147). While this hierarchy points to some social distinctions, other important qualifications should be made. First, to be socially meaningful the aggregate data cited need to be disaggregated and related to family income. Second, earned income must be related to other significant variables such as status, education and social interaction before any firm sociological conclusion may be drawn.

As individuals live in families, in households, it is usual to consider income on a family basis. Real income is then calculated by adding the earnings of all bread-winners and dividing the total by the number of persons in the household unit. Following such a calculation, we achieve quite a different picture for Hungary to that put forward by Parkin. Table 4 shows a hierarchy with a per capita income hierarchy running from non-manual through manual to agricultural workers. These three groups are again sub-divided by level of skill. Study of the figures in the table shows that while clerical workers receive slightly less per household than skilled manual workers (2,856 forints: 3,024 forints), the smaller size of family results in per capita income being some 9 per cent greater. The table brings out the clear income advantage of non-manual groups. A second explanation of the apparent incongruity between this result and the quantitative data cited by Parkin and Matthews is to be found in the combined occupational status of spouses. The male members of the first two strata defined in Table 4 tend to marry girls either in the same category or in category 3 which is predominantly female. Male skilled manual workers (category 4) most frequently marry girls who are semi-skilled manual or who are employed in agriculture (see below, p. 186). The net overall 'income' effects of inter-marriage tend to bring up the average of non-manual households and to reduce the average for the skilled manual households. (Even more important is the social significance of inter-marriage – to be discussed below.) Similar quantitative data are available for Poland. A study of the distribution of income per

person per month among manual and non-manual households showed that at the lowest level (less than 600 zl.) there were 8 per cent of manual households and 0·7 per cent of non-manual; in the top income bracket (over 1,500 zl.) were 19·3 per cent of the manual

Table 4

Income level by average per capita and per household income,
Hungary 1963

		Average monthly income in forints	
Type of activity of the head of household	Average size of household	Per capita	Per household
1. Leading officials, intellectuals	3·39	1,265	4,288
2. Professionals	3·17	1,050	3,332
3. Clerical workers	2·91	983	2,856
4. Skilled manual workers	3·37	899	3,024
5. Semi-skilled manuals	3·53	778	2,746
6. Unskilled operators	3·38	678	2,296
7. Agricultural manuals	3·48	719	2,498
8. Pensioners and others	2·06	689	1,423
Total	3·18	823	2,612

Source: Hungarian Central Statistical Office (hereafter: HCSO, 1967), *Social Stratification in Hungary* (Budapest, 1967), 46.

households and 34·8 per cent of the non-manuals (Lane and Kolankiewicz, 1973: 124). Parkin's hierarchy is confirmed for the top and bottom groups, but not for the middle two.

One can be fairly confident that income distribution does follow the broad occupational aggregate of income groups defined by Parkin, but it is true to say that there remains income advantage to non-manual groups. What is relevant for our purposes, is that one cannot *a priori* discount claims for income redistribution by manual workers. Indeed, as Lane and Kolankiewicz (1973) have shown, demands for greater income by some groups of manual workers were important in Poland in the 1960s and early 1970s. In addition, however, the study of the pattern of social stratification must include consideration of the distribution of other values, including status, access to education and the consumption of services in kind.

Let us therefore consider various forms of income in kind. Some top directing personnel have access to official cars, and have the opportunity to shop in 'special' stores which are stocked with desirable goods (Matthews, 1972: 93; Katz, 1973: 44). Other kinds of

'perks' are holidays and rest cures at sanatoria. Such forms of income do not affect a large number of people, and certainly not the broad bands of strata that we have been discussing. But differential access to housing is a structural phenomenon. Housing is cheap and subsidised. Thus those who have the most housing space receive the highest subsidy. Szelenyi has pointed out that in Hungary the greatest housing subsidy is given to those earning the highest incomes, and the least subsidised are those earning less than the average income (Szelenyi, 1972: 282). He points out that those 'in need' are far too large in number to be satisfied by the amount of housing available, and that the principle of merit is employed by the authorities to select between claimants for housing space. Here, then, we fall back again on the criterion (merit) utilised to justify differential pay awards, and in fact the non-manual strata received both higher salaries and greater housing subsidies. One study of expenditure on housing showed that the higher the income group, the lower was actual expenditure on housing, as shown below (Hegedüs and Markus, 1972: 47).

Income Group	*Expenditure on housing (forints)*
Upper	51,000
Upper Middle	47,000
Middle	69,000
Lower Middle	82,000
Lower	73,000

This does not mean that the housing standards were poorer; on the contrary, the housing situation of the upper income groups was 'much better, and this applies to density as much as to equipment and location'. The authors calculated that 'certain groups of executives and professionals' obtain a housing subsidy 'roughly equal to 5–10 years' wages of an average worker' (*ibid*, 47).

Similar results have been found in Poland. In Lodz in 1965, for instance, there was found to be a strong correlation between nonmanual occupation and low housing density. The density of accommodation by number of persons per room varied from the intelligentsia with 93·4 per cent of the respondents being up to 2 persons per room, to skilled manual workers, of whom 57 per cent were in this category, and the proportion fell to 44.4 per cent of the unskilled workers. It is quite clear that the non-manual groups are advantaged and that the three manual-worker categories are distinctly under-privileged having much greater density of accommodation even than clerks. (For other data on Poland, see Lane and Kolankiewicz, 1973: 127–8.)

We have now disposed of the first part of the thesis concerning the replacement of the distinction between manual and non-manual workers by that between skilled and unskilled. We must now consider the second set of objections by examining the system of stratification in terms of status, educational opportunity and social mobility.

Occupational Prestige

Data collected in surveys of Soviet refugees after the Second World War suggested that occupational prestige in the Soviet Union followed a similar pattern to that in western capitalist countries (Rossi and Inkeles, 1957). This conclusion has been verified in numerous ways in other state-socialist societies (see Lane, 1971: 79–86). One of the best surveys of occupational hierarchies is that of Slomczynski. Three thousand persons in Poland were interviewed between 1965 and 1967 and were asked to rank forty different occupations in terms of their prestige. The top ranks were nearly all professional–technical employees: 1. liberal arts professionals and creative artists; 2. teachers; 3. engineers and architects; 4. physicians and dentists; 5. natural scientists; 6·5 lawyers and economists; 6·5 medium-level medical assistants; 8. managers of political and economic life; 9. steel workers and lathe operators; 10. laboratory assistants (Slomczynski, 1970: 33). It will be noted that the ninth rank was occupied by skilled manual workers; this again echoes the Inkeles and Rossi report which found that 'workers' were ranked higher in the USSR than in capitalist countries. But this does not affect all workers. The bottom ten occupations listed by Slomczynski were: 40. unskilled workers in construction; 39. unskilled workers in heavy industry; 38. unskilled workers in light industry; 37. unskilled workers in transport; 36. unskilled workers in the sector of service; 34.5 semi-skilled workers in transport; 34.5. service workers; 33. semi-skilled workers in construction; 31·5. homeworkers; 31·5. private shopkeepers and tradesmen. Here we see a definite grouping of manual unskilled occupations at the bottom of the hierarchy. Data for the Soviet Union on prestige scales are more difficult to come by, but studies of job preferences by school-leavers conducted between 1962 and 1970 show a similar ranking of manual and non-manual occupations. In one study eighty occupations were ranked on a ten-point scale. The top occupations were put in the following order: physicist (7·64), pilot (7.62), radio technician (7·62), mathematician (7·34), geologist (7·2), physician (7·2), employees in literature and art (7·04), teachers in higher education (6·75). The bottom jobs were: clerks (2.27), workers in municipal enterprises (2·27), book-keepers (2·56), shop assistants (2.75), carpenters (2·96), smiths and press operators (3·14),

workers in restaurants (3·24), bricklayers (3·57) (Omel'yanenko, 1973 : 120).

Differences in styles of life also characterise these social strata. What we are considering here is the consumption of different services and commodities which give rise to various life-styles. A study of three levels of family income in the USSR has been reported by Matthews (1972 : 94). The average per capita income of these three family groups in the early 1960s was: 44 rubles, 82 rubles and 113 rubles. Matthews shows that the rich families spend proportionately less on food and housing; on cultural amenities and transport, the richest families 'spend more than three times as much as the poorest' (*ibid*, 95). Another study of the uses of time showed that of three different income groups, those in the richest spent half as much time on domestic duties as the poorest. While richer families worked longer hours they also spent less time on servicing everyday needs and occupied themselves for longer hours with leisure pursuits (*ibid*, 100–1).

Table 5

Consumption of various cultural items, by occupation of head of household, Hungary (%)

Occupation of head of household	Households subscribing to newspapers/ periodicals	Radio owners	Cinema-goers	Tele-vision owners	Visitors to theatre	Frequent book-readers
Leading officials, intellectuals	96	91	81	33	75	69
Professional non-manual workers	91	91	84	28	68	64
Clerical workers	92	88	81	20	65	66
Skilled manuals	87	84	76	20	48	40
Semi-skilled manuals	80	77	78	8	41	27
Unskilled operatives	68	69	70	4	30	21
Agricultural manuals	71	63	55	1	17	12
Pensioners and non-earners	—	71	—	5	—	—

Source: HCSO, 1967: chapter IV.

More specific data on various aspects of consumption are provided by the Hungarian survey mentioned above (HCSO, 1967). This survey points to consistent differences in consumption between

occupational strata. A summary of its conclusions is shown in Table 5. The table shows that as we move down the list of occupations, the proportion of households with various cultural commodities declines. This is particularly the case with television sets: 33 per cent of leading officials' and intellectuals' families, 20 per cent of skilled manuals, 4 per cent of unskilled operatives and 1 per cent of agricultuarl manuals, have a set. The percentage of the groups visiting the theatre and frequently reading books follows a similar pattern, and there are sharp breaks between manual, non-manual and agricultural strata. Such breaks can also be detected in the proportions of cinemagoers, but they are less distinct and point to the greater mass appeal of the film.

Many studies of patterns of friendship show that individuals choose friends in a similar socio-occupational group. A Hungarian study showed that 86 per cent of young chemical engineers' best friends were engaged in the same profession and their wives were from similar backgrounds (Lane, 1971: 102). In the Soviet Union, Shkaratan has shown that members of various strata choose friends from the same or from similar occupational groups. (Shkaratan, 1970: 428. See also Lipset and Dobson, 1973: 138.) In the three highest strata, some 60–70 per cent of the respondents had friends from the same groups; of the unskilled manual workers, more than 78 per cent had their best friends in the manual worker stratum (*ibid*).

Marriage follows a similar social pattern. In the Hungarian survey it was found that most marriage partners were selected within the same occupational groups: 65 per cent of non-manual husbands took non-manual wives; 50 per cent of industrial manual husbands married industrial manual wives; 96 per cent of agricultural manual husbands had agricultural manual wives (cited in Lane, 1971: 102). In a Leningrad survey, it was found that the correlation coefficient between the educational levels of spouses was $+0.8$, and that the differences between educational levels are diminishing between generations. (A. N. Baranov, *Sotsial'nye issledovaniya*, 7th edn (1971): 80. Cited by Lipset and Dobson, 1973: 138n.)

Status is a dimension of stratification quite separate from economic class, though it is linked with occupation and cultural background. As Gordon and Klopov have put it: 'in the workers' milieu, strata are being distinguished ever more distinctly . . . by their level of culture in the broad sociological sense . . . In other words, "conditions of the life situation" . . . in the contemporary stage . . . take on a relative autonomy' (cited by Lipset and Dobson, 1973: 141). I have argued that the major 'breaks' in the stratification system are between industrial-manual, non-manual and agricultural-manual

workers rather than between skilled and unskilled. These distinctions become more important when we consider access to the various echelons of the educational system.

Educational Opportunity
The educational system has been singled out as a dominant institution by writers as diverse politically as Bell (1973) and Althusser (1971: 145). Halsey, writing in 1958, pointed to the importance of the differentiation and functioning of educational institutions, and asserted that 'the educational system comes to occupy a strategic place as a central determinant of the economic, political and cultural character of society . . .' (Floud and Halsey, 1958: 170).

In the absence of inherited wealth, educational opportunity comes to be of great importance in state-socialist society because the educational system is the filter through which social position is allocated; it is a mechanism crucial to social mobility. It is my contention that non-manual strata have much advantage in educational opportunity and thereby strengthen their status position. The superior access of non-manual workers to higher educational institutions may be illustrated by data from many social surveys.

A well-known study by Shubkin (1965) of the aspirations and consequent fulfilment of school-leavers' plans shows a differential rate of social accessibility to educational institutions for school-leavers. Examination of the school-leavers' aspirations shows that an extremely high proportion of children wanted to continue to study – an average of 83 per cent, ranging from 76 per cent of agricultural workers' children to 93 per cent of the offspring of the urban intelligentsia. Throughout there was very little aspiration to start work immediately – the range being from 2 per cent to 12 per cent. In studying the subsequent realisation of the children's ambitions it was found that there was a definite relationship between social origin and educational opportunity. Eighty-two per cent of the urban intelligentsia stayed on to study; at the other end of the scale only 10 per cent of the children of agricultural workers continued in education. Of the children of workers in industry and building 83 per cent wanted to continue to study and 61 per cent succeeded in doing so. Arutyunyan found that in the Tartar Republic there was a positive correlation co-efficient of 0·7 between the educational level of parents and children (cited by Lipset and Dobson, 1973: 167).

Another study (Sennikova, 1967) has shown the social background of students entering the three different departments (day, evening and correspondence) of the Urals University (named after Gorky) in 1966 – see Table 6. Here we observe that in the day and evening departments over half (66 per cent and 54 per cent respectively) of

Table 6

Composition of students entering the Urals University in 1966 (%)

| | Social origins | | | | | Education of parents | | | | | |
	Manual workers	Peasants	Non-manual workers Specialist	Others		Illiterate	Primary	Incomplete secondary	Secondary	Secondary specialist	Higher
Day department	28·4	0·7	39·5	26·5	4·9	1·6	13·7	21·3	0·7	26·0	26·7
Evening department	33·2	4·1	40·5	13·8	8·4	4·6	13·8	31·6	17·4	18·7·	13·9
Correspondence dept.	36·7	13·4	25·5	12·9	11·5	7·4	23·3	32·2	16·7	10·5	10·3

Source: Sennikova, 1967: 135.

the students were of non-manual (including specialist) origin. Many more correspondence course students were from manual and collective farm strata.

We may now return to consider the social background of students at the various institutes of higher education. A study by Sennikova (1967: 133) of evening-class students of higher educational institutions at Sverdlovsk found some important differences between the social background of students at various institutions. Over two-thirds of the students at the university, conservatory, and teacher training college were non-manuals, but at the polytechnic, mining institute, railway institute and economics institute, over half the students were manual. More than 52 per cent of the evening-class students were manual workers or the children of manual workers.

In Table 7 we have summarised the results of a similar study carried out in day departments of various institutes of higher education in Sverdlovsk in 1968. The pattern of recruitment is similar to Sennikova's findings: note the large proportions of non-manual workers at the medical institute (72 per cent), and at the polytechnic (64.4 per cent). Students of collective farmer origin accounted for 34.4 per cent of the intake at the agricultural institute.

Table 7

Social origins of first-year students in various day departments of higher education institutions in Sverdlovsk in 1968

	No. of students	*Percentage of total*		
		Manual workers	*Non-manual workers*	*Collective farmers*
Teacher Training	783	41·8	56·2	2·0
Economics Institute	525	49·5	47·3	3·2
University	600	43·7	52·5	3·8
Law Institute	500	43·0	44·2	12·8
Agricultural Institute	325	43·1	22·5	34·4
Medical Institute	500	26·8	72·0	1·2
Railway Institute	575	58·7	39·2	2·1
Forestry Institute	900	49·8	47·0	3·2
Polytechnic	2,250	34·1	64·4	1·5
Mining Institute	850	62·6	37·0	0·4
Total	7,808	43·5	52·1	4·4
Population of USSR		54	24	22
Population of Sverdlovsk Province		63	35	2

Source: Rutkevich and Filippov, 1970: 135.

The Hungarian survey mentioned above (HCSO, 1967) collected interesting statistics on the numbers of students at school after the compulsory leaving age and at university. Table 8 shows the numbers of children continuing their education as a percentage of the children in various social groups. Here again we perceive sharp breaks between non-manual, manual and agricultural workers. In the non-manual groups an average of 77 per cent of the children stay on at school, and 23 per cent go to the university. Within this group the 'leading officials and intellectuals' had the highest ratios – 83 per cent

Table 8

Social background of senior secondary school and university students[a]

Group according to type of activity of head of household	*Percentage of secondary school students as compared to all children of secondary school age (14 to 17 years)*			*Percentage of university students as compared to all persons of university age (18 to 22 years)*		
	Males	*Females*	*Total*	*Males*	*Females*	*Total*
Leading officials, intellectuals	77	88	83	35	34	34
Professional non-manuals	57	79	68	27	7	16
Clerical Workers	79	80	79	32	11	17
Total of non-manuals	71	84	77	31	17	23
Skilled manual workers	26	48	37	10	4	7
Semi-skilled workers	20	30	25	5	2	3
Unskilled operatives	11	19	15	1	3	2
Total of non-agricultural manual workers	20	34	27	6	3	4
Agricultural manual workers	13	25	18	4	1	3

[a] Excluding households where head of household is a pensioner or non-earner.
Source: HCSO, 1967: 86.

and 34 per cent. Of the manual workers, the numbers of children staying on at school fell to 27 per cent, and only 4 per cent attended university. In the agricultural manual workers' group the proportions fell to 18 per cent and 3 per cent at school and university respectively.

Similar statistics may be cited for Poland. In the 1969–70 academic year, 48 per cent of students entering the first year of higher education were of non-manual social origin, 32 per cent were of manual, and 16 per cent peasant (Lane and Kolankiewicz, 1973: 129). Furthermore, as we saw in the Soviet Union, different kinds of higher education were variously stratified. In 1969, 32 per cent of manual working-

class students were represented on full-time courses, 47 per cent on correspondence courses and 59 per cent on evening courses (*ibid*, 210). At the secondary level, there was a strong tendency for the vocational schools to be attended by the children of manual workers and for the secondary schools (which lead to higher education) to be a preserve of the non-manual strata (*ibid*, 129).

While the existence of greater educational opportunity for non-manual strata is clear, the reasons for this inequality need to be explored. Unlike ruling class or ruling elite theorists, we do not seek the causes of privilege of the non-manual strata in the political intentions or self-interest of the political elites. There is much evidence that the elites have sought to encourage and to favour applications of manual workers and peasants to higher educational institutions. A points system or quotas favouring under-privileged groups has been introduced in some of the countries discussed here. In the Soviet Union, higher educational institutions give greater weight to work experience and to evidence of poor facilities for education. Students who lack formal education may be proposed by their factory or farm and may be admitted without a formal test to a preparatory department. In 1970, about 4 per cent of students were admitted in this way. The most important source of inequality of educational opportunity lies in the *cultural situation* of various social strata. The unequal initial distribution of cultural resources in the home puts the children of manual workers at a great disadvantage when in competition with children from a non-manual background. Children are socialised at home into patterns of motivation and ambition; they also learn various intellectual skills – particularly language – informally as well as formally. Thus what Safer (1971: 205) calls the 'cultural orientation' to education is a major determinant of social mobility.

The different motivation to higher education may be studied by considering the parents' ambitions for their children. Although desire to stay on at school is socially widespread, the aspirations of parents for their children also vary according to their social background. This may be illustrated by a study carried out in Sverdlovsk. Some 2,500 parents were asked what education they desired for their children. The results are shown in Table 9. Examination of the table shows the relatively low levels of expectation of collective farmers, some 60 per cent of whom sought less than higher education. As we consider the other three groups we note the gradation of the very large proportions seeking higher education – 65 per cent of the manual workers, 71 per cent of the lower non-manuals and 89 per cent of non-manuals having specialist qualifications.

These aspirations by parents are linked to cultural background.

Table 9

Education desired for their children by parents of various social groups

Social position of parents	Total in group	Incomplete middle	Secondary	Secondary specialist	Higher	Secondary specialist or higher	Don't know
				Desired education for children (% of group)			
Manual workers	1,395	4·2	8·5	19·9	64·9	1·5	1·0
Collective farmers	501	16·6	24·4	20·4	36·2	—	2·4
Non-manual (with no specialist qualifications)	133	—	0·8	28·6	70·6	—	—
Specialists	488	0·2	0·2	10·6	89·0	—	—
Total	2,518	5·7	9·7	18·7	64·0	0·9	1·0

Source: Tkach, 1967: 145.

They have tangible effects in that parents procure private tuition for their children to help them prepare for entrance examinations to higher educational institutions. One study has shown that of first-year students at Gorky University in 1967, 25 per cent with non-manual education had had private tuition; the proportions were 5 per cent of the manual students and 0 per cent of the peasants. In terms of the educational background of parents having higher education, 36 per cent of students with parents having higher education had received private tuition. The proportions fell to 17·2 per cent of those with middle special and 2·5 per cent of those with only four years' education (Matthews, 1975: 89). Obviously, ability to pay for private tuition is important here and in this respect the higher earnings (and smaller family) of the more educated strata are relevant considerations. All these factors, however, are part of the cultural situation which is a major determinant of educational achievement.

The Hungarian survey (HCSO, 1967) considered the performance of children in school against their social background. If we examine Table 10 we see in the first part of the table that as we move down the occupational hierarchy, the percentage of pupils with good marks steadily falls: in the first four classes of the primary school the share falls from 61 per cent to 18 per cent, in the last four classes from 50 per cent to 13 per cent. For those who stay on in the secondary school, the proportion of the bottom three groups with good marks increases. This trend may be accounted for by the smaller proportion of students continuing their studies in the lower groups – and these included those students with the better grades.

This kind of research has been repeated in 1970 and has been reported by Ferge who in general confirms the results of the earlier study. She shows that within each class of non-streamed children the influence of social origin is clear. The higher the social class, the higher the average school grades and the greater the proportion of children having good marks (i.e. an average of 4 out of 5). As children progress through the school, the decline in average marks falls more for the children from lower social backgrounds than from higher ones (Ferge, 1972: 233). Ferge also shows that if the school is in a more urban area and includes large numbers of children of non-manual workers, the standards of those from manual homes are raised slightly. But these data would seem to cast some doubts on the extreme claims sometimes made by many advocates of comprehensive education: mixed-ability groups and mixed social groups in learning units do not eradicate (though they do slightly reduce) the initial differences in the cultural endowment of various social strata.

Table 10

Ratio of children with excellent and good school results and average school achievements[a]

Group by types of activity of head of household	Ratio of pupils with excellent and good results to all pupils in			Average school achievements in			
	1-4 classes	5-8 classes	Secondary school	1-4 classes	5-8 classes	Secondary school	
	of the primary school			of the primary school			
	percentage						
Leading officials, intellectuals	61	50	41	4·52	4·37	4·14	
Professional non-manual workers	54	37	33	4·38	4·09	3·96	
Clerical workers	50	36	19	4·37	4·10	3·78	
Skilled manual workers	35	22	23	4·01	3·68	3·81	
Semi-skilled manual workers	22	15	26	3·70	3·45	3·89	
Unskilled operatives	16	12	19	3·39	3·37	3·73	
Agricultural manual workers	18	13	28	3·54	3·40	3·92	

[a] Excluding households where head of household is a pensioner or non-earner.

Source: HCSO, 1967: 90.

Male and Female Differentiation

One of the most traditional forms of social stratification is that between man and woman. Feminists such as Millett consider that 'sexual domination' (that is of men over women) is 'perhaps the most pervasive ideology of our culture and provides its most fundamental concept of power' (1969: 25). Marxists recognise that sexual domination is a feature of non-communist human society but consider that this form of inequality be approached in class terms. Sexual or gender liberation and the equality of women are bound up with human liberation and the socialist revolution. The abolition of private property enables the family to be based on equal partnership and mutual love between the partners. Public ownership of property and state control of the economy make possible supportive arrangements for the family and for the upbringing of children. Only in this socio-political context is the liberation of women possible. Feminists, however, reject this line of argument. They see the oppression of women as being caused by the family as such, rather than by the capitalist or feudal type of family (see Reed, 1972). Millett, in discussing women in the Soviet Union, explicitly remarks that 'Marxist theory had failed to supply a sufficient ideological base for a sexual revolution . . .' (*ibid*, 169). Rather than in a ruling class rooted in the means of production, Millett locates the domination of the male in the 'needs and values of the dominant group and dictated by what its members cherish in themselves and find convenient in subordinates. . . . This is complemented by a second factor, sex role, which decrees a consonant and highly elaborate code of conduct, gesture and attitude for each sex' (*ibid*, 26). From this point of view, the October Revolution did not achieve the liberation of women because the goals of women's liberation were either not held, or were not thought to be sufficiently important, by the Marxists who led the movement.

Such a feminist position, in my view, is overstated, though it must be recognised that there is considerable male domination. What is true is that women in state-socialist societies are not equal or in a *minority group* in the sense of being treated differentially and unequally in some important respects because of their sexual characteristics. The reasons for this are, as Millett asserts, cultural rather than biological. What many feminists ignore, however, are the very positive advances which have been made in state-socialist societies, and the limitations which the low level of the productive forces and the hostile traditional culture imposed in providing an alternative to the patriarchal family. This may be shown by considering the position of women and the family in Soviet Russia and China.

In both these countries, legislation was passed by the Communist

governments giving women legal equality with men and equal rights. The Marriage Law of the People's Republic of China (passed in 1950) defined the 'new democratic marriage system' as being 'based on free choice of partners, on monogamy, on equal rights for both sexes, and on protection of the lawful interests of women and children' (Article 1; reprinted as Appendix in Yang, 1959). As in Soviet Russia after 1917, marriage was to be freely contracted, divorce was easily available to both partners, and children born out of wedlock had the same rights as those of married parents. (For early Soviet legislation, see Schlesinger, 1949.) Women had the right to abortion and the same rights to employment and education as men. Homosexuality was not made a criminal offence. The intention of this legislation was to destroy the *traditional* family structure and to replace it with an equalitarian socialist family structure.

Feminist critics point out quite correctly that many of those early provisions of Soviet law were changed under Stalin and that women in fact continue to be under-privileged. Laws against homosexuality (between males, not females) were reinstituted in the USSR in 1934; in 1936 abortions of first pregnancies were prohibited and in 1944 the right to abortion was completely denied to women.* In 1935 divorce was made more difficult and expensive. In 1944, 'common law' marriages were no longer recognised and children born out of wedlock did not have the same claims to their father (e.g. use of his name) as did 'legitimate' children. The Soviet Union, like Communist China and other state-socialist societies, began to strengthen the family and to use it as an instrument of socialisation. The position of the family in society, however, and the role of women had undoubtedly changed to the advantage of women – and this is why many feminist critics are unrealistic in their appraisal. The position of women *in society* is more equal to that of men than in capitalist states, but within the family much of women's traditional under-privilege remains.

The non-implementation of many of the goals of the early revolutionaries in the Stalin era occurred because they had proved impractical in the circumstances of Soviet power. The provision of kindergartens and child care for young children could have been achieved only at the cost of lowering considerably the rate of industrial growth. The need for manpower was undoubtedly an important factor in the restriction of the right of abortion and of the new emphasis put on the value of motherhood in 1936. These policies, it must be conceded, made women, rather than men, carry the greater burden for the upbringing of children; but they have to be seen in

*It has subsequently been legalised in 1955.

relation to the political priorities of the Soviet Union in the 1930s, rather than interpreted in terms of sexual politics. At the same time, women's employment opportunities were considerably widened.

We might compare the economic and educational position of women in the USSR with the picture drawn by Kate Millett:

> One of the most efficient branches of patriarchal government lies in the agency of its economic hold over female subjects. . . . In modern reformed patriarchal societies, women have certain economic rights, yet the 'woman's work' in which some two thirds of the female population in most developed countries are engaged is work that is not paid for. . . . Just as their social position is vicarious and achieved (often on a temporary or marginal basis) through males, their relation to the economy is typically vicarious or tangential. (Millett, 1969 : 39–40.)

Since the revolution, women have increased their absolute and relative share in the employed population. In the USSR in 1922, only 1·56 million women were in paid employment – 25 per cent of the total; by 1973 some 50 million (51 per cent of the total) were in such employment (*Zhenshchiny*, 1974 : 4). In many branches of industry, women make up more than half the employees – in communications 68 per cent, in housing and domestic service 53 per cent, in health, physical culture and social insurance 85 per cent, in education and culture 73 per cent, in credit and insurance 79 per cent and in various organisations of administration 63 per cent. The number of women with 'specialist' qualifications has risen from 151,000 in 1928 to 11·2 million in 1972 : from 29 per cent of the total to 59 per cent of the total. In 1972, 72 per cent of all physicians were women. In 1972, women made up 39 per cent of the scientific workers – 13 per cent of the Doctors of Science and 27 per cent of the Candidates of Science. These figures show that women are still less than equally represented in many industries : in transport only 24 per cent of the workers are women and in forestry they account for only 21 per cent. But in general, women face no serious structural limitations on their employment or education. (For more fragmentary data on women's occupations in China, see Yang, 1959 : 144–9.)

This does not mean that women's labour is as well paid as men's. If we consider the industries in which women are largely employed we see that they are below the average industrial wage. For instance, the average wage was 130 rubles in 1972 : in communications it was 103r., in housing and domestic service 97r., in health, physical culture and social insurance 96r., in education and culture 112r., in credit and insurance 118r., and in various organisations of administration 124r. (*Narkhoz*, 1973 : 516–17).

Women are most unevenly represented among those with responsible positions. Although amongst the heads of junior schools, 74 per cent are women, of heads of 8-year schools their share falls to 30 per cent and of middle schools 26 per cent; of assistant heads of the last two types of schools, their proportion rises to 62 per cent and 63 per cent respectively (*Zhenshchiny*, 1974: 9). Women do not figure very prominently among the chiefs of industrial enterprises; despite the fact that 30 per cent of Soviet engineers are women, they make up only 6 per cent of factory directors, 16 per cent of chief engineers and 20 per cent of foremen (*Zhenshchiny i deti*, 1969: 102). In politics about a third of all elected deputies are women: 31 per cent of the Supreme Soviet USSR (1970), 35 per cent of the supreme soviets of the Union republics (1971) and 47 per cent of the local soviets (1973) (*Zhenshchiny*, 1974: 3). Just over a third of judges in district people's courts are women. In 1974 there was only one woman among 100 men in the Council of Ministers of the USSR; in 1963, at the republican level, there were 9 women chairmen and vice-chairmen, out of a total of 114 (Lennon, 1971: 50). In the Communist Party, the number of women falls as one rises in the hierarchy. Of Party members about a quarter are female; this falls to 4 per cent of the Central Committee, and there are no women in the Politbureau. (In People's China in 1956, only 10 per cent of Party members were women, and 4·7 per cent (8 out of 170) members of the Party's Central Committee were female (Waller, 1973).)

Within the family, women have a particularly hard task. In addition to paid employment, women take the brunt of domestic chores and child-rearing. In a very detailed study of the use of time after work, Gordon and Klopov (1972: 98) point out that women workers spend on housework $2-2\frac{1}{2}$ times as much time as men, and have correspondingly less time for leisure and for the improvement of their qualifications. Another study, reported by Lennon (1971: 54–5), reported that 44 per cent of Leningrad working women found it 'difficult to combine family obligations with work on the production line', and another 25 per cent found it 'very hard'. While the structure of the family has changed towards smaller, more 'democratically' oriented units, traditional male chauvinist attitudes still linger on. In a rural area outside Moscow it was found that 30 per cent of a sample of people interviewed 'thought it better for the wife to devote herself exclusively to the home and children'. Another study even found that 25 per cent of the intelligentsia thought it 'proper for a husband to punish his wife' (data cited in Lipset and Dobson, 156). (Perhaps it is fair to add that 75 per cent did *not* approve.)

While it cannot be properly argued that women are an exploited under-class subordinate to men, there is sufficient evidence to show

the persistence of structural inequality, particularly in politics. The element of truth in the feminist analysis (see Salaff and Merkle (1973), on Russia and China) is that changes in ownership relations are a necessary but not a sufficient condition for female liberation. Cultural artefacts, particularly tradition, have an independent effect on conditioning attitudes and these call for more than economic changes. Thousands of years of history of the subjection of women influence the attitudes which men learn, and while communist governments may significantly alter the institutional arrangements of society, it is much more difficult to change attitudes to get women accepted in authority roles on the same basis as men. As shown in Table 8 above, the access of women to higher education varies by social origin, and this is a reflection of social attitudes. Marxist feminists are probably correct when they argue that special efforts are necessary for the full liberation of women even in a socialist society. The high cost of liberation in poor countries such as China today and Russia in 1917 together with the male chauvinistic culture of these societies means that the struggle for equality for women continues for a considerable time, and for its implementation women need to articulate their specific demands. While we have seen that on an objective basis there is considerable sexual inequality in state-socialist societies, there is no consciousness of sexual oppression and no movement for women's liberation. One of the most important reasons for this is that women's advancement has been considerable under communist rule: the provision of educational and occupational opportunity far outweighs the inequality which remains, and this cannot be understood independently of social background. Secondly, politically active women are being successfully incorporated into the ruling Party and are increasingly being brought into the formal political apparatus.

Social Mobility
We have argued above that a break in the system of social stratification occurs betwen manual and non-manual strata; this is reflected in differential incomes, availability of housing, patterns of consumption, occupational status, patterns of social interaction, access to education and opportunities for women. Sociologists in capitalist countries define movement between statuses, or social positions, in terms of horizontal or vertical mobility. Vertical mobility assumes that there is a hierarchy of superior and inferior statuses, and vertical mobility measures upward and downward movement between these status positions. Soviet sociologists deny the relevance to state-socialist society of the concept of vertical mobility in the sense of upward and downward mobility between social statuses in a hierarchy. They

consider the differences between strata, which we have examined above, to be unrelated to notions of higher or lower, and see them simply as socially differentiated groups. These are equal in social value and are viewed as standing side by side, rather than above and below, each other. As Rutkevich has put it: 'The concept of "lower" and "higher" social strata is fundamentally inapplicable to Soviet socialist society.' Such sociologists conceive of mobility in terms of 'interchanges' (*peremeshcheniya*) between occupational positions rather than between social statuses related to various dimensions of inequality. Rutkevich and Filippov, however, do recognise the existence of 'vertical gradations' in socialist society. These are determined by the varied kinds of labour skills and education required for different jobs. It is these differences which justify differentials in income discussed earlier. Movement to a position requiring greater skill and education is regarded by Rutkevich and Filippov as a form of vertical movement, though different in quality to that of 'vertical mobility' in capitalist societies (Rutkevich and Filippov, 1970: 41–2). In my opinion, movement between occupational positions does involve more than simply an occupational change, because, as has been demonstrated above, it is also associated with different forms of life style and life chances. The extent of social mobility has important implications for the character of the social order. If there is considerable self-recruitment within strata, the system of social stratification is rigid and inequality and privilege are perpetuated from one generation to the next. Sociologists of capitalism tend to equate the openness or 'democracy' of a society with high rates of upward and downward mobility. This viewpoint sees hierarchy and inequality as endemic and democracy in a social sense as providing a means by which the most talented or qualified gain positions ensuring high income, or status or power, or combinations of these attributes. From a more narrowly political point of view, a tendency towards internal stratum recruitment may weaken the capacity of the elites to rule, because capable, and possibly aggrieved, individuals may pose a political threat to them (Bendix and Lipset, 1959: chapter 1).

It is widely recognised that a political revolution has an important but relatively small impact on the system of *social* stratification as a whole. While recruitment to the leading political, administrative and property-related statuses is significantly altered, the occupational structure remains relatively unchanged. We might distinguish between 'exchange' mobility when the number of positions remains the same and the occupants change, and 'structural' mobility which is caused by the number of statuses actually increasing and calling for an inflow. A political revolution *per se* creates exchange mobility

which is relatively modest and takes place within somewhat narrow spans of occupations. This may be illustrated by research (Lane, 1973) on Soviet Russia between 1917 and 1928 during which time very little, if any, industrial growth took place. In 1923–4, in higher educational institutions in the Russian Republic, workers and the children of workers accounted for only 19·4 per cent of the university students, whereas intellectuals and their children provided over 50 per cent (Lane, 1973: 245). Workers from production gave rise to the largest contingent at industrial-technical institutions (25·2 per cent) – closely followed by members of the 'working intelligentsia' (24·7 per cent). In arts faculties the working class also did badly, having 21·6 per cent of the places compared to 64 per cent of the intelligentsia. Similar rankings occurred in 1927–8. Workers and their children are more easily able to gain access after a revolution to the more practical and applied institutions of education than to those requiring abstract learning and theoretical skills.

Political revolutions led by the Communist Party are followed by an induced *industrial* revolution from which stem important changes in the occupational structure. This engenders what has been defined above as 'structural' mobility. The number of industrial, commercial and administrative jobs increases considerably and this involves an inflow of men from agricultural occupations to industrial and from manual to non-manual. In 1928, in the Soviet Union, for example, only 18 per cent of the population was made up of manual and non-manual workers; this proportion rose to 50·2 per cent in 1939, 68·3 per cent in 1959, 77·7 per cent in 1968 and 81·3 per cent in 1973. The total number of employed persons rose from 11·4 million in 1928 to 95·2 million in 1972, and of these, non-manual workers were 2·7 million in 1928 and 27·7 million in 1972. However, the marginal *rate* of growth of the working class and its sub-groups has declined. Between 1922 and 1926 for the non-manual strata as a whole the average rate of increase was 14·1 per cent, rising to 34·25 in the years 1928–32 (Fig. 4). Since 1932, there has been a downward trend in the average growth rate, both for the non-manual strata as a whole and for specialists in particular. As the rates of economic and occupational growth fall, there is a tendency for the *rate* of social mobility to decline and for the system of social stratification to become more crystallised. This does not mean, it should be emphasised, that patterns of social recruitment are inflexible or that the system of social mobility is rigid, but rather that the inflow caused by 'structural' mobility declines and that the amount of 'exchange' mobility does not compensate for it.

A comprehensive picture of inter-generational mobility accompanying rapid industrialisation is given by a study of the Yugoslav

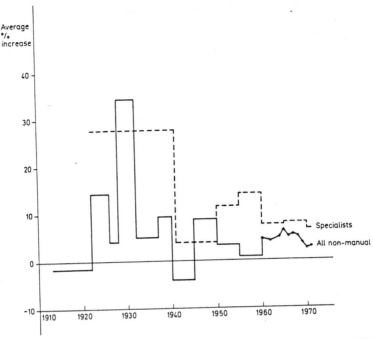

Figure 4. Annual average rate of growth on non-manual specialist employees, USSR

census carried out in 1960 (Milic, 1965). Milic shows that considerable upward mobility took place. Of the non-manual workers, the largest single group (40·4 per cent) had fathers who were peasants; this was also the case with the manual workers – 57·3 per cent originated in the peasant stratum. The doubling of the industrial population between 1953 and 1961 was largely due to an inflow of peasants from the countryside. At the same time, however, there was considerable self-regeneration of each stratum. This is particularly apparent for the peasantry: 92·6 per cent of the peasant respondents had peasant fathers; of the children of manual industrial fathers, the largest group (58·3 per cent) also became industrial workers – though they formed but a third (36·8 per cent) of the total of that group. The children of non-manual workers also largely (67·3 per cent) became non-manuals, though again they formed less than a third (30 per cent) of the total number of non-manual workers.

If we examine in more detail the internal characteristics of the very widely defined 'manual industrial' and 'non-manual' strata we

see that the inflow of men from lower strata fills the least skilled positions. For instance, Milic shows that of the total of unskilled manual workers, 74·5 per cent were of peasant origin, the proportion falling to 48 per cent of the skilled and highly-skilled manual workers (*ibid*, 124). In white-collar jobs, 84·2 per cent of the low-grade office employees and auxiliaries were of peasant or manual industrial origin; but of those with the highest qualification, 51·1 per cent were the offspring of non-manual parents.

Similar trends have been found in Poland. Zagorski (1974) in 1972 studied a 0·5 per cent sample of Poland's economically active population. Some of the major results are shown in Table 11. The study shows a predominantly 'upward' profile of mobility. There is a large outflow of farmers' sons to manual (31·3 per cent) and a lesser number (12·1 per cent) to non-manual occupations. While 61·5 per cent of the children of manual workers also became manual workers, 27·5 per cent entered non-manual jobs, and formed the largest group (38·8 per cent) among such workers; and of non-manuals' sons, 68·3 per cent became non-manual workers. The sons of non-manual workers, however, also experienced downward mobility – some 27·3 per cent became manual workers, though they accounted for only 5·8 per cent of the total number of manual workers.

Taking recruitment to specific professions, Zagorski also shows that there is a definite tendency towards internal recruitment. Physicians and stomatologists make up 0·4 per cent of the economically active population, though a quarter of this occupational group also had fathers who were physicians and stomatologists; scientific workers and teachers account for 0·2 per cent and 1·9 per cent of the economically active population, and the proportion of workers in these fields who also had fathers in them is 17·4 per cent and 19·6 per cent respectively (Zagorski, 1974: 17).

Considering mobility to different kinds of non-manual jobs between 1950 and 1972, Zagorski shows that there is a tendency for internal self-recruitment to decline over time. For instance, the percentage of children of administrative and managerial fathers starting their first jobs in the same occupational group was 33·9 per cent in 1950–4, 22·8 per cent in 1965–9, and 21·7 per cent in 1970–2; children of 'specialists in technical fields' entering the same socio-occupational group were 22·7 per cent of the cohort in 1950–4, 17·9 per cent in 1965–9 and 19 per cent in 1970; the children of 'specialists in non-technical fields' entering similar posts fell from 39·3 per cent in 1950–4 to 35·2 per cent in 1965–9 (it was 35·3 per cent in 1970–2). On the other side of the coin, the proportions of the children of non-manual workers entering manual jobs has increased as shown in Table 12.

Table 11

Inter-generational mobility of economically active population, Poland 1972

Fathers' occupation (%)	Respondents' occupation (%)*				
	Individual farmers	Working on own account	Manual	Non-manual	Total
Individual farmers	87·6 / 55·0	41·8 / 1·0	38·4 / 31·3	26·8 / 12·1	51·7 / 100
Working on own account	1·2 / 14·7	17·3 / 7·6	2·7 / 41·9	3·9 / 34·4	2·7 / 100
Manual	9·0 / 8·9	28·9 / 1·0	48·0 / 61·5	38·8 / 27·5	32·9 / 100
Non-manual	0·7 / 2·4	7·7 / 1·0	5·8 / 27·3	26·3 / 68·3	9·0 / 100
Total	100 / 32·5	100 / 1·2	100 / 42·2	100 / 23·3	100 / 100

*Owing to residual categories and rounding, the total percentages do not sum to 100.
Source: Zagorski, 1974: 12 (data rearranged).

Table 12

*Children of non-manual workers taking up their first job
in industrial manual employment*

Father's occupational group	Year of starting first job	Percentage of children taking up industrial manual employment
Administrative managerial	1950–4	15·6
	1965–9	27·8
	1970–2	21·7
Specialists in technical fields	1950–4	16·0
	1965–9	31·4
	1970–2	22·7
Specialists in non-technical fields	1950–4	8·5
	1965–9	13·4
	1970–2	14·7

Source: Data derived from Zagorski, 1974: 15.

With the maturation of the industrialisation process there is a tendency (a) for the replenishment of occupational strata from within those strata (i.e. children 'inheriting' their parents' social position), (b) for upward mobility to continue, but at a slower rate, and (c) for downward mobility from non-manual to manual to increase. There is no evidence to support a thesis that the able children of manual workers are denied education and therefore may present some actual or potential political opposition.

While we have brought out a tendency for crystallisation of the social structure, it must be emphasised that this does not preclude considerable upward mobility through education. In Table 6 (p. 188) we saw that from 28 per cent of students in the day department at the Urals University were of manual worker origin; the proportion was 33 per cent in the evening department and 37 per cent in the correspondence section. In the evening departments at Sverdlovsk University, 53 per cent of the students were manual workers or children of manual workers. The social origin of students entering day departments of six higher educational establishments in Sverdlovsk between 1950 and 1969 has been studied by Rutkevich and Filippov (1970: 128–32). They show that the share of manual workers actually increased from 30·5 per cent in 1950 to 47·3 per cent in 1969 – though, as we have noted above, the non-manuals invariably had a higher relative and absolute number of places. But

the point must not be lost sight of that around two-fifths of the students are of manual-worker social origin, and that therefore the possibility of upward social mobility is very real for the offspring (and especially for ambitious sons) of manual workers. In Poland, the number of students of manual social origins entering higher educational institutions averaged about 27 per cent between 1960 and 1966; in 1967 it fell to 25·8 per cent, whereupon a 'points' system, including social origin, was introduced as a basis of selection, and between 1968 and 1970 the intake of manual workers averaged nearly 32 per cent (Lane and Kolankiewicz, 1973: 129).

The tendency for replenishment from within a particular stratum may be illustrated by the Hungarian survey and by investigations carried out in localities of the Soviet Union. The Hungarian study (HCSO, 1967) was conducted only some twenty years after the formation of a socialist type of society and therefore one might not expect crystallisation of statuses to have taken place. The recruitment to various strata by age group gives a picture of the changing bases of social origin. Mobility into the stratum of leading officials and intellectuals would not appear to differ very much by age group. Of officials aged 50–59, 57 per cent had fathers who were either manual workers or peasants; the proportion of those aged 30–39 was 72 per cent (see Table HCSO: 117). The figures cited here do not substantiate the case that the *top positions* have as yet become the preserve of a hereditary group. Table 13, however, does show a more distinct tendency for the children of parents in a given group to gravitate to that group. Consideration of the top three non-manual groups in Table 13 shows that more than half the children of these strata were occupied only in non-manual posts (63 per cent, 51 per cent and 51 per cent) but that a considerable number (from a quarter to over a third) had careers in manual work. The greater part of the offspring of members of the three industrial manual strata also took up manual positions (51 per cent, 52 per cent, 53 per cent). Those from agricultural manual families experienced considerable upward mobility: the largest single group of children (37 per cent of the total) became industrial manual workers.

If we consider mobility between three generations, we discover that manual and non-manual strata reproduce themselves to a surprising extent. This is particularly the case with non-manual families. In Table 14 we see that where the head of household is non-manual, 56 per cent of the children are non-manual; where the grandfather is also non-manual, the share of non-manual children rises to 71 per cent. Considering the industrial manual households, 52 per cent of the children become industrial manual workers; but if we go back another generation, of those children with non-manual grandfathers,

Table 13

Percentage of households by career of employed children, Hungary

Group by type of activity of the head of household[1]	Non-manual only	of which: leading official, intellectual only	Non-manual and some manual	Non-agricultural manual only	Manual and agricultural manual	Agricultural manual only	Total	of which: there are agricultural manuals among children
Leading officials, intellectuals	63	19	9	24	1	3	100	5
Professional non-manuals	51	10	12	35	1	1	100	1
Clerical workers	51	6	9	37	2	1	100	4
Skilled manuals	30	4	14	51	2	3	100	6
Semi-skilled manuals	18	2	11	52	7	12	100	20
Unskilled operatives	13	2	13	53	10	11	100	24
Agricultural manuals	8	2	10	37	18	27	100	49
Total	19	15	11	44	11	15	100	28

[1] Including active earner heads of household only.
Source: HCSO, 1967: 120.

Table 14

Mobility between three generations in Hungary

Group by type of activity of the father of the head of household	Main group by type of activity of the head of household[1]	Percentage of households by career of employed children					
		Non-manual only	Non-manual or some manual	Industrial manual only	Manual and agricultural manual	Agricultural manual only	Total
Non-manual	Non-manuals	71	10	18	—	1	100
Manual		57	10	31	1	1	100
Agricultural		41	11	42	2	4	100
Total		56	10	31	1	2	100
Non-manual	Industrial manuals	36	10	46	3	5	100
Manual		26	11	56	3	4	100
Agricultural		17	14	49	8	12	100
Total		21	13	52	6	8	100
Non-manual	Agricultural manuals	—	—	—	—	—	—
Manual		8	11	49	18	14	100
Agricultural		8	9	37	18	28	100
Total		8	10	37	18	27	100

[1] Including active earner heads of household only.
Source: HCSO, 1967:121.

36 per cent reverted to non-manual status; of those with manual grandfathers 26 per cent became non-manual and only 17 per cent did so of those with grandfathers who were agricultural manuals.

We are not fortunate enough to have at our disposal comparable data for other state-socialist societies. For the Soviet Union we have a number of studies which show the social background of various social strata analysed by age. A study by Rutkevich and Filippov (1970: 60) has drawn up a social profile of the 'specialists' working at a Sverdlovsk gas turbine factory. Of the total, 44·4 per cent came from the families of manual workers; when they are analysed by age, however, we perceive a tendency for the share of manual workers to fall as the age of specialist falls: of those aged over 50, 55·2 per cent were of manual origin, whereas only 47·2 per cent were from this stratum of those aged under 31. The share of peasants also fell from 27·4 per cent of those aged over 50 to 14·8 per cent of those aged under 31. The proportion of men with a non-manual social origin increased from 14·5 per cent of the over-50 age group to 31·2 per cent of the under-31 age group. The children of specialists made up only 6·8 per cent of the under-31 age group; however, when we consider the age structure of men with such a background, we find that 47·6 per cent are under 31, 35 per cent are aged between 31 and 40, 12·7 per cent are aged between 41 and 50, and only 4·7 per cent are over 50.

Another study of engineering technical workers at the Pervourals tube factory showed similar tendencies to be prevailing. Table 15 shows the social origins of engineers, technicians and *praktiki** by age group. Considering the social origins of engineers, we see that nearly half (48·4 per cent) are the sons of non-manual workers. There is a tendency, fully brought out by the youngest group, for engineers to be increasingly recruited from this social stratum. There would appear to be no slackening-off of working-class men becoming technicians, and the share of workers' children becoming *praktiki* is on the increase – probably a 'safety net' for those who do not succeed in the formal educational process.

A study of inter-generational mobility at the Sverdlovsk wood-working factory illustrates a tendency for manual workers to be increasingly drawn from working-class backgrounds and for fewer to come from peasant and collective-farm families. Among the specialists, there is a tendency for the younger men to be drawn from the families of non-manuals (*see* Table 16). The proportion of fathers of manual workers increases from 41·6 per cent for those over 45 to 69·7 per cent for those under 20; likewise the percentage of grandfathers in this category increases from 13·3 per cent to 42·9

Praktiki are men who do specialist work but have no paper qualifications.

Table 15

Social composition of engineering-technical staff at the Pervourals tube factory by age

Age group	Engineers (%)			Technicians (%)			Praktiki (%)		
	Manual workers	Peasants	Non-manual	Manual workers	Peasants	Non-manual	Manual workers	Peasants	Non-manual
21–30	31·6	8·4	60·0	60·7	18·1	21·2	63·7	12·1	24·2
31–40	28·5	39·9	31·6	45·2	42·7	12·1	49·9	42·5	8·1
41–50	34·9	23·8	41·3	34·4	39·1	26·6	44·2	42·1	13·7
50–	26·1	35·7	38·2	40·9	40·9	18·2	40·0	44·9	15·1
Total	30·8	20·8	48·4	47·7	35·2	17·1	47·5	39·9	12·6

Source: Rutkevich and Filippov, 1970: 168.

Table 16

Changes in social position of workers over three generations at the Sverdlovsk woodworking enterprise

Social position of respondents	Age groups of respondents	Social position of fathers (%)				Social position of grandfathers (%)			
		Workers	Non-manuals	Specialists	Peasants or collective farmers	Workers	Non-manuals	Specialists	Peasants
Manual worker	−20	69·7	6·1	—	24·2	42·9	21·4	—	35·7
	20–25	60·7	3·6	3·6	32·1	18·2	—	—	81·8
	26–35	53·6	8·0	4·8	33·6	31·9	4·3	2·1	61·7
	36–45	50·5	10·3	—	39·2	13·7	2·0	—	84·3
	46–	47·6	2·4	—	50·0	13·3	6·7	—	80·0
	Average	54·0	7·4	2·1	36·5	23·2	5·1	0·7	71·0
Non-manual	26–35	50·0	50·0	—	—	—	—	—	100·0
	36–45	66·7	—	—	33·3	50·0	—	—	50·0
	46–	22·2	—	—	77·8	25·0	—	—	75·0
	Average	41·7	20·8	—	37·5	22·2	—	—	77·8
Specialists	20–25	—	100·0	—	—	—	50·0	—	50·0
	26–35	46·6	40·0	6·7	6·7	—	14·3	—	85·7
	36–45	50·0	30·0	10·0	10·0	25·0	—	—	75·0
	46–	50·0	25·0	—	25·0	33·3	—	—	66·7
	Average	45·2	38·7	6·4	9·7	15·0	10·0	—	75·0

Source: Rutkevich and Filippov, 1970: 89.

per cent. The social origin of specialists has become quite markedly non-manual: of the oldest age group, 25 per cent were the children of white-collar workers, whereas all of the youngest group were in this category. In Shkaratan's study of workers in the Leningrad machine-tool industry, data are given on the occupation of the children of different grades of worker. Of the members of the top two social groups in the factory (managers and highly qualified specialists) 82 per cent and 74 per cent of their adult offspring became non-manual workers of one kind or another: of the first group, 35·6 per cent were specialists or students, and of the second group 57·8 per cent were in these two categories. Examining the offspring of the unskilled manual workers, the largest single category of occupations was manual worker (37·3 per cent); however, more than half of their children (62·7 per cent) became non-manuals of one kind or another, and 16·3 per cent were students (Shkaratan, 1970: 437). These data bear out the effects of macro occupational changes outlined above. There is a tendency for internal recruitment of strata. The rate of movement upwards has declined but in absolute terms is still substantial. Let us now draw some general conclusions.

Educational selection is an important pivot around which social stratification and social mobility are balanced. We have seen that there is a tendency for educational selection based on merit to favour the non-manual strata. The question is sometimes put as to whether educational policy in state-socialist societies should not rely on merit (in the form of educational attainment) but should adopt a more discriminating egalitarian policy of admission with the selection of students proportional to the occupational groupings of the population. Such views are sometimes advanced by social democrats in England who favour using the educational system as a lever of social change. It is perhaps interesting to note here that such views when advanced in state-socialist society are dubbed 'reactionary'. In the first place they are considered to be put by conservatives wishing to deny places at higher educational institutions to the more outspoken and politically critical children of professionals. Secondly, it is thought to be discriminating against particular classes of person. Under socialism it is considered morally indefensible to deny a university place to a student because his father is a professional worker, as it is reprehensible to deny him a place because of a national or racial characteristic. Thirdly, it must be conceded that the role of the educational system is to transmit 'accumulated culture' and to make possible further advances in science, so that the admission of students with considerably lower educational qualifications would slow down the transmission and

improvement of cultural standards. It seems a more realistic as well as a more just solution to the problem to attempt to ameliorate the 'educability' of the deprived strata through greater state provision for their children in general and through an extension of preparatory courses for those whose secondary education is deficient. Greater equality could also be achieved through a reduction of the rewards earned by the professional strata, though this in turn might lead to a reduction in the efficiency of certain professional workers if income fell below an acceptable relative minimum. The data we have examined on social mobility indicate that from a political point of view there appears to be very little evidence to suggest that the class structure has crystallised into two hereditary, socially differentiated groups. While it is true that professional strata are socially privileged and tend to 'perpetuate' themselves, at the same time there continues to be considerable inflow to these groups from the manual working class and from the lower non-manual. We feel justified in concluding that while there are new forms of social inequality and unequal opportunity, the thesis of the privileged forming an hereditary social group has been much exaggerated (see Bauman, 1971).

Bibliography

This bibliography lists all works cited in the text. Students seeking guidance about further reading should first consider the following books and journal articles which treat the subject of state socialism in an introductory way; full references to these can be found in the alphabetical list.

Bociurkiw: 'Political Dissent in the Soviet Union'
Brown: *Soviet Politics and Political Science*
Brzezinski and Huntington: *Political Power USA/USSR*
Hazard: *The Soviet System of Government*
Hollander: *Soviet and American Society*
Ionescu: *The Politics of the European Communist States*
Ionescu: *Comparative Communist Politics*
Lane: *Politics and Society in the USSR*
Meyer: *The Soviet Political System*
Moore: *Self-Management in Yugoslavia*
OECD: *Jugoslavia*
Schram: *Mao Tse-Tung*
Seton-Watson: *The East European Revolution*
Singleton and Topham: *Workers' Control in Yugoslavia*
Staar: *The Communist Regimes in Eastern Europe*
Wheelwright and McFarlane: *The Chinese Road to Socialism*

An asterisk against an entry in the list which follows signifies a good study of a particular topic which serious students should read.

Alekseev, G., 'Otkrytoe pis'mo grazhdanam Sovetskogo Soyuza', *Posev*, January 1969.
Almond, Gabriel A., and Verba, S., *The Civic Culture* (Princeton University Press, 1963).
Althusser, Louis, *For Marx* (Penguin Books, 1969).
——, *Lenin and Philosophy and Other Essays* (New Left Books, 1971).
Amalrik, A., *Will the Soviet Union Survive Until 1984?* (Harper and Row, 1970).
Anon, 'Rossiya i Tserkov segodnya', *Vil'noe slovo, Khronika tekushchikh sobytiy*, vyp. 27. Frankfurt 1972.
'Appeal from the Dissident Baptists', *Religion in Communist Dominated Areas*, Vol. IX, Nos. 3-4 (February 1970).
Arendt, Hannah, *The Origins of Totalitarianism* (Harcourt, Brace, 1966).
Aron, Raymond, 'Social Structure and the Ruling Class', *British Journal of Sociology*, Vol. 1 (June 1950).
*Barton, Allen H., Benitch, B., and Kadushin, C. (eds), *Opinion-Making Elites in Yugoslavia* (Pall Mall, 1973).
Bauman, S., 'Social Dissent in the East European Political System', *European Journal of Sociology*, Vol. 12 (1971).

*Beck, Carl, 'Leadership Attributes in Eastern Europe: The Effect of Country and Time', in Beck, Carl, *et al., Comparative Communist Political Leadership* (David McKay Co., 1973).

Bell, Daniel, *The End of Ideology: on the exhaustion of political ideas in the fifties* (Collier Books, 1961).

——, 'The "End of Ideology" in the Soviet Union?' in M. M. Drachkovitch (ed.), *Marxist Ideology in the Contemporary World – Its Appeals and Paradoxes* (Praeger, 1966).

——, *The Coming of Post-Industrial Society* (Heinemann, 1974).

Bendix, Reinhardt, and Lipset, S. M., 'Political Sociology', *Current Sociology*, Vol. VI, No. 2 (1957).

——, *Social Mobility in Industrial Society* (University of California Press, 1959).

——, *Class, Status and Power,* 2nd edn (Routledge, 1968).

*Bicanic, Rudolf, *Economic Policy in Socialist Yugoslavia* (Cambridge University Press, 1973).

Blumberg, Paul, *Industrial Democracy: The Sociology of Participation* (Constable, 1968).

Bochenski, Joseph M., 'Marxism in Communist Countries', in M. M. Drachkovitch (ed.), *Marxist Ideology in the Contemporary World – Its Appeals and Paradoxes* (Praeger, 1966).

Bociurkiw, Bohdan R., 'Political Dissent in the Soviet Union', *Studies in Comparative Communism*, Vol. 3, No. 2 (April 1970).

Bourdeaux, Michael, *Religious Ferment in Russia: Protestant Opposition to Soviet Religious Policy* (Macmillan, 1968).

*——, *Patriach and Prophets: Persecution of the Russian Orthodox Church Today* (Macmillan, 1970).

*Bronfenbrenner, Uria, *Two Worlds of Childhood* (Allen and Unwin, 1971).

Brown, A. H., *Soviet Politics and Political Science* (Macmillan, 1974).

Brzezinski, Z. K., and Huntington, S., *Political Power USA/USSR* (Chatto & Windus, 1964).

Burrowes, Robert, 'Totalitarianism: The Revised Standard Version', *World Politics*, Vol. XXI (1968-9).

Carr, E. H., *Socialism in One Country 1924–26*, Vol. 1 (Macmillan, 1958).

Chang Peng-Ya, 'Soviet Revisionist Leading Clique Restores Capitalism', *Peking Review*, No. 48 (25 November 1966).

Chornovil, Vyacheslav, *The Chornovil Papers* (McGraw-Hill, 1968).

Churchward, Lloyd G., 'Theories of Totalitarianism', *Arena* (Australia), Vol. 12 (1967).

*——, *The Soviet Intelligentsia* (Routledge, 1973).

*Cliff, Tony, *Russia: A Marxist Analysis* (Socialist Review Publishing Co., n.d. (1964)).

——, *State Capitalism in Russia* (Pluto Press, 1974).

Cohen, A. K., 'The Study of Social Disorganisation and Deviant Behaviour', in R. K. Merton *et al., Sociology To-day* (Basic Books, 1959).

Connor, Walter D., 'Juvenile Delinquency in the USSR: Some Quantitative and Qualitative Indicators', *American Sociological Review*, Vol. 35, No. 2 (April 1970).

*——, *Deviance in Soviet Society: Crime, Delinquency and Alcoholism* (Columbia University Press, 1972).

Constitution of the People's Republic of China (1954), reprinted in Winberg Chai (ed.), *Essential Works of Chinese Communism* (Bantam Books, 1969).

Converse, P. E., 'The Nature of Belief Systems in Mass Politics', in D. Apter (ed.), *Ideology and Discontent* (Free Press, 1964).

Dahrendorf, R., 'Out of Utopia: Toward a Reorientation of Sociological Analysis', *American Journal of Sociology*, Vol. 64 (1958–60).

Davis, Kingsley, and Moore, Wilbert W., 'Some Principles of Stratification', *American Sociological Review*, Vol. 10, No. 2 (1945).

Donaldson, Robert H., 'The 1971 Soviet Central Committee: An Assessment of the New Elite', *World Politics*, XXIV, No. 3 (April 1972), 382–409.

Dore, Ronald, *British Factory – Japanese Factory* (Allen & Unwin, 1973).

Dunning, E. G., and Hopper, E. I., 'Industrialisation and the Problem of Convergence: A Critical Note', *Sociological Review*, No. 14 (1966), 163–86.

Dzyuba, Ivan, *Internationalism or Russification? A Study in the Soviet Nationalities Problem* (Weidenfeld & Nicolson, 1968).

Ello, Paul, *Dubcek's Blueprint for Freedom* (William Kimber, 1969).

Ellul, Jacques, *The Technological Society* (Cape, 1965).

*Farrell, R. Barry, *Political Leadership in Eastern Europe and the Soviet Union* (Butterworth, 1970).

Fedoseyev, P., 'Theoretical Foundations of Leninist Party', *Kommunist*, No. 17 (1973). Translation in: *Socialism: Theory and Practice*, No. 9 (September 1974).

Feiwel, George, *New Economic Patterns in Czechoslovakia* (Random House, 1968).

Feldman, Arnold S. and Moore, W. E. 'Industrialisation and Industrialism, Convergence and Differentiation', *Transactions of Fifth World Congress of Sociology* (Washington, D.C., 1962).

Ferge, S., 'Some Relations between Social Structure and the School System', *Sociological Review Monograph*, No. 17 (Keele, 1972).

*Fleron, F. J. (ed.), *Communist Studies and the Social Sciences* (Chicago, 1969).

Floud, J., and Halsey, A. H., 'The Sociology of Education', *Current Sociology*, Vol. 7, No. 3 (1958).

Frank, Peter, 'The CPSU Obkom First Secretary: a Profile', *British Journal of Political Science*, Vol. 1, No. 3 (1971).

Friedrich, Carl J., and Brzezinski, Z. K. *Totalitarian Dictatorship and Autocracy* (Praeger, 1st edn 1956, rev. edn 1965).

*Friedrich, Carl J., Curtis, M., and Barber, B. R., *Totalitarianism in Perspective: Three Views* (Praeger, 1969).

Friedrich, Carl J., 'In Defence of a Concept' in Leonard Schapiro, *Political Opposition in One-Party States* (Macmillan, 1972).

Galbraith, J. K., *The New Industrial State* (Hamish Hamilton, 1967).

Gardner, J., and Idema, W., 'China's Educational Revolution', in S. R. Schram (ed.) (1973). (see below.)

*Gehlen, M. P., and McBride, M., 'The Soviet Central Committee: an Elite Analysis', *American Pol. Sci. Rev.*, Vol. LXII, No. 4 (1968). Also reprinted in R. E. Kanet (ed.), *The Behavioral Revolution and Communist Studies* (Free Press, 1971).

Giddens, Anthony, *The Class Structure of The Advanced Societies* (Hutchinson, 1973).

Gluckstein, Y., *Mao's China* (Allen & Unwin, 1959).

*Golan, Galia, *The Czechoslovak Reform Movement* (Cambridge University Press, 1971).

——, *Reform Rule in Czechoslovakia* (Cambridge University Press, 1973).

Goldthorpe, John, 'Social Stratification in Industrial Society', in Reinhardt Bendix and S. M. Lipset (eds), *Class, Status and Power* (Routledge, 1968).

Gordon, L. A., and Klopov, E. V., *Chelovek posle raboty* (Moscow, 1972).

Gray, Jack, 'Mao Tse-Tung's Strategy for the Collectivisation of Chinese Agriculture: an Important Phase in the Development of Maoism', in E. de Kadt and G. Williams, *Sociology and Development* (Tavistock, 1974).

Griffith, William T., *Communism in Europe* (M.I.T. Press, 1965).

Habermas, Jurgen, *Towards a Rational Society* (Heinemann, 1971).

Hammer, Darrell P., 'The Dilemma of Party Growth', *Problems of Communism*, Vol. 20 (July/August, 1971).

*Harasymiw, Bohdan, '*Nomenklatura*: The Soviet Communist Party's Leadership Recruitment System', *The Canadian Journal of Political Science*, Vol. 2, No. 3, 493–512.

Harper, Paul, 'Workers' Participation in Management in Communist China', *Studies in Comparative Communism*, Vol. 4, Nos 3 and 4 (July/October 1971).

Hayward, Max, *On Trial: Soviet State versus Abram Tertz and Nikolai Arzhak* (Harper & Row, 1966).

Hazard, John N., *The Soviet System of Government*, 3rd edn (University of Chicago Press, 1964).

*Hegedus, Andras, and Markus, Maria, 'Values in the Long Range Planning of Distribution and Consumption', in Halmos, *Hungarian Sociological Studies* (Sociological Review Monograph, No. 17) (Keele, 1972).

Hoffman, George W., and Neal, Fred Warner, *Yugoslavia and The New Communism* (Twentieth Century Fund, 1962).

Hoffmann, Charles, 'Work Incentives in Communist China', *Industrial Relations*, Vol. 3, No. 2 (1964).

Hollander, G. D., *Soviet Political Indoctrination* (Praeger, 1972).

Hollander, Paul, *Soviet and American Society* (Oxford University Press, 1973).

*Howe, Christopher, *Wage Patterns and Wage Policy in Modern China 1919–1972* (Cambridge University Press, 1973).

Hughes, T. J., and Luard, D. E. T., *The Economic Development of Communist China 1949–1960*, 2nd edn (Royal Institute of International Affairs, 1961).

Hungarian Central Statistical Office (HCSO, 1967), *Social Stratification in Hungary* (Budapest, 1967).

ILO, *Workers' Management in Yugoslavia* (Geneva, 1962).

*Inkeles, Alex, and Bauer, Raymond A., *The Soviet Citizen* (Harvard University Press, 1959).

Ionescu, Ghita, *The Politics of the European Communist States* (Weidenfeld & Nicolson, 1967).

——, *Comparative Communist Politics* (Macmillan, 1972)

Istoriya vsesoyuznoy kommunisticheskoy partii (bol'shevikov). Kratki kurs (Moscow, 1950).

Johnson, A. Ross, *The Transformation of Communist Ideology: The Yugoslav Case, 1945–53* (M.I.T. Press, 1972).

Johnson, Chalmers, 'Comparing Communist Nations', in *Change in Communist Systems* (ed. Chalmers Johnson) (Stanford University Press, 1970).

Kaplan, F. I., *Bolshevik Ideology and the Ethics of Soviet Labour 1917–1920: the Formative Years* (Philosophical Library, 1968).

Karalasingham, V., 'The War in Korea', in *The Fourth International, Stalinism and the Origins of the International Socialists. Some Documents* (Pluto Press, 1971).

Katz, Zev, *Soviet Dissenters and Social Structure in the USSR* (Cambridge, Mass.: Centre for International Studies, 1971).

——, 'Sociology in the Soviet Union'. *Problems of Communism*, Vol. 20, No. 3 (1971A).

——, *The Nachalnik (Executive) Class in the USSR* (MIT Center for International Studies, May 1973).

——, *Patterns of Social Mobility in the USSR* (MIT Center for International Studies, 1973B).

*Kautsky, J. *Communism and the Politics of Development* (Wiley, 1968).

Keller, Suzanne, *Beyond the Ruling Class* (Random House, 1963).

Kerr, Clark, Dunlop, J. T., Harbison, F. H., and Mayers, C. A., *Industrialism and Industrial Man. The Problems of Labour and Management in Economic Growth* (Heinemann, 1962).

Kohoutek, Miloslav, 'On Problems of the Plan and the Market', *Czechoslovak Economic Papers*, Vol. 10 (1968), 125–37.

*Kolaja, Jiri, *Workers' Councils: The Yugoslav Experience* (Tavistock Press, 1965).

Kolankiewicz, G., Review of L. Churchward, *The Soviet Intelligentsia*, in *Anglo-Soviet Journal*, Vol. 34, No. 1 (1973).

Kollektiv Kolkhoznikov (Moscow, 1970).

Kon, Igor S., 'The Concept of Alienation in Modern Sociology', in Peter Berger (ed.), *Marxism and Sociology* (Appleton-Century-Crofts, 1969).

Konstitutsii zarubezhnykh sotsialisticheskikh gosudarstv Evropy (Moscow, 1973).

Koval, Anton, 'An Open Letter', *Studies in Comparative Communism*, Vol. 3, No. 2 (1970).

'KPSS v tsifrakh', *Partiynaya Zhizn'*, No. 14 (1973).

*Kusin, Vladimir V., *Political Grouping in the Czechoslovak Reform Movement* (Macmillan, 1972).

Kuusinen, O. (ed.), *Fundamentals of Marxism-Leninism*. (Moscow: Foreign Languages Pub. House, 1961).

Lakatos, Michal, 'Some Problems of Socialist Democracy from the Viewpoint of the Citizen's Position in our Society', *Pravny Obzor*, 3 (1966), translated in *Czechoslovak Press Survey*, No. 1780.

Lane, Christel, 'Some Explanations for the Persistence of Christian Religion in Soviet Society', *Sociology*, Vol. 8, No. 2 (May 1974).

Lane, David, *Politics and Society in the USSR* (Weidenfeld, 1970).

*——, *The End of Inequality? Stratification under State Socialism* (Penguin, 1971).

——, 'The Impact of Revolution: The Case of Selection of Students for Higher Education in Soviet Russia, 1917–1928', *Sociology*, 7, No. 2 (May 1973).

——, 'Leninism as an Ideology of Soviet Development', in E. de Kadt and G. Williams (eds.), *Sociology and Development* (Tavistock Press, 1974).

——, 'Ethnic and Class Stratification in Soviet Kazakhstan, 1917–39', *Comparative Studies in Society and History*, Vol. 7, No. 2 (1975).

*Lane, D. and Kolankiewicz, G. (eds.), *Social Groups in Polish Society* (Macmillan, 1973).

Lasswell, H. D., *et al., The Comparative Study of Elites* (Stanford University Press, 1952).

Lemert, Edwin M., *Human Deviance, Social Problems and Social Control* (Prentice Hall 1972).

'Leninism or Social Imperialism', *Peking Review*, 24 April 1970.

Lennon, Lotta, 'Women in the USSR', *Problems of Communism*, No. 20 (July/August 1971).

Levytsky, Borys, *The Soviet Political Elite* (Munich, 1969; distributed by Hoover Institution, Stanford University, California).

*Lipset, S. M., and Dobson, R. B., 'Social Stratification and Sociology in the Soviet Union', Survey, Vol. 19 (Summer 1973).

Lowenthal, Richard, 'Development v. Utopia in Communist Policy', in Chalmers Johnson, *Change in Communist Systems* (Stanford, 1970).

Mandel, Ernest, *Marxist Economic Theory* (Merlin Press, 1968).

——, *The Inconsistencies of State Capitalism* (International Marxist Group Pamphlet, 1969).

Mann, Michael, 'The Social Cohesion of Liberal Democracy', *American Sociological Review*, Vol. 35, No. 3 (1970).

Mao, Tse-Tung, 'On Contradiction' (1937), *Selected Works*, Vol. 1 (Peking, 1964).

——, 'Stalin is our Commander' (1939), printed in Stuart R. Schram, *The Political Thought of Mao Tse Tung* (Penguin, 1969).

——, 'On the People's Democratic Dictatorship' (1949), *Selected Works*, Vol. 4, 411–24.

——, 'Revolutionary Forces of the World Unite, Fight Against Imperialist Aggression!' (1948), *Selected Works*, Vol. 4 (Peking, 1961).

Marcuse, Herbert, *Soviet Marxism: A Critical Analysis* (Routledge, 1958).

——, *One Dimensional Man* (Sphere Books, 1968; first published 1964).

Marksistko-leninskaya filosofiya: istoricheski materializm (Moscow, 1972).

*Matthews, Mervyn, *Class and Society in Soviet Russia* (Allen Lane, 1972).

——, 'Soviet Students – Some Sociological Perspectives', *Soviet Studies*, Vol. 29, No. 1 (January 1975).

'Memorandum demokratov verkhovnomu sovetu SSR o nezakonnom zakhvate vlasti rukovodstvom KPSS i ego antikonstitutsionnoy deyatel'nosti', *Khronika tekushchikh sobytiy*, vyp. 21 (Posev, 1972).

Meyer, Alfred A., *The Soviet Political System* (Random House, 1965).

Mickiewicz, Ellen, *Handbook of Soviet Social Science Data* (Free Press, 1973).

Milic, Vojin, 'General Trends in Social Mobility in Yugoslavia', *Acta Sociologica*, Vol. 9 (1965/6).

Millett, Kate, *Sexual Politics* (Hart-Davis, 1969).

Mills, C. Wright, *The Power Elite* (Oxford University Press, 1956).

Minagawa, Shugo, 'The Functions of the Supreme Soviet Organs, and Problems of their Institutional Development', *Soviet Studies*, Vol. 27, No. 1 (January 1975).

Mlynar, Zdenek, 'Problems of Political Leadership and the New Economic System', *World Marxist Review*, Vol. 8, No. 12 (1965), 58–64.

Moore, Roy, *Self-Management in Yugoslavia* (Fabian Research Series No. 281, 1970).

Narodnoe Khozyaystvo SSSR 1922–72 gg (*Narkhoz* 1972) (Moscow, 1972).

Narodnoe Khozyaystvo SSSR v 1972 g (*Narkhoz* 1973) (Moscow, 1973).

Nauchno-technicheski progress i sotsial'nye izmeneniya na sele (Minsk, 1972).

Nove, Alec ' "Market Socialism" and its Critics', *Soviet Studies*, 24, No. 1 (July 1972).

OECD, *Jugoslavia* (April 1974).

Omel'yanko, B. L., *Tekhnicheski progress i sovremennye trebovaniya k urovnyu kvalifikatsii i podkotovke rabochikh kadrov* (Moscow, 1972).

The Origin and Development of the Differences between the Leadership of the CPSU and Ourselves (Peking, Foreign Languages Press, 1963).

On Khrushchev's Phoney Communism and its Historical Lessons for the World (Peking, Foregin Languages Press, 1964).

Osnovy nauchnogo kommunizma (Moscow, 1969).

Parkin, Frank, *Class Inequality and Political Order* (MacGibbon & Kee, 1971).

——, 'System Contradiction and Political Transformation', *European Journal of Sociology*, Vol. 13 (1972).

Parry, Albert, *The New Class Divided: Science and Technology versus Communism* (Macmillan, 1966).

Parsons, Talcott, 'Characteristics of Industrial Societies', in *Structure and Process in Modern Societies* (Glencoe, 1960).

——, 'On the Concept of Political Power', *Proceedings of the American Philosophical Society*, Vol. 107, No. 3 (June 1963). Reprinted in R. Bendix and S. M. Lipset, *Class, Status and Power* (Routledge, 1966).

——, *Societies: Evolutionary and Comparative Perspectives* (Prentice Hall, 1966).

——, 'Social Classes and Class Conflict in the Light of Recent Sociological Theory' (1949). *Essays in Sociological Theory* (Collier Macmillan, 1964a).

——, 'Communism and the West: The Sociology of the Conflict' in A. and E. Etzioni, *Social Change: Sources, Patterns and Consequences* (Basic Books, 1964b).

——, *The System of Modern Society* (1971).

——, 'Petition to U.N. Commission on Human Rights, May 20, 1969', reprinted in *Studies in Comparative Communism*, Vol. 3, No. 2 (April 1970), 114–16.

Poulantzas, N., *Political Power and Social Classes* (New Left Books, 1973).

The Programme of the League of Yugoslav Communists (International Society for Socialist Studies, 1959).

'A Proposal Concerning the General Line of the International Communist Movement', *Peking Review*, No. 25 (21 June 1963).

Pye, L. W. and Verba, S., *Political Culture and Political Development* (Princeton University Press, 1965).

Reddaway, Peter, 'Freedom of Worship and the Law', *Problems of Communism*, Vol. 17, No. 4 (July/August 1968).

——, 'The Soviet Spiritual and Intellectual Ferment' (two documents), *Frontier*, Vol. 12, No. 2 (May 1969).

——, *Uncensored Russia; the Human Rights Movement in the Soviet Union* (Cape, 1972).

Reed, Evelyn, 'In Defence of Engels on the Matriarchy', in L. Jenness, *Feminism and Socialism* (Pathfinder Press, 1972).

Renmin, Ribao, *Is Yugoslavia a Socialist Country?* (Peking, Foreign Language Press, 26 Sepember 1963).

Riddell, David S., 'Social Self-Government: The Background of Theory and Practice in Yugoslav Socialism', *Brit. J. Sociol.*, 19, No. 1 (March 1968).

*Rigby, T. H., *Communist Party Membership in the USSR 1917–67* (Princeton University Press, 1968).

Rigby, T. H., 'The Soviet Political Elite 1917–1922', *British Journal of Political Science*, Vol. 1 (1971a), 415–36.

——, 'The CPSU Elite: Turnover and Rejuvenation from Lenin to Khrushchev', *Australian Journal of Politics and History*, Vol. XVI, No. 1 (1971b), 11–23.

——, 'The Soviet Politburo: A Comparative Profile 1951–1971', *Soviet Studies*, Vol. 24, No. 1 (July 1972).

Riordan, J. W., 'The Olympic Games as a Mirror of Society', *Anglo-Soviet Journal*, XXIX (1969).

Ross, J. A., 'The Composition and Structure of the Alienation of Jewish Emigrants from the Soviet Union', *Studies in Comparative Communism*, Vol. 7, Nos. 1 and 2 (1974).

Rossi, P. H., and Inkeles, A., 'Multidimensional Ratings of Occupations', *Sociometry*, Vol. 20, No. 3 (1957).

Rutkevich, M. N., and Filippov, F. R., *Sotsial'nye peremeshcheniya* (Moscow, 1970).

Safer, Z., 'Different Approaches to the Measurement of Social Differentiation in the Czechoslovak Society', *Quality and Quantity*, Vol. 5 (June 1971).

Sakharov, Andrei D., *Progress, Co-existence and Intellectual Freedom* (Andre Deutsch, 1968).

——, 'How I Came to Dissent', *New York Review of Books*, Vol. 21, No. 4 (1974).

Salaff, J. W., and Merkle, J., 'Women and Revolution: The Lessons of the Soviet Union and China', in M. B. Young (ed.), *Women in China* (Ann Arbor: Center for Chinese Studies, 1973).

Schlesinger, R., *The Family in the USSR* (Routledge, 1949).

Schram, Stuart R., *Mao Tse-Tung* (Penguin, 1966).

——, *The Political Thought of Mao Tse-Tung* (Penguin, 1969).

*——, (ed.), *Authority, Participation and Cultural Change in China* (Cambridge University Press, 1973).

Schueller, George K., *The Politburo* (Stanford University Press, 1951).

Schurmann, Franz, *Ideology and Organization in Communist China*, 2nd edn (University of California, 1971).

Sennikova, L. I., 'Vechernee i zaochnoe obuchenie i vysshey shkole kak faktor izmeneniya sotsial'nogo polozheniya', in *Protsessy izmeneniya sotsial'noy struktury v Sovetskom obshchestve* (Sverdlovsk, 1967).

Seton-Watson, H., *The East European Revolution* (Methuen, 1956).

Shaffer, Harry G., 'An Economic Model in Eclipse', *Problems of Communism*, Vol. XVII, No. 6 (1968), 50–6.

Shkaratan, O. I., *Problemy sotsial'nye struktury rabochego klassa SSSR* (Moscow, 1970).

Shubkin, V. N., 'Molodezh' vstupaet v zhizn' ', *Voprosy filosofii*, No. 5 (May 1965), 57–70.

Sik, Ota, 'Czechoslovakia's New System of Economic Planning and Management', *World Marxist Review*, Vol. 8, No. 12 (1965), 15–21.

——, *Plan and Market Under Socialism* (International Arts and Sciences Press, 1967).

Singleton, F. B., *Workers' Self-Management in Yugoslavia* (National Association of Soviet and East European Studies, duplicated paper, 1970).

Singleton, F. B., and Saksida, S., *Workers' Self-Management in Yugoslavia*, duplicated paper, n.d.

Singleton, F. B., and Topham, A. J., *Workers' Control in Yugoslavia* (Fabian Society, 1963).

Skilling, H. Gordon, and Griffiths, F., *Interest Groups in Soviet Politics* (Princeton University Press, 1971).

Skolimowski, Henryk, 'Open Marxism and its Consequences', *Studies in Comparative Communism*, Vol. 4, No. 1 (January 1971).

Slomczynski, K., *Socio-Occupational Differentiation and Education, Authority, Income and Prestige* (Varna: World Congress of Sociology, 1970).

Sokol, M., 'Changes in Economic Management in Czechoslovakia', *Czechoslovak Economic Papers*, No. 8 (1967).

Solzhenitsyn, A., *The Gulag Archipelago* (Collins, Fontana, 1974).

Sorokin, P. A., *Russia and the United States* (Dutton, 1944).

Staar, R. F., *The Communist Regimes in Eastern Europe* 2nd edn (Stanford: Hoover Institution, 1971).

Stouffer, Samuel A., *Communism, Conformity and Civil Liberties* (Doubleday, 1955).

Strauss, G., and Rosenstein, E., 'Workers' Participation in Management: A Central View', *Industrial Relations*, Vol. 9, No. 2 (February 1970).

Sweezy, Paul M., and Bettelheim, Charles, *On the Transition to Socialism* (New York: Monthly Review, 1971).

Szczepanski, Jan, *Polish Society* (Random House, 1970).

*Szelenyi, Ivan, 'Housing System and Social Structure', in Paul Halmos (ed.), *Hungarian Sociological Studies. The Sociological Review* Monograph 17 (Keele, 1972).

Talantov, B. V., 'Sovetskoe obshchestov (1965–68gg)', *Posev*, Vol. 25, No. 9 (September 1969).

'Text of the 1970 Draft of the Revised Constitution of the People's Republic of China', in *Studies in Comparative Communism*, Vol. 4, No. 1 (1971).

Thomson, George, *From Marx to Mao Tse-Tung: A Study in Revolutionary Dialectics* (London: China Policy Study Group, 1971).

Ticktin, Hillel H., 'Towards a Political Economy of the USSR', *Critique*, No. 1 (1973).

——, 'Political Economy of the Soviet Intellectual', *Critique*, No. 2 (1973).

Timasheff, N. S., *The Great Retreat* (Dalton, 1946).

Tkach, Ya. M., 'Roditeli o sud'bakh svoikh detey', in *Protsessy izmeneniya sotsial'noy struktury v Sovetskom obshchestve* (Sverdlovsk, 1967).

Tökes, Rudolf L., 'Dissent. The Politics for Change in the USSR', in H. W. Morton and R. L. Tökes, *Soviet Politics and Society in the 1970s* (Free Press, 1974).

Trotsky, L., *The Revolution Betrayed, The Soviet Union, what it is and where it is going?* (written 1936) (New York; Pioneer Publishers, 1958).

'The USSR: Non-Proletarian and Non-Bourgeois State?' (written 1937), printed in *The Class Nature of the Soviet Union* (London: W. I. R. Publications, n.d.).

United States Senate, Committee on Government Operations: United States Senate (88th Congress), *Staffing Procedures and Problems in the Soviet Union* (Washington: US Government Printing Office, 1963).

Vaculik, L., '2,000 Words to Workers, Farmers, Civil Servants, Scientists, Artists and Everyone' (1968). Reprinted in Committee on the Judiciary, United States Senate, *Aspects of Intellectual Ferment and Dissent in Czechoslovakia* (Washington: US Government Printing Office, 1969).

*Waller, Derek J., 'The Chinese Communist Political Elite: Continuity and

Innovation' in C. Beck *et al, Comparative Communist Leadership* (David McKay, 1973).

Waller, Derek J., 'Elite Composition and Revolutionary Change in China: 1965–69' *Asian Studies: Occasional Paper,* No. 7 (Southern Illinois University, 1973a).

Warner, M., 'Bureaucracy, Participation and Self-Government in Organisations', in *Participation and Self-Management,* Vol. 2 (Zagreb: First International Sociological Conference on Participation and Self-Management, 1972).

Weinberg, E. A. *The Development of Sociology in the Soviet Union* (Routledge, 1974).

Weinberg, Ian, 'The Problem of the Emergence of Industrial Societies: A Critical Look at the State of a Theory', *Comparative Studies in History and Society* (1969), 1–15.

Wheelwright, E. L., and McFarlane, Bruce, *The Chinese Road to Socialism* (Penguin, 1973).

*White, Stephen, 'Contradiction and Change in State Socialism', *Soviet Studies,* Vol. 26, No. 1 (January 1974).

Wittfogel, Karl A., *Oriental Despotism* (Yale University Press, 1957).

Yang, C. K., *The Family in The Chinese Revolution* (MIT Press, 1959).

*Yanowitch, Murray, and Fisher, Wesley, *Social Stratification and Mobility in the USSR* (International Arts and Sciences Press, 1973).

Yesenin-Volpin, A., 'The Tragic Ordeal', in *The Humanist* (January–February 1973).

Zagorski, K., *Changes of Socio-Occupational Mobility in Poland* (Jablonna: G.U.S. (Central Statistical Office), March 1974).

Zaninovich, M. George, *The Development of Socialist Yugoslavia* (Johns Hopkins Press, 1968).

Zhenshchiny i deti v SSSR (Moscow: Statistika 1969).

Zhenshchiny v SSSR (Moscow: Statistika 1974).

Index